12/2013

CYCLE WORLD

THE TOTAL MOTORCYCLING MANUAL

CYCLE WORLD

THE TOTAL MOTORCYCLING MANUAL

MARK LINDEMANN
AND THE EDITORS OF *CYCLE WORLD*

weldon**owen**

CONTENTS

RIDING

WHEN I WAS THREE YEARS OLD,

my parents took me to an AMA Supercross race in Dallas, Texas. We had to leave the event early because I threw a fit; they wouldn't let me ride during intermission with the KTM Junior Supercross kids. Even at that young age, I was hooked. I got my first motorcycle two years later, and I rode it every day after school, around the backyard or on the trails close to my mom's house.

In the beginning, I just wanted to ride a dirt bike. Then I had to learn how to do a wheelie. After that, I wanted to drag my knee. I didn't stop riding until my knee touched the ground. When it finally did, I nearly fell off the bike because I was so scared. Once I started road racing, I walked around the pits asking everybody for their lap times so that I could compare my times with theirs.

When you're first learning to brake or use a clutch or blip the throttle between downshifts, remember to take baby steps—and keep taking them—in order to become a better rider. If you try to make a big jump, you'll miss things that are really important. Also, don't skimp on your equipment. At my level, I can choose what I wear. If you don't have a lot of money, wait until you can at least afford to buy the most protective gear.

I've worked very hard to achieve my racing goals, but riding isn't always about competition. When I retire from racing, I'll probably buy a motocross bike or a cruiser and take a long trip with a few of my buddies. That's something I've never done, and always wanted to. Whatever I decide, motorcycles will always be a part of my life. I hope you have as much fun on your bike as I've had on mine.

BEN SPIES
AMA Superbike Champion
Superbike World Champion
MotoGP race winner

WHAT IS IT ABOUT MOTORCYCLES?

I started riding because bikes were exciting, all about danger and freedom. Motorcycles promised performance, practicality, affordability. Transportation changed from something passive into something active. A motorbike turned my commute from drudgery into the best part of my day. It was economical too—part of the solution, not the problem.

But then something else happened. I discovered that motorcycling demanded more focus and concentration than anything I'd ever experienced. Riding well was incredibly rewarding; riding poorly delivered immediate consequences. Twisting the throttle was like turning the focus ring on a camera's lens: If I found my mind wandering, opening that throttle brought everything into sharp clarity. You want to learn about personal responsibility? Here are the keys.

For me, proficient motorcyclists need to develop six key skills:

- They need to ride with a degree of facility.

- They need to be able to navigate, especially true for off-road riders.

- They need to be able to perform basic maintenance and repairs.

- They need to know some first aid and how to respond at accidents.

- They need to know how to ride with a group.

- They need to ride critically and be aware—to be able to provide conscious feedback about their bike and how it performs.

I hope this book whets your appetite—to start riding, to become a better rider, to develop those six skills. I hope you learn a trick or two. And I hope your time on two wheels proves as rewarding for you as it has for me.

Enjoy the ride.

MARK LINDEMANN
Cycle World

MOTORCYCLE MASTERPIECES

Fourteen seminal bikes that define 100 years of riding.

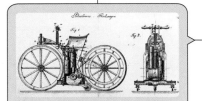

1885 DIAMLER EINSPUR
264cc • 0.5 Horsepower • Germany
The original motorcycle: Wooden frame, single-cylinder four-stroke engine, gear final drive. *(see sidebar)*

1909 HARLEY-DAVIDSON
810cc • 7 Horsepower • USA
The first Harley to use the V-twin layout (previously singles). H-D is now one of the most powerful brands in the world.

1922 BMW R32
494cc • 8.5 Horsepower • Germany
The original Bay-Em-Vay, incorporating the iconic shaft drive and horizontally-opposed-twin engine layout.

1946 VESPA 150
145cc • 7 Horsepower • Italy
The epitome of a motor scooter, the Vespa ("Wasp", for its bulbous rear end and the buzz from its two-stroke engine) is a fashion and design icon.

1950 MOTO GUZZI FALCONE
499cc • 23 Horsepower • Italy
Today, Moto Guzzis are known for their longitudinal V-twin engines. But it was the modest Falcone that motorized Italy and got the company on its feet after the war.

1949 VINCENT BLACK SHADOW
998cc • 55 Horsepower • UK
Gorgeous and high performance, with one of the best names ever, this bike also offered technology like stressed-member construction that eliminated conventional frame elements.

1959 TRIUMPH BONNEVILLE
650cc • 46 Horsepower • UK
The iconic British twin, a descendent of Edward Turner's 1937 Triumph Speed Twin, one of the most influential designs of the century.

1960 BSA GOLD STAR
499cc • 340 Horsepower • UK
The peak of single-cylinder Britbike design, and beloved of café racers.

1958 HONDA 50 SUPER CUB
49cc • 4.0 Horsepower • Japan
Also known as the C100, while not Honda's first bike, this was the machine that gave the company a toehold worldwide. Hugely significant because it's gone on to become the most-produced motor vehicle in the world, surpassing Ford's Model T.

1975 HONDA GL1000
999cc • 80 Horsepower • Japan
The Gold Wing has grown over the years, but it still uses the horizontally opposed engine and shaft drive.

1922 MEGOLA SPORT
640cc · 14 Horsepower · Germany
Born of WWI technology, the stylish Megola's front-wheel rotary engine was a design cul-de-sac.

1946 VELO SOLEX
49cc · 0.8 Horsepower · France
With millions of units sold, this moped was a modest bicycle with its front wheel driven by a two-stroke engine.

1968 YAMAHA DT1
246cc · 22 Horsepower · Japan
The first real Japanese dirtbike instead of a converted street scrambler.

1972 KAWASAKI H2
748cc · 74 Horsepower · Japan
These early two-stroke triples could be both terrifying and exhilarating.

TAKE A HISTORIC RIDE

Right after reproduction, locomotion stands as one of mankind's oldest obsessions. The first proto-cowboy probably climbed onto a horse 6,500 years ago. Steam engines reached a practical degree of evolution by the late 1700s. The modern bicycle is a child of the middle-to-late 1800s, and the end of the 19th century was a hotbed of development for internal-combustion engines, with a variety of fuels—natural gas, petrol, diesel oil, even coal dust.

Inventors tried steam-powered bicycles with predictably scalding results, but the first practical motorcycle clearly appeared in 1885. Built by those crafty Swabian inventors Gottlieb Daimler and Wilhelm Maybach of Bad Cannstatt, a suburb of Stuttgart, Germany, the Reitwagen ("riding wagon") or Einspur ("single track") harnessed a petroleum-fueled internal-combustion engine, two wheels, and the desire to ride like the wind (or at least at its top speed: 7 miles per hour, or 11 kph).

With its wooden frame, single-cylinder engine, and driven rear wheel, the Reitwagen is instantly recognized as the precursor to bikes we all ride today. The original was destroyed in a 1903 factory fire, but you can enjoy several great replicas in Stuttgart's Mercedes Museum, Munich's Deutsches Museum, the Honda Collection Hall in Japan, or the AMA Motorcycle Hall of Fame in Ohio.

Note: The first officially recorded motorcycle accident occurred on November 18, 1885, when the Reitwagen's hot-tube ignition set fire to the seat while Daimler's 17-year-old son was riding from Bad Cannstatt to Untertürkheim, no doubt to show off in front of his girlfriend. Teenagers and bikes: some things never change!

1 FALL IN LOVE ...
CAREFULLY

Sometime between adolescence and adulthood, you define your ideals in beauty, art, love—and your perfect bike. For me it was the Moto Guzzi 850 Le Mans. It was fast, dangerous, exotic, expensive, red—and completely unattainable. I lusted after one with all my soul, even though I'd only seen it in photos.

Fast-forward a decade: I was a test rider for a major magazine, and guess what showed up, unannounced, with the keys in the ignition and a full tank of gas: an 850 Le Mans III. Hands shaking, I went for a ride.

It was a total disaster. The brakes were weird, the handling trucklike and evil. Torque reaction and driveshaft jacking were shameful. The throttles were stiff, and the bike revved like a tractor. I was mortified. Progress had left the Le Mans behind.

I felt betrayed, like a jilted lover. The object of my youthful desire had let me down. Lesson learned? Lust alone makes a poor basis for a long-term relationship.

Those old Le Mans are still drop-dead gorgeous to my eye—I just don't want to ride one anymore.

2 KNOW WHY YOU
WANT TO RIDE

Learning to ride a motorcycle is no casual undertaking. Motorbikes are fun, but you need to be dedicated and capable of understanding a load of new information. If you're looking at getting into bikes because they're fast or cool, that's just the tip of the iceberg. If you're trying to impress someone or to fit in, you're likely going at it the wrong way. Ride for yourself, for fun, for freedom on the open road . . . but do it safely, and do it because it's the thing that *you* really want to do.

3 FIND YOUR FIRST BIKE

So you think you want to ride. What's next? There are plenty of ways to get started. Maybe you catch a ride as a passenger with a friend or family member. Next thing you know, you're eyeballing the piggy bank. You'll want to see what's available, and probably ride a range of bikes yourself. (Be sure you're street legal, and know your local licensing and insurance laws.) You can search the classifieds or buy a bike from a buddy, but it's better if you can test ride a variety of bikes first. That way you can find out what you really like, then go back to the ads. But you'll be a much more informed consumer.

DEALERSHIPS	USED BIKE LOTS	BIKE SHOWS
Motorcycle showrooms are full of new machines. And more and more dealerships house more bikes from more than one maker.	Not as plentiful as used-car lots in most countries, but another option that could pan out well.	Most major markets have travelling bike shows that let you see hundreds of new bikes all in one location.
UPSIDES You'll find plenty of new machines—and there's free coffee, too.	**UPSIDES** Could be a screaming deal, and an inexpensive way for you to get started.	**UPSIDES** The latest new machines, factory-fresh. Demo rides are sometimes available.
DOWNSIDES Mostly new bikes, aggressive sales staff . . . and the coffee's always bad.	**DOWNSIDES** Even worse coffee, uneven inventory.	**DOWNSIDES** Little one-on-one time. Yearly shows in big cities, only new models, and no free joe.

4 START OUT RIGHT

In the bad old days, we learned to ride a motorcycle without much professional input: We just stumbled into it with no real instruction, thrashed around awkwardly, tried to avoid disaster, and counted ourselves lucky if we could hang on for more than a couple of minutes. Today, though, there are much better ways. Here are some good places to start.

THE MOTOR VEHICLE DEPARTMENT In most countries you need some sort of license. That motor vehicle department is also a good place to ask about rider-training resources. If nothing else, they usually have literature telling you what to expect on the test.

MANUFACTURERS Every major motorcycle manufacturer has a website, and most of them have links to rider-training information. It doesn't matter which brand you start with, although some will offer free or discounted training courses if you purchase one of their bikes.

A DEALER Your local dealers probably won't offer training, but may know who does in your area.

YOUR LOCAL AUTOMOBILE CLUB Clubs like the American Automobile Association ("Triple A") in America, the AA or RAC in the UK, the ADAC in Germany, and many more often cater to motorcyclists as well as auto drivers. Invariably they can steer you towards insurance, licensing, and training solutions.

5 GET YOUR LICENSE

Motorcycle laws vary greatly from state to state and country to country, but one truth is profoundly evident: Riders without a license are far more likely to end up involved in an accident than licensed riders. And you may find you have difficulty getting insurance without a license, too.

You'll want to start by visiting your local Department of Motor Vehicles, either online or in person. Find out whether your local laws require you to take a written test, a riding test, or both. While you're there (or on the website), determine whether they have any pre-test materials you can study—they often do, at no charge.

Find out if there's any specific training you will need before you take the test, and what equipment you need to have for the test: helmet, gloves, boots, jacket, and/or a bike? Also, inquire with the DMV whether attending a certified riding school can substitute for all or part of the test.

Next, study the laws, and take some rider training if you decide this is right for you (it is). Practice your skills, especially low-speed maneuvering and, when you're ready, go for it. Good luck!

6 FIND A RIDING SCHOOL

Motorcycle riding schools fall into several categories. Make sure you pick the right one for your skill level.

BASIC RIDER LICENSING AND TRAINING This instruction is the most common. It'll take you from zero to applying for your license. Most of the time these classes are geared for streetbike riders. Very often they will provide all the safety equipment you need—and a bike as well.

ADVANCED RIDER TRAINING These schools are for street riders who want to advance their skills to the next level. They can be operated either by the same foundations that set up the basic schools, or they can be offered on racetracks by various expert riders.

RACING ASSOCIATION SCHOOLS Many racing associations will require you to take one of their school courses before you can participate in an event. These classes are often held at your local racetrack. You'll need your own equipment and a track-prepped bike.

RACING SCHOOLS Separate from the association schools, these are typically run by former racers who either tour the country or operate out of a home track. The classes can last several days and are often a nice vacation opportunity for advanced riders: You get to meet a famous racer, hang out with him for a couple of days, and get first-hand riding tips. You also get lots of track time on a new course.

DIRTBIKE SCHOOLS These courses can be either basic or advanced. Like the roadbike schools, you may want to pick one at an exotic location and make a vacation out of it. This training is becoming more and more popular for the big twin-cylinder adventure bikes like the BMW GS series and the KTMs. Your dealership can probably give you a good idea of what's out there.

GEAR

WHAT DRAWS ANYONE TO A MOTORCYCLE?

The freedom? The excitement? The danger? The way a bike looks? The rebellious aspects? The clothing? The practicality? The challenge? It's different for everyone, but one thing never changes: it all starts with the bike.

My mom only knew that there were red bikes and black bikes, and that some were louder than others. You'll need to know a lot more. This chapter is designed to give you a solid foundation in the different types of motorcycles out there, and the equipment you'll need as a rider.

Three pieces of advice: First, be honest with yourself about why you want to ride, and what you're looking for in a bike. If you are, you'll end up choosing a machine that you'll enjoy. On the other hand, if you base your choice on someone else's criteria, or if you get blinded by chrome and paint and sound, you may end up bitterly disappointed when it actually comes time to wheel the thing out of the garage.

Second, don't obsess and fixate on the gear, especially if you're just getting started. Today's motorcyclists are extraordinarily fortunate in how many good bikes there are on the market, and how much great equipment too. You'll need a certain amount of gear to be safe and comfortable, but it's always more important to ride than to own.

Third, while bikes get crashed and gear wears out, memories last forever. Concentrate on your experiences and you'll never go wrong.

7 CHOOSE THE RIGHT BIKE FOR YOU

When it comes to picking a new bike, there are a lot of options, and the next few pages of this book will take you through them one by one. Start by being brutally honest with yourself. Are you really going to be taking weeklong road trips through the Alps, or are you more likely to commute to the train station every workday? Both plans are fine, but they will point you to two different types of bike. As you start this process, there are two schools of thought: Call them left brain and right brain.

LEFT BRAIN
- Decide your primary use.
- Identify a budget.
- Decide if you want to go new or used.
- Go for a test ride.
- Compare varying brands.
- Perform online searches for the benefits and liabilities of a particular model.
- Calculate amortized cost/benefit of fuel, insurance, parking, and savings.
- Decide on a service contract.
- Ask spouse/parent/ significant other/ neighbor for opinions.
- Ask experienced riders for opinions.
- Research specific models online.

RIGHT BRAIN
- Pick the bike that makes your heart beat the fastest.

8 GET MORE INFORMATION

Want to find out more about your dream bike? It's as easy as 1-2-3.

STEP 1 Check out general information in magazines and in authoritative online sources. Magazines such as *Cycle World* in the U.S. offer a wide range of facts, figures, and opinions in print and digital versions, will set you up with publications in other countries/languages.

STEP 2 Identify the bikes you're most interested in, Google them, and find the info you need for your country. Make sure you visit your local dealerships, too. They'll probably have your dream (new) bike sitting in the showroom, as well as brochures and other literature for you to take home and study.

STEP 3 Ask around, both on the web and wherever the riders in your area hang out. Social media is fine—as far as it goes. But nothing beats real socialization. Motorcycles aren't virtual—they're real.

9 TREAT A LADY RIGHT

Which bike is the right choice for a female rider? The answer, of course, is any bike she wants.

Motorcycling is wonderfully gender-neutral, and every year more women discover how much fun riding can be. At present in the U.S., more than seven million women ride, which is over 10 percent of all active motorcyclists. And the number continues to rise.

That said, many women may want a bike with a lower seat height, lighter weight, or lower center of gravity. Cruisers offer some of the lowest seats of any bikes. One- or two-cylinder machines also tend to be narrower, and a narrow bike often feels lower and lighter. In the 750cc and smaller displacements, women will find plenty to choose from.

10 PICK A NUMBER (OF WHEELS)

Everyone knows a motorcycle has two wheels, right? Not so fast, partner. What about sidecars, like today's Ural? Or trikes like the old Harley-Davidson Servicar (aka the Meter Maid Special), or the popular conversions for Gold Wings? And what about three-wheelers with two wheels up front and one in the rear, like the Can-Am Spyder?

Three-wheelers can be a lot of fun in their own

right. And for riders with physical limitations or disabilities they can provide a way to get out and ride when those same riders might not be able to operate a more conventional bike.

That said, trikes are almost always heavier and wider. On the plus side, three-wheelers often have better carrying and towing capacity, and they take balance out of the equation.

11 UNDERSTAND BIKE TYPES

Manufacturers and riders keep coming up with new terms to describe types of bikes. Here are the seven most common categories you'll see, and the pluses and minuses of each type for the new or experienced rider.

STANDARD BIKES

+ Minimal bodywork
+ Neutral seating position
+ Often weigh less
+ Do almost everything well
+ Often cost less
− Might look old-fashioned

DIRTBIKES

+ Light
+ Simple
+ Excellent way to learn
− Not street legal
− May need more maintenance

TOURING BIKES

+ Excellent wind protection
+ Comfortable for long trips
+ Can carry a lot
− Bigger bikes can be heavy
− Top-of-the-line bikes are pricey

ADVENTURE BIKES

+ Can ride on street and dirt
+ Versatile
+ Rugged construction
+ Often come with luggage
+/− Tall seat heights
− Varying levels of comfort

CRUISERS

+ Low seat height is a great choice for first-time riders
+ Plenty of style
+ Wide choice of models
+ Often inexpensive
− Less comfortable for long rides

DUAL-SPORTS

+ Legal on both street and dirt
+ Light yet rugged construction
+ Great for rural areas
+ Great for tall riders
− Compromised performance on both pavement and dirt

SPORTBIKES

+ Sporty, aggressive seating
+ Full-coverage bodywork
+ Excellent handling
+ Superior engine performance
+ Powerful brakes
− Seating may be uncomfortable
− Too powerful for some beginners

BREAK THE RULES

Remember, there's no law that says you can't commute on a touring bike, or ride your scooter across the continent, or take your sportbike to Sturgis. In fact, the more places you ride your new bike, the better you'll understand what you want in your next one.

LEARN MOTORCYCLE ANATOMY

Entire books have been written on understanding the parts of your bike (some of them we call "owners manuals"). Here's a basic primer, so you can read a "for sale" ad or talk to a dealership saleperson without feeling like—or worse, being treated like—a total newbie.

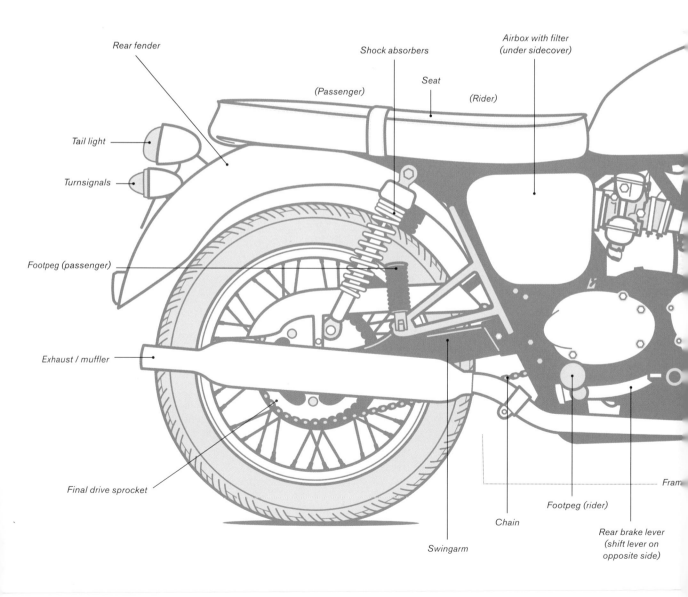

Rear fender

Shock absorbers

Airbox with filter (under sidecover)

(Passenger)

Seat

(Rider)

Tail light

Turnsignals

Footpeg (passenger)

Exhaust / muffler

Final drive sprocket

Frame

Footpeg (rider)

Chain

Swingarm

Rear brake lever (shift lever on opposite side)

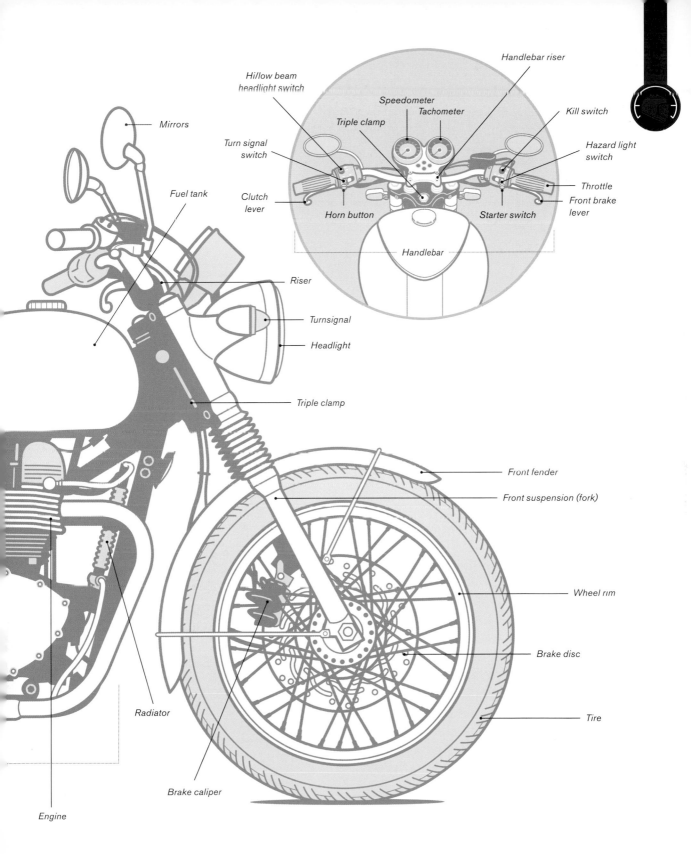

Mirrors

Hi/low beam headlight switch

Handlebar riser

Speedometer

Tachometer

Triple clamp

Kill switch

Turn signal switch

Hazard light switch

Fuel tank

Clutch lever

Throttle

Horn button

Starter switch

Front brake lever

Handlebar

Riser

Turnsignal

Headlight

Triple clamp

Front fender

Front suspension (fork)

Wheel rim

Brake disc

Radiator

Tire

Brake caliper

Engine

14
KNOW YOUR STREET BIKES

In the beginning, a motorcycle was a motorcycle was a motorcycle, and most of the streets were dirt. But like any species destined to survive, bikes began to mutate and evolve. At the same time, great ribbons of pavement began to crisscross the globe, from Germany's Autobahns to Great Britain's M1 to America's Route 66 and eventually the grandest superslab of them all, California's Interstate 5.

Today, bikes are designed to operate primarily on pavement or in the dirt: streetbikes and dirtbikes. And this is where you need to start your journey: Where do you want to ride?

Let's start with streetbikes. Here are some of the major categories:

STANDARD The jack-of-all-trades; motorcycles with neutral seating positions and minimal bodywork.

CRUISER With low-slung seats, forward-positioned footpegs, and chrome, they often have a retro style.

TOURING Bikes designed primarily for long trips, often featuring integrated luggage and big fairings.

SPORT/SUPERSPORT Machines designed for racetrack-like performance, with a premium placed on power and handling.

SUPERBIKE Technically this refers to a 1000cc racing-class machine, but the term is frequently used to mean any sportbike of 1000cc or over, especially a four-cylinder model.

SPORT-TOURING A sporty machine fitted with bags and a windshield for longer trips.

CAFÉ RACER A now-dated term for a standard modified for sporting use—think of them as a retro sportbike.

NAKED Term used to refer to sportbikes without any bodywork.

COMMUTER Typically smaller machines with a high emphasis on fuel economy and low price.

CHOPPER A special breed of cruiser with an extended front suspension and all extraneous elements removed.

CUSTOM One-off rolling art projects.

15 START WITH A STANDARD

Standards are the decathletes of the two-wheeled world, machines that haven't become so specialized that they sacrifice versatility. They're often the best "starter bike" for new riders.

ENGINE SIZE Standards come in a wide variety of displacements, and you need to choose an engine that's big enough for the kind of riding you plan, but not so large as to get poor mileage or add unnecessary weight.

OPEN SEATING A good standard will let you sit upright; you don't slouch as on a cruiser or lean forward like on a sportbike.

FOOTPEG POSITION Look for a model where the pegs fall pretty much right under your seat or a little farther forward. You should be able to stand up on the pegs with no difficulty, just as you can on a dirtbike or a dual-sport.

ACCESSORIES The key to making a standard work for you is to add any accessories you need, but not too much. A trunk or tankbag lets you carry gear, and a windshield makes winter or wet-weather riding more pleasant.

FUEL CAPACITY Most standard riders want a fuel tank that holds at least 3.5 gallons (13.25 liters) of fuel—enough for them to ride up to 150 miles (240 km) or more.

PASSENGER CAPACITY Even if you don't plan on regularly carrying a passenger, you'll want the option. Find a seat comfortable enough that your partner doesn't hate you after a long ride.

TRANSMISSION Most standards feature standard transmissions (of course), but a growing number of options (like automatics and dual-clutch transmissions) are appearing on the market.

STYLE Many standards—though not all of them—evoke the classic bikes of the 1960s and '70s.

Be Elvis. Or Brando. Or the Fonz. Whether you're embracing your inner Easy Rider or just want an easy-riding bike, cruisers are the most popular single class of motorcycles.

ENGINE V-Twins are the archetypal cruiser powerplants. Sizes vary from 750cc to more than double that.

FORWARD-SET FOOTPEGS These will let you stretch out in comfort, but some riders feel this posture lessens their ability to control the bike with their bodies, forcing greater emphasis on steering with the bars.

LONG WHEELBASE The long look adds to the bike's straight-line stability, but detracts from cornering capability.

LOW SEAT You sit *in* these bikes, more than *on* them. This relaxed posture can be a good thing for first-time riders, and makes it easy to put your feet down at stoplights, too. It's also true, however, that this low, laid-back position can translate into backache after an extended ride.

REASONABLY PRICED As with any piece of high-performance machinery, you can end up spending big bucks, but many cruisers are priced for those who don't want to break the bank.

PULLBACK HANDLEBAR This design reduces or eliminates weight on the wrists.

ACCESSORIES Take parts off. Put parts on. Cruisers are all about customization to express yourself.

CHROME Cruisers are as much about the way they look as how they work. Shiny objects attract, whether you're a packrat or a rider.

CUSTOM PAINT For most cruiser riders, a gas tank is just a blank canvas for self expression.

17 GET INTO SPORTS

Sportbikes are all about performance, speed, and handling. Here are some of the characteristics they offer.

STRONG BRAKES Slowing down is just as important as gaining speed. Sportbikes' brakes afford better stopping power.

STIFF FRAME The curves on tracks or mountain roads put a lot of stress on the bike's chassis. Reinforced frames help the bike handle well.

HIGH CORNERING CLEARANCE A sportbike's superior ground clearance allows the rider to lean more during turns without dragging bike or body parts.

LOW HANDLEBARS These controls aren't made for cruising. The handlebar arrangement tucks the rider in low to cut down on wind resistance.

ADJUSTABLE SUSPENSION The action of the suspension can be fine-tuned for different roads and rider weight.

MINIMAL SEAT Comfort is a secondary consideration for many models; speed matters more.

LOW-PROFILE TIRES Wide, low tires give better road response.

AERODYNAMIC BODYWORK Sleek body panels provide some wind protection and reduce drag.

POWERFUL ENGINE Two-, three-, or four-cylinder engines rev higher than most cruisers or touring bikes—up to 15,000 rpm!

COMPACT RIDING POSITION On a sportbike, your arms and legs are tucked in, your body's tilted down close to the tank, and your head's just peering over the windscreen. Athletic riders will find it gives them maximum control, but others may find it confining.

18 TOUR THE ROADWAYS

Who hasn't dreamed about taking a trip on a motorcycle? The right bike can make all the difference.

WINDSHIELD A full-protection windshield is a must for long-distance riding.

FULL-COVERAGE BODYWORK Helps provide protection from both wind and weather.

SHAFT FINAL DRIVE Not a necessity, but reduces maintenance on the road and runs cleaner.

SMOOTH-RUNNING ENGINE Lower revs for longer mileage. Four- and six-cylinder engines tend to be the smoothest.

LUGGAGE Can be removable or integrated. Lets you carry clothes, groceries, small animals.

COMFORTABLE SEAT Wide and supportive seating for those long hours in the saddle.

OPEN RIDING POSITION Not too leaned over, not too laid back.

PASSENGER SEATING If your passenger isn't happy, your trip won't be long. Touring bikes offer comfortable passenger seating and a significant backrest.

SOUND SYSTEMS Lets you listen to music while you ride. The system may also incorporate a CB radio or GPS navigation.

LARGE FUEL TANK Increases your bike's range. To calculate your touring range, you'll need to take into account both tank size and fuel efficiency.

TRAILER HITCH This is an option suitable for advanced riders only. Before you decide on this option, ask yourself if you really need to take that much stuff with you.

19
KNOW YOUR OFF-ROAD BIKES

For most riders, taking a streetbike off-road is the definition of a crash in progress. But if you want to explore riding off-road, there are some great ways to do it. In fact, we believe that most motorcyclists should probably start off in the dirt first—you'll learn how to control skids and find traction, there's no traffic to worry about, and in most places you don't even need a special license.

Dirtbikes (or off-road bikes—the terms are largely interchangeable) fall into two major groups, and then some subcategories. The first are dirtbikes you can also ride on the street:

DUAL-SPORTS Think of these as dirtbikes with lights and a license plate; fully street legal, but designed to ride primarily in the dirt, or at least 50/50. When choosing, be aware that a good off-road machine will still be decent on pavement, but the reverse may not be true.

ADVENTURE BIKES Larger machines, typically with two cylinders, designed for longer trips. Maybe 80 percent street and 20 percent dirt usage.

RALLY/RAID A special class of adventure bike that's been fitted out for multi-day competition.

Then we come to the pure dirt machines, bikes which are for off-road riding only:

MOTOCROSS High-performance machines designed for competition. If you want to get into racing, this is the bike type you'll need.

TRIALS BIKES Specialized bikes designed for slow-speed riding over tricky obstacles.

TRAIL BIKE/ENDURO Technically an enduro is a specific type of competition, but these bikes are designed for casual off-road riding— think of them as the standard bikes of the off-road world.

PLAYBIKE A motorcycle designed for younger riders and typically 150cc or smaller. Great starter bikes for kids.

20 HIT THE DIRT

Dirtbikes are some of the best machines to learn on, but only if you pick the right one. Here's what to consider.

HIGH-QUALITY SUSPENSION These bikes are meant to handle rough terrain, and often need a foot (30 cm) of suspension travel in order to do it right.

RUGGED CONSTRUCTION Meant to ride through mud, sand, dust, dirt, gravel, and many other punishing conditions, dirtbikes need to be sturdy.

SIMPLE DESIGN You don't need turn signals, flashy lights, or aerodynamic panels; you just need a strong, simple machine that will roar across the dirt.

TOUGH TIRES Built for pure off-roading, dirtbikes need tires that are going to claw into the terrain for traction.

VERSATILE Dirtbikes are available in a wide range of engine and chassis sizes, from 50cc bikes for kids to 500cc machines for adults. When in doubt, you can't go wrong with a smaller bike for newbies.

GREAT STARTER BIKES The lower price, light weight, simple construction, and the fact that you don't have to contend with traffic make dirtbikes great for beginners.

EASY TO HANDLE While recreational dirtbikes don't have the high-performance components found on motocross machines, that's actually better (and cheaper!) for most casual riders. Their broader powerbands also make them more forgiving than racing bikes that require serious precision.

HIGH MAINTENANCE Dirtbikes have a simple construction that makes them ideal for the DIY mechanic, but the beating they tend to take also means that mechanic will be doing more wrenching than the average street rider.

21 GO BOTH WAYS (ON A DUAL-SPORT)

The key to choosing the right model is to know how much off-road riding you'll do compared to how much on-road riding, since individual models are usually biased one way or another.

SUSPENSION In general, the more suspension travel you have, the better. Six inches (15 cm) is a bare minimum, 12 inches (30 cm) is about the maximum.

OVERALL CONSTRUCTION Dual-sports take a beating in the dirt. Bodywork, windshields, and so on are all prone to damage. Follow the KISS principle here: Keep It Simple, Stupid.

CRASH PROTECTION Any off-road bike needs some sort of a skidplate to protect the engine.

APPROPRIATE GEARING Dual-sports need a first gear low enough for rock crawling and a top gear high enough for highway rides.

TIRES Good off-road tires are a compromise when on the street, especially under braking, while street tires are worthless in the dirt. When in doubt, look for DOT-approved knobbies (or the equivalent in your region).

ENGINE Almost all dual-sports use single-cylinder engines, and the best are derived from true dirt machines. A bonus: Dual-sports almost always get superior gas mileage and make great urban commuters, especially if your city government seems to think that potholes add character.

STREET-LEGAL FEATURES A dual-sport needs to have a headlight, turnsignals, mirrors, horn, taillight, and a mounting for your license plate.

EXHAUST You need a high pipe and muffler, tucked up out of the way. More important, the exhaust needs to be fitted with an approved spark arrestor if you ride off-road.

22 HAVE AN ADVENTURE

Designed for multiday trips over paved and dirt roads. When you win the lottery, quit your job, and decide to ride around the world or down to the tip of South America, this is the kind of bike you want.

ENGINE Big distances mean you need a bigger engine, between 600cc and 1200cc. And you're going to want to make it at least a two-cylinder. They're smoother on the highway and offer more power.

LUGGAGE The classic adventure-bike choice is the hard-sided aluminum box. You'll need a rack as well, so you can lash down that goat you bought for dinner at the local souk.

SUSPENSION As with a dual-sport, more is better, at least 9 to 10 inches of travel (23–25 cm).

TIRES Long trips mean a hard tire with a more closed pattern. The trade-off is less traction in the dirt.

LARGE FUEL TANK Who wants to run out of gas in Timbuktu (or anywhere else)? Fuel availability can be a real issue on some trips. A bigger tank, around 5 or 6 gallons (19 to 23 liters) is what most riders want. Bigger than that and your bike gets too heavy when full.

WINDSHIELD Most of these bikes offer some sort of short/narrow windshield to deflect the windblast on long highway sections.

EXHAUST As on a dirtbike or dual-sport, it needs to be up high and out of the way.

GROUND CLEARANCE As a general rule, more is always better, but too much means you won't be able to reach down with your feet at stoplights. This is where a serious test ride can be your friend.

HIGHER PRICE TAG This is what the phrase "you get what you pay for" was invented to describe. You're getting a high-performance, versatile machine. Expect to pay a little more in most cases.

23 DON'T LET THEM BORROW YOURS

Some things just aren't done in polite society. You never ask to borrow someone else's toothbrush. And you never ask if you can ride someone else's bike. Unfortunately, some less-civilized soul may ask exactly this. Best be prepared to fend it off. Here are some useful responses.

THE DEFLECTION "Sure—got a helmet? Hop on the back and I'll take you for a spin."

THE MECHANICAL LIE "Okay, but there's some knocking sound coming from the engine. I need to get that looked at first."

MAÑANA "Hey, how about next week after I put some new tires on? It'll handle better then."

MISDIRECTION "No problem. But first, how about the (local or college sports team)? Think they're going to make it to the playoffs this year?"

LEGAL EAGLE "Sure. Whoops, I just remembered—my insurance lapsed yesterday. How about after I get it straightened out?"

PAPERS, PLEASE "I'm still making payments. My bank says I've got to see a driver's license, insurance, certificate of rider training, character references..."

OUTTA TIME "Look at the time. I gotta go. Maybe next week."

THE DIRECT APPROACH "I'm really not comfortable letting anyone else ride my bike."

THE MORE DIRECT APPROACH "No."

THE EVEN MORE DIRECT APPROACH "What part of 'No' don't you understand?"

PERFECTLY CLEAR "If I ever even catch you sitting on my bike, I'll break your arm."

24 SHARE THE WEALTH— KIND OF

Lending someone your bike is the fastest way to lose a friend. Taking someone for a ride is one of the best ways in the world to introduce someone to motorcycling. So go with the latter plan.

25 RENT A RIDE

Renting a motorcycle can be an excellent way to revive a bland vacation or to make a great holiday even better. It's also a good way to experience new bikes. If you're travelling in most places, the Internet should be your first stop. And the closer you are to a major vacation destination, the more luck you're going to have. The farther you get from civilization, though, the more you'll have to improvise.

Airports are a good place to start your search, since they're geared toward automobile rentals already. Local bike shops may rent you a ride informally, especially in developing countries. Some clubs, organizations and owners' groups offer rental deals in other cities. (Or they offer lower rental rates. Always ask.) Automobile associations may have helpful information on who rents bikes and where. It may pay to join up, even if you're only going to be in the country for a short time.

The most effortless way is to book a package deal, which may include a bike, a guide, and accommodations. Be prepared to pay as much in insurance/security deposit as you do for the rental. You may get some of it back if you and the bike return in one piece.

Rent a bike appropriate for the venue: Big Harleys make sense in America, Royal Enfields in the Hindu Kush, Vespas in Rome, Honda Cubs in Saigon, mopeds in the Peloponnese. Don't rent some enormous touring bike if you've never ridden anything bigger than a scooter, unless your idea of a great vacation is sampling foreign hospital cuisine. Wherever you are, familiarize yourself with local road signs and laws.

26 KNOW WHAT TO BRING

Sure, you're renting a bike, but that doesn't mean they'll give you all the extras and options, too. Here are a few important things you should bring with you when renting, especially overseas.

- ☐ Your own helmet. (Do you really want to wear a rental helmet?) Or at least bring a thin silk or nylon helmet liner.
- ☐ Your license, with a motorcycle endorsement.
- ☐ An international driver's license.
- ☐ Any pertinent insurance, although be prepared that this won't be accepted overseas.
- ☐ Cash.
- ☐ A battery-powered GPS.
- ☐ An open mind, a positive attitude, and a sense of adventure.

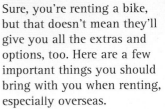

27 THE INSIDE LINE
LAGUNA SECA

NUMBER OF TURNS: **11**

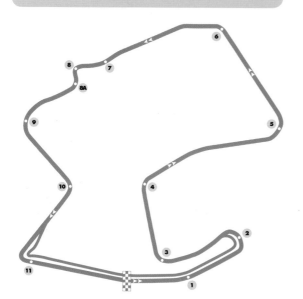

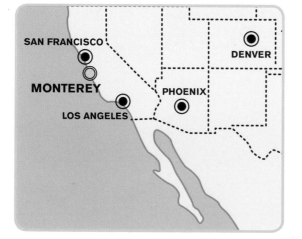

FAST FACTS

OFFICIAL NAME Mazda Raceway
Laguna Seca

LOCATION Monterey, California,
U.S.A., south of San Francisco

TRACK LENGTH 2.238 mi (3.602 km)

NUMBER OF TURNS 11

DATE OPENED 1957

FAMOUS FEATURE Turn 8 and 8A,
better known as the "Corkscrew," a
plunging five-and-a-half-story drop
with a blind entry.

TRIVIA Named for the dry lake bed
around which the track was built,
Laguna Seca is one of the most
beloved racetracks in America, by
riders, racers, and fans.

Nestled in the foothills east of
Monterey, California, the location
offers moderate weather. The roads
leading to the track are a rider's
dream, and the food and wine in
town are spectacular.

An easy day's ride from Los Angeles
or San Francisco, the track follows the
natural, rolling terrain of the northern
California countryside—a classic
roadcourse in contrast with the more
current road-course practice.

The track originally featured nine
turns in 1.9 miles (3.1 km), but was
lengthened to its present configuration
in 1988 to host the USGP.

Though several concessions are
offered, the best track food here is,
without a doubt, the fried calamari.

28 BUILD AN ADVENTURE BIKE SURVIVAL KIT

On a long ride or in a foreign country, you never know what might go wrong. If your bike breaks down in the middle of nowhere or the weather suddenly turns nasty, you'll need more than just luck to survive. When you're heading off the beaten track, pack a survival kit, and be ready for the unexpected.

KNIFE You don't need some big Rambo pig sticker here. At the very minimum, a multitool with a good blade will do. A Swiss Army knife with a locking blade is also a great choice.

TRASH BAGS These are your wilderness get-out-of-jail-free cards. Stuffed with leaves or pine needles or cattail fluff, they're a mattress. You can also slit them open to make a tarp or cut holes to make a poncho, or just use one as a short-term sleeping bag.

ROPE You should already have some tow rope, ideally 25 feet (7.5 meters) of one-inch (2.5 cm) flat nylon strap. But 50 to 100 feet (15.25 to 30.5 meters) of parachute cord (aka 550-cord) takes up less space.

TARP A tarp can shelter against sun and rain. Wrap yourself up in it, spread it out, or use it as a hammock. The best are ripstop or silcoat nylon.

FLASHLIGHT A headband-mounted light frees up your hands for bike repairs or shelter-building in the dark. Also, know that your bike's taillight or turnsignal bulb draws less battery power than the headlamp.

COMPASS When your GPS fails, you'll need to navigate on your own. Keep your compass on a cord around your neck and tucked into your riding jacket, and know how to use it, too. Don't forget a map of your riding area, either.

COFFEE CAN You can use it as an improvised digging tool, to transfer gas from one bike to another, or slosh parts in gas to clean them. But most of all, it's a great impromptu cooking pot.

WATER PURIFICATION You should always have water with you, but you can only carry so much. Regardless, you need to purify whatever you find. Instead of a filter, just use iodine-based tablets and follow the directions on the label.

FOOD You don't need much—3,000 calories will seem like a feast and will see you through a couple of days or give you enough energy to walk out. Pack a double handful of snack bars and bouillon cubes or instant cocoa to drink.

WALKING SHOES When all else fails, the best plan is to hoof it out. Hiking some serious distance in motocross boots might cripple you, but in decent footwear you can manage it with ease. Throw in a pair of clean hiking socks, too.

29 APPRAISE A USED BIKE

What should you look for in a used bike? Few are perfect, but here's what to look at to pick a winner.

OVERALL CONDITION Eyes wide open here—look at several models in the same year if you can, to get a feel for what's out there

MILEAGE Lower is always better, but it's best to pick a bike that's been run regularly instead of one with lower miles that sat for five years and needs work.

FIRST OWNER If he or she bought it new, maybe they took better care of it.

FOOTPEGS Scraped footpegs mean the bike was leaned over vigorously. Not the end of the world, but a sign that the bike has been ridden hard.

TIRES Bald, hard tires equal neglect. Tires worn flat in the center speak of freeway droning. Tires worn clean to the edge signify aggressive sport riding. New tires mean a significant sum you won't have to spend.

OIL Is it full? Is it clean? If there's a dipstick, be sure to feel for grit.

MAINTENANCE RECORDS You're looking for regular maintenance from a certified shop.

PAPERWORK/REGISTRATION Is it all in order? Is it current? If not, the DMV is going to take their pound of flesh from you one way or another.

MISSING PARTS Motorcycle parts can be astonishingly expensive. Missing or damaged parts can double the cost of a bike, or halve its worth.

30 KNOW WHY THAT BIKE'S FOR SALE

Used bikes can be a bargain or a nightmare. But the choice between buying used and riding or not buying and not riding at all is a no-brainer. And especially for new riders who are looking for an introduction to bikes before they move up in displacement, a used bike is a great choice. Not all used bikes are thrashers, crashers, lemons, or time bombs. So why would anyone sell a perfectly good bike?

LIFE CHANGES The owner gets married and his or her spouse isn't keen on the bike. The first kid is born, and hey, the college fund needs money. The owner gets divorced—while you're in the garage checking out his former pride and joy (the bike, that is), make an offer on that SCUBA gear in the corner, the boat in the driveway, and his gun collection, too.

BAD CHOICES He read too many bike magazines and thought the latest, greatest bike would make his life more worth living. It was way faster than he imagined, resulting in said life flashing in front of his eyes. Or, it just didn't live up to the hype.

REALITY CHECK The owner dreamed of quitting his job, chucking it all, and riding 'round the world. Bought new adventure bike, and only rode to the bagel shop on Sunday. Back to work on Monday, and bike's for sale! Or maybe he thought a new bike would make him faster, but now his friends only laugh at him harder since he's still dead last on the Sunday-morning ride.

TOUGH TIMES Some of us would rather sell that second kidney we only use on the weekends before unloading our bikes, but not everyone has their priorities in order.

LOST LICENSE Use caution here—if it's a sportbike, the owner probably lost their license while riding the wheels off the thing.

31 TAKE A TEST RIDE

This bike looks like a keeper, but you wouldn't buy a pair of shoes without trying them on first—so why would you do the same with a bike? On the other hand, the seller is rightfully worried that you might steal the bike, drop it and damage it, or otherwise ruin his day.

What you want to do is offer him peace of mind. Leave him your driver's license (or spouse, or kid) as security. You can also have him ride along as a passenger (although this might just turn his fear of theft into a potential hostage situation). Finally, if he won't agree to any of these ideas, and you really want the bike, go ahead and buy it but insist on getting a written right of return from the seller.

32 IDENTIFY YOUR DEAL-BREAKERS

It's easy to be blinded by a great deal—which is why you need to be very clear on what your deal-breakers are, and stay firm. Any major flaw is an instant "no"—that includes a bike that doesn't run, won't shift, smokes (or catches fire), leaks, or has severe corrosion. Same deal for evidence of crash damage (such as scrapes or mismatched parts) or of submersion (like carp in the airbox).

How it rides is important too. If it wobbles or shakes, has excessive vibration, or makes odd noises, especially deep knocking, just walk away. If the seller says "It started up fine yesterday," or "It just needs a tune up," and you fall for that, you probably deserve what you get.

Finally, if anything seems at all sketchy about the legality of the deal, bail. Don't ever accept, "I'll send you the title later." Not even from your grandma.

33 READ THE FINE PRINT

In the United States, (and other countries, too), there are several kinds of titles (aka "pink slips"). Unless the title is in order, the motor vehicle department will make your life an expensive, living hell.

CLEAR The name on the bike and the owner's name match. The most desirable situation.

COUNTERSIGNED The title is in someone else's name, but signed off by that person. (Think of a two-party check). The problem is that you have no guarantee the signature is genuine.

ATTACHED The title is held by a second party, typically a finance company or lienholder. You'll need them to sign off on it as well.

JOINT Two names on the title, husband and wife. Both need to sign. Especially important if a divorce is involved, or you may find yourself married (at least financially) to the former owner's ex.

SALVAGE This means the bike was wrecked, and re-purchased from a salvage company. Nothing wrong with this per se, as long as the repairs were done correctly, but it may complicate insuring the new bike, especially for collision (repair damage). A salvage title typically lowers the bike's value substantially.

LOST No title? No deal, unless you intend to break the bike up for parts. Even then you may be on the hook for receiving stolen property. Tell the owner to get the paperwork in order, or you're outta there.

34 HIDE A NEW BIKE FROM YOUR SPOUSE

Sometimes opportunity knocks so loudly you just can't say no. So here you sit, with a new motorcycle's title warming the inside of your wallet, and facing the specter of a spouse or other family members who may suffocate you in your sleep if they find out. What to do? The easiest way out is to hide the new sled at a buddy's house. Look for a friend who's already divorced and has plenty of room since there's no furniture left.

He won't go for it? Try telling the better half that it's not your bike—you're storing it for a buddy since his spouse took him to the cleaners in the recent divorce (see left) and he's been reduced to sleeping in his van down by the river and surviving on uncooked hot dogs and ramen noodles. Of course you'll have to start it and run it every weekend for him so it won't be ruined. Sure it's an inconvenience, but you're just a nice guy.

35 PREP YOUR BIKE FOR SALE

As much as we hate to admit it, even the biggest garage (or budget) can only hold so many bikes. Here's what to do before that sucker—er, proud new owner—shows up to ride off on your former beauty.

WASH AND WAX Even if it doesn't run, at least clean it up. You may see a diamond in the rough; everyone else just sees the rough.

TUNE IT UP Unless you're willing to unload it for pocket change, money spent getting a bike to run right is almost always recovered in the sale.

CHARGE THE BATTERY Nothing kills a sale like a bike that won't start.

AIR UP THE TIRES Costs nothing, but can make a huge difference in the way a bike rides.

TOP OFF THE OIL If you see a bike with low oil, it's an instant pass—who knows how bad that engine is?

GET THE PAPERWORK Be sure you have the current registration and a blank bill of sale from your local motor vehicle department. And, finally, always fill out a transfer of ownership/liability form. Doing so will protect you from legal consequences if the buyer gets in a wreck 10 minutes after you sell the bike.

SHOW YOUR WORK Gather any maintenance records that show the bike was serviced regularly. If you do your own work, record it in the back of the owner's manual or shop manual.

FUEL UP Nothing says respect like a full tank of gas. With some of the beaters we've sold, a full tank probably doubled its value.

36 SELL YOUR BIKE FOR THE RIGHT REASONS

Why on earth would you sell your bike? The only really good reason, of course, is to raise the money to buy a new bike. Also acceptable are getting the money to repair your other bike, funding a racing career, or paying for that life-saving surgery (if you absolutely must).

So, what counts as a bad reason to sell a bike? Glad you asked. Silly little things like needing money for rent or food. Anything involving a parent, spouse, or boss. Fear, age, depression, or winter. In fact, every real rider knows that a motorcycle is a sure cure for the last four.

37

WEAR YOUR ROAD ARMOR

Smart riders know the bike is just the start. At bare minimum you'll also need the following items.

HELMET Your head is your most important asset. Find more detail on what to look for in items #40–43.

EYE PROTECTION A flying bug or a stone in the eye will ruin your day. Wear goggles or make sure your helmet has a face shield.

JACKET Leather is the traditional choice, but anything that offers warmth and abrasion/impact protection will do.

GLOVES Leather for protection and comfort. Some are also made with reinforced knuckle guards.

LONG PANTS Leather or textile for protection from wind and abrasion.

STURDY BOOTS OR SHOES A non-skid sole is essential. Solidly built for good support.

38 FIND 5 POCKET ESSENTIALS

When heading out, you know you've got your spectacles, your wallet, and other essentials. But here are a few more things you should make room for.

First, carry a spare key (A), preferably tucked into an inside pocket or somewhere else that it'll be hard to misplace. Next, a small pen-sized air-pressure gauge (B). One you can keep in your riding jacket is convenient, and if it's convenient, you'll use it. Another

item is a multitool or pocket knife (C), like the popular Leatherman or its competitors/knockoffs. It doesn't replace a proper tool kit, but can be a big help. A small pocket type flashlight (D) can make a big difference. Carry a penlight or an LED-type attached to your keychain for reading maps or nighttime repairs. Lastly, bikes can be loud, and wind noise even louder. If they're legal in your area, protect your hearing with earplugs (E).

39 CONSIDER THESE EXTRAS

A luggage rack or set of panniers can carry spare clothing, camping gear, fuel, tools, or whatever else you need on a long trip. Crash bars or frame sliders will help keep your bike from taking some nasty damage if you do end up taking a fall. Cold or rainy weather can mean frigid hands; heated grips will ward off the chill and give back control of your fingers. A reflective vest or similar clothing will improve your conspicuity, and more is always better here. For your passenger, a backrest will mean greater comfort on a long ride, for both them and for you, since they won't have to lean on you the whole time.

40 DRESS LIKE A RIDER

In the pages that follow, we'll go into the details of how to gear up from head to toe. Here are the basics. Essentially, you want to be protected from the elements and from the road, but have the flexibility to move.

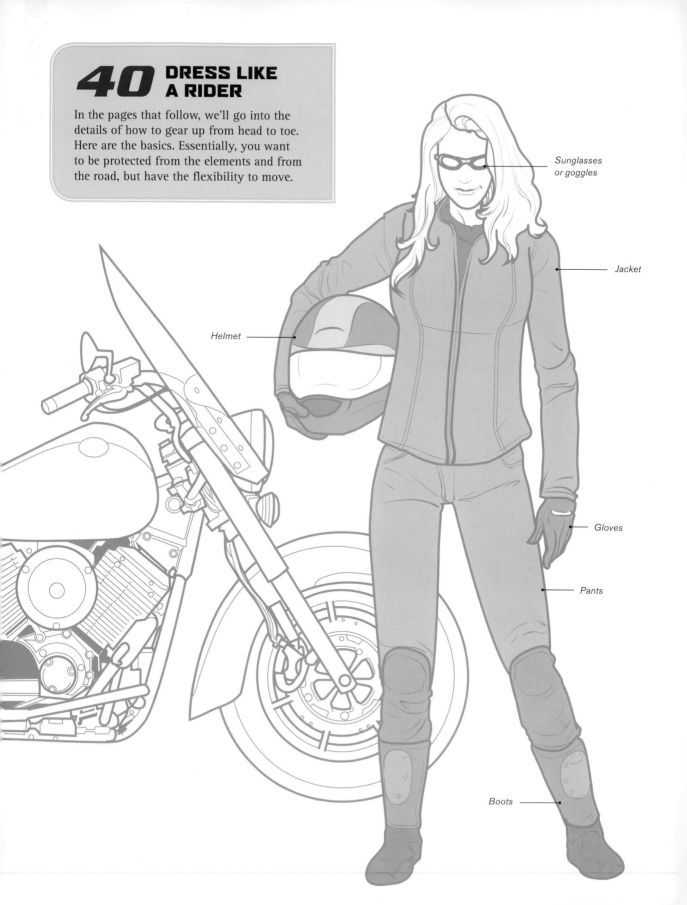

Sunglasses or goggles

Jacket

Helmet

Gloves

Pants

Boots

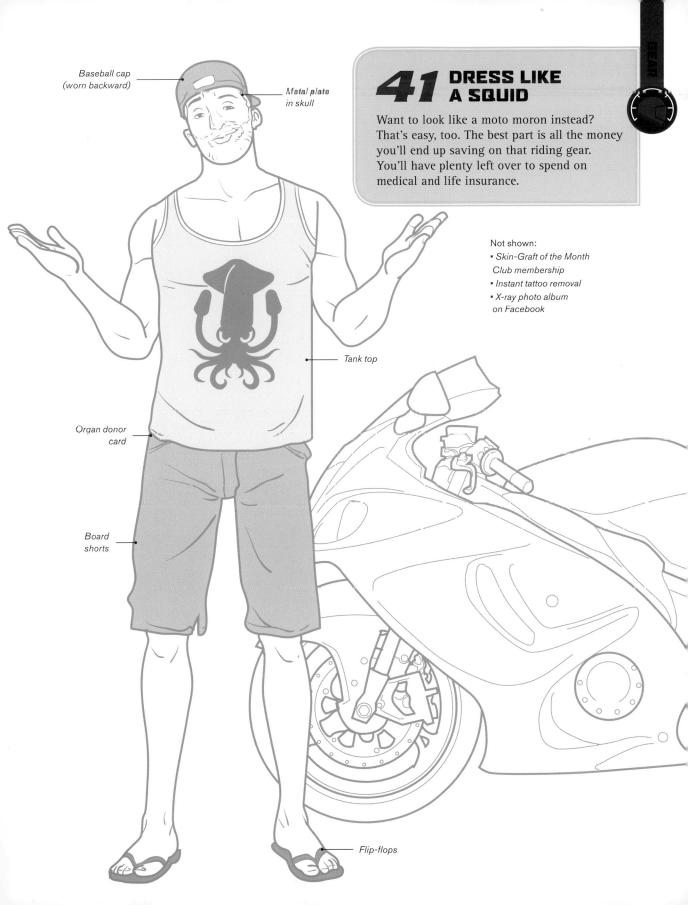

Baseball cap
(worn backward)

Metal plate
in skull

41 DRESS LIKE A SQUID

Want to look like a moto moron instead?
That's easy, too. The best part is all the money
you'll end up saving on that riding gear.
You'll have plenty left over to spend on
medical and life insurance.

Not shown:
- *Skin-Graft of the Month Club membership*
- *Instant tattoo removal*
- *X-ray photo album on Facebook*

Tank top

Organ donor
card

Board
shorts

Flip-flops

42 KNOW A JACKET'S SAFETY FEATURES

On- or off-road riders should look for jackets with the following features.

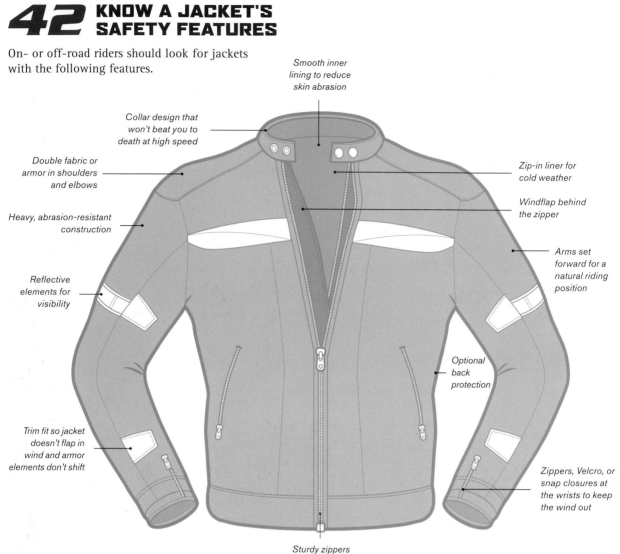

Smooth inner lining to reduce skin abrasion

Collar design that won't beat you to death at high speed

Double fabric or armor in shoulders and elbows

Heavy, abrasion-resistant construction

Reflective elements for visibility

Trim fit so jacket doesn't flap in wind and armor elements don't shift

Zip-in liner for cold weather

Windflap behind the zipper

Arms set forward for a natural riding position

Optional back protection

Zippers, Velcro, or snap closures at the wrists to keep the wind out

Sturdy zippers and stitching

43 GROW AN EXOSKELETON

The elements can take a serious toll on you while you ride. The proper protection can go a long way toward keeping you warm and safe, and if you should happen to take a spill, keep your skin where it belongs—on your body. Think of a jacket as a suit of armor and you're on the right track.

Sportbike and streetbike riders can choose between leather, which provides excellent abrasion protection, flexible comfort range, and is long-lasting; and textile, which is good for hot weather, and may be lighter and offer superior venting.

Dirtbike and adventure-bike riders usually prefer textile jackets, which tend to be a little longer than leather models. Look for one with plenty of ventilation, and a belt that lets you cinch up the waist. You want lots of pockets for all the extra gear a trail rider needs. Detachable sleeves for extra air are good in hot weather.

44 PUT ON THE RIGHT GLOVES

It's critical that your gloves fit correctly while you're holding on to a handgrip—pay particular attention to whether the thumb is long enough to fit right.

MATERIALS Leather is the number-one choice for versatility, protection, grip, and comfort. Look for carbon fiber or plastic armor in the knuckles and the heel of the palm. Thin gloves give less protection, but better control feel. Strap closures help keep the gloves on your hands in a crash. Deer- or elkskin stays supple after getting wet. Interior seams should be placed where they don't chafe. Going cheap? Hardware-store leather work gloves can be a good value, and if you have heated grips you can use thinner gloves.

VERSATILITY No one glove will do it all—you'll need at least two pair—one for warm weather, one for cold. Shorter gloves may be more comfortable in warm weather; long gauntlet-style gloves overlap jacket sleeves to keep wind out. You only need insulation on the back of the glove and fingers. Fabric panels on the sides of fingers and back add ventilation in warm weather. Choose long, thicker-insulated fabric gloves with leather palms for cold weather, and add a thin liner to increase your glove's warmth.

FIT Your gloves and your jacket need to work together, but your jacket is a bigger investment. Take your jacket with you when you're glove shopping, and make sure the jacket's sleeve and the glove's cuff don't fight against each other.

45 BOOT UP FOR SAFETY

At the very minimum, your boots need to be sturdy. Beyond that, you'll want to look at some specific characteristics depending on how (and what) you ride.

STREETBIKE RIDERS You have a pretty wide range of options, but leather construction is a must, as is over-the-ankle protection. Stay away from laces (they can get caught in your bike's mechanicals); zip-up boots are faster to get on and off, and are often more waterproof. Firm synthetic soles grip pavement well during stops, and let you push down on the footpegs with less discomfort. Heels should be wide and low, but with enough height to hook over the footpegs. The toe needs to fit under the shift lever comfortably. A shifter patch isn't a necessity, but adds to boot life where the shift lever rubs the top of the left shoe. Traditional black shows dirt less and shrugs off shifter scuffs.

DIRTBIKE RIDERS Look for specialized boots with plenty of plastic armor and epic ankle support. Steel or reinforced shanks are a must. A smoother sole lets you put your foot down in corners during flattrack-style slides. Stout shin protection defends against sticks and rocks. Ski-boot-style buckles (usually four) let you adjust fit quickly. Special grip panels on the left boot match the shift lever. An elastic top gasket keeps debris out. A separate inner bootie provides better fit and comfort.

ADVENTURE-BIKE RIDERS You'll want many of the same features as a dirt boot, but shorter and lighter; you need a boot that's more comfortable to walk in, too—get one with a sole that's more flexible and that offers more traction. It should be weatherproof as well—look for a Gore-Tex lined model.

ROADRACERS Specialized footwear takes you through severe lean angles—good race boots will offer replaceable plastic sliders on the outside of the boot toes.

46 GET THE RIGHT HELMET FOR YOU

When it comes to motorcycle helmets, plenty of riders get all wrapped around the axle discussing helmet laws. We're smart enough not to wade into that mess, but our opinion is that no matter what the law says, you gotta protect your coconut, and that means wearing a helmet.

FULL FACE

- Offers the most protection
- Quietest design
- Integrated faceshield for eye protection
- Trade-offs: Expensive, limited sensory input
- Heavier design can mean more neck fatigue

OFF-ROAD OR MOTOCROSS

- Open face port lets your wear goggles to protect your eyes from dust
- Chin bar for mouth/jaw protection
- Long visor for sun protection and to deflect branches
- Trade-offs: Visor catches wind at higher speeds

HYBRID

- Combines the best of full-face and off-road helmets; also called a "dual-sport" helmet
- Intended for on- and off-road use
- Wider peripheral vision and space to wear optional goggles
- Longer chin bar and added visor, like off-road helmets
- Trade-offs: Potential noise or visor wind-resistance issues

MODULAR

- Also known as a "flip-up" helmet
- Chin bar pivots to allow open-face configuration
- Safety of moveable chin bar not widely studied
- Some hybrids are fully functional as both full- and open-face
- Popular for motorcycle police and commuters, for ease of conversation and snacking

OPEN FACE

- Also known as ¾ (three-quarter) helmet
- Acceptable combination of head protection and freedom
- Plus: Puts you in touch with the elements
- Minus: Puts you in touch with the elements (you can add a face shield if you wish)

HALF HELMET

- Cool, light, inexpensive
- Minimal legal coverage—check your local laws
- Trade-offs: Low safety ratings; many counterfeit helmets on the market offer unacceptably low protection

47 KNOW YOUR HELMET'S ANATOMY

Just like your head, a helmet has plenty of parts that need to work together to protect your brain. These are the things to look for.

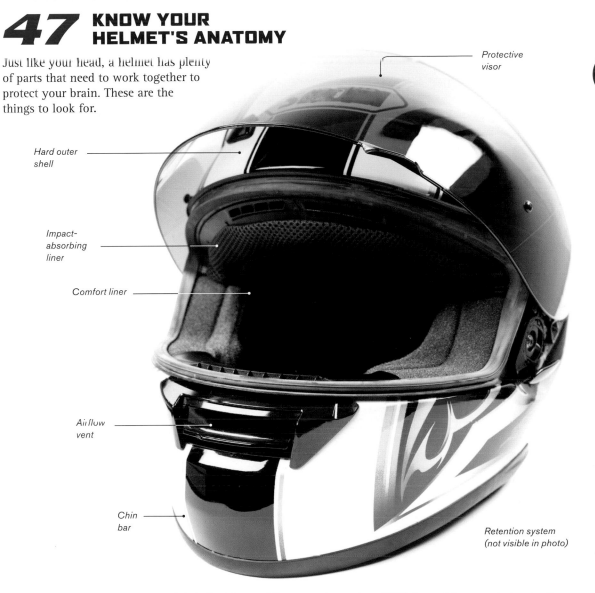

Protective visor

Hard outer shell

Impact-absorbing liner

Comfort liner

Airflow vent

Chin bar

Retention system (not visible in photo)

VISOR Shields face/eyes from sun/wind. Provides a mild level of crash protection. Helps reduce noise.

AIRFLOW VENTS The best designs feature vents in the chin bar, over the brow, and exhaust vents in the back. All of these should open and close.

CHIN BAR A chin bar with an inner liner not only stiffens overall helmet construction, it protects this vulnerable area.

HARD OUTER SHELL Plastic, Kevlar, fiberglass or carbon fiber can all do a good job. The shell helps prevent penetration and presents a smooth, non-snag surface.

IMPACT-ABSORBING LINER The one part of your helmet you typically don't see. Sandwiched between the tough outer shell and the soft inner liner, the expanded polystyrene/

polypropylene (EPS) foam deforms and absorbs the energy of a blow. Never reuse a helmet that's suffered a major blow: the liner is one-time-use only.

COMFORT LINER Some helmets feature removable liners you can launder; others let you add or remove padding to fine-tune fit.

RETENTION SYSTEM Usually a tough nylon strap and a pair of "D" rings. Use it every time.

 A quality helmet should display a sticker showing it's been tested. In the United States, DOT is acceptable; Snell is generally viewed as better. In Europe, look for an ECE-certified lid. When in doubt, go with a major brand and avoid buying any used helmet.

48 FIT IT RIGHT

No helmet should be uncomfortable, especially across the crown of your head or your brow—if it is, it's probably too small. A little tight in the cheeks is usually the sign of a good fit. Too loose and your helmet will lift at speed and flop around—neither is optional.

To try a helmet on, buckle it down, grab it with both hands, and see if you can push it around on your head. If you can, try another. Different brands fit differently, so keep trying until you find the perfect fit for you.

49 STRAP IT DOWN

Fastening a helmet with double D-rings can be confusing. Here's how to do it right. First, pass the strap through both rings from inside to outside (A) of the helmet. Separate the rings, grasp the strap's free end and pass it back through the inside ring only (B). Pull comfortably tight (C).

50 DON'T GO UNPLUGGED

Say "motorcycle noise" and most people think of loud exhaust pipes. But savvy riders know there's a much greater enemy—wind. Exposure to sound louder than 95 decibels (dB) can cause permanent hearing damage. Street riders on quiet bikes can expect wind roar to exceed 110dB even inside a good helmet; racers can expect 115 dB. Fifteen minutes of 110dB a day, five days a week (can you say commute?) can cause up to a 30-percent hearing loss within a year. Your options: never ride faster than you can walk, use earplugs, or face a future with one of those ear trumpets glued to the side of your head. Are earplugs legal? Consult your local authorities.

EARPLUGS

	FOAM	RUBBER	CUSTOM-MOLDED
PLUSES	• Inexpensive, especially if bought in bulk. • Available at any hardware store. • Soft enough to be comfortable under helmet. • Disposable.	• Good balance between price and quality of performance. • Readily available at any decent hardware store.	• Very effective, with up to 30dB sound reduction. • Most riders find them very comfortable.
MINUSES	• Depending on style, may fit well or not. • Effectiveness varies between models.	• Fit is very fussy. • Firmer models may be not be very comfortable under a helmet. • Need cleaning between uses.	• Expensive. • Need to be custom fit. • Need to be well cleaned after each wearing.

51 TUNE IN, RIDE ON

Portable audio gets better and better every year, and the iPod was a real revolution. Earbuds generally fit under a helmet with no trouble. But you don't want to just blast your Beethoven louder than the wind roar—that'll just make you go deaf faster. Better choice: A sports-style earbud that seals better and fits tighter. Best choice of all: An earplug with a built-in speaker.

Some touring bikes come with sound systems pre-installed, and some riders choose aftermarket sound systems. Don't want to go that route? Get a handlebar-mounted add-on speaker system that integrates with your iPod or other portable media player.

A note on safety: Music can make a good long ride even better for some, but it can also distract and insulate you from traffic. Beginning riders should just forget about the tunes and concentrate on riding instead. And every rider should check their local laws to make sure they don't end up singing the blues due to a big fat traffic citation.

52 MAINTAIN YOUR GEAR

Ever been in the Army? Or even seen a movie where a drill instructor yells at a recruit for having a dirty rifle? When it comes to motorcycling, you need to be your own drill instructor.

Maintaining your bike is a no-brainer—your safety depends on properly functioning brakes, properly inflated tires, correctly tensioned chain, and all the rest. But cleaning and maintaining the rest of your gear is just as important. A small tear can turn into a ruined garment when you're talking about a 60-mph (96-kph) wind flapping it to pieces.

The steps are simple, but important. First, air out your helmet after every ride, and store it in a dry place with plenty of air circulation where it won't get accidently knocked over. (Every blow the helmet absorbs is one fewer blow it can protect you from.) Next, turn your riding jacket inside-out after a hot day's ride. Finally, a little talcum powder in your gloves can freshen them in hot weather.

Never, ever, put leather items away wet, or dry them over artificial heat. Stuffing sleeves or pantlegs with towels or crumpled newspaper can help the garment retain its form while drying. For hard-finished leather, saddle soap is the external cleaner of choice. At least once a year, give your leather items a rubdown with a good leather treatment like Lexol or Pecard. Even Vaseline can help to restore suppleness. Retouch scuffed leather with shoe dye and shoe polish.

53
CLEAN YOUR HELMET

It's a hot summer afternoon, and you're sweating like a sinner on judgment day. When you get home you can jump in the shower and grab a cold drink, but what about your helmet? Just toss it in the closet and it'll start looking like a portable mushroom farm—and smell even worse. Here's the fix.

INTERIOR Use baby shampoo to gently clean the helmet's inner lining. You know the drill: lather, rinse, repeat. Stuff a towel up inside to get most of the water out, then let dry someplace with plenty of air circulation. Some helmets feature removable liners—they make cleaning easier, and dry fast.

EXTERIOR Mild detergent only—think dish soap—and a soft washcloth. If your lid's covered with dried bugs, wet down a cloth with warm water, drape it over the helmet's shell, and let it soften the crud for a few minutes. Most modern helmets feature tough clear-coat finishes, but you might as well top it off with a quick touch of some quality car wax.

FACE SHIELD Never use anything but warm water, mild soap, and a soft cotton washcloth, and always clean the shield under lots of running water to prevent scratches. It's easier if you've removed the shield from the helmet shell. Avoid glass cleaners or any product containing ammonia—they can lift the shield's anti-scratch coating. Pat dry, and be sure to store extra shields in a soft bag.

54 STAY WARM

It's hard to pick the right line when your teeth are chattering. Any warm body—including yours—loses heat through five mechanisms: radiation, respiration, conduction, convection, and perspiration. Here's how to combat them.

STAY DRY Water conducts heat about 200 times better than dry air; ergo, a wet rider is a cold rider. A rainsuit or Gore-Tex oversuit is the fix. Added bonus: Even in dry weather, a rainsuit adds plenty of warmth and wind protection.

GET BEHIND THE WINDSHIELD Choosing a bike with bodywork or a windscreen can add a lot of comfort. Consider adding a small aftermarket windscreen for chilly autumn or winter climates.

STAY PLUGGED IN Electric gloves, grips, vest, and even socks can turn you into a four-season rider. The best systems feature a quick-disconnect between you and the bike as well as a rheostat to control temperature. Make sure your bike's electrical system has enough juice to power it.

SEAL THE DEAL Air blowing up your sleeves or pantlegs can feel like an arctic blast. Pants and jackets that zip up tight are the answer. Even better: gloves and boots that overlap the gap and let those sleeves/legs tuck in.

WEAR A ONESIE One-piece overall-style riding suits eliminate the jacket-pants gap. Snowmobile suits are wind- and weather-resistant and offer good insulation. The best advice is to dress in layers, making it easy to adjust your temperature.

55 GET SOME HEAT ON THE CHEAP

If you're trying to save money (or if you spent it all on your bike and gear) there are plenty of ways to keep warm that won't break the bank.

Want to go old-school? Stuff your jacket with some crumpled newspaper. You can also use with a hot-water bottle (or the new school version, a CamelBak-style hydration bladder removed from its insulating sleeve) filled with hot water. Slip it inside your jacket and stay toasty for about an hour. Fill it with hot coffee to sip and you get warmth inside and out.

You can also try using a couple of those chemical hand and foot warmers used by hunters and skiers.

57 PLAY IT COOL

Those same five heat-loss mechanisms you may remember from item #54 (radiation, respiration, conduction, convection, and perspiration) can also work to cool you down in hot weather.

STAY COVERED Ever seen a picture of a Touareg tribesman in the Sahara? He's covered from head to foot. Only soon-to-be-broiled tourists go out wearing shorts and a T-shirt. Riding a bike through hot air is like standing in front of a blow dryer. Cover up, or you'll end up as beef jerky.

VENT YOUR ANGER Controlled airflow is your friend—especially through your helmet, gloves, and jacket. Look for clothing with vents you can zip open. Even better are nylon mesh jackets with removable cold weather liners.

HYDRATE YOUR CLOTHING Soak your clothes before you hit the road. And if you can't water down everything, then pay special attention to your neck. A damp bandana can make a big difference.

HYDRATE YOURSELF When your bike runs low on fluids, it seizes up. So do you. Your brain will shrink to the size of a pinto bean and start rattling around in your skull. Poor decisions immediately follow. The big get-off will follow soon after that.

TAKE FREQUENT BREAKS Need to wait for your buddies who are back down the trail flopping like carp and blowing bubbles? Find some shade, unzip your jacket, and take off your helmet.

56 COOL OFF WITH CHEAP TRICKS

Motorcycles don't come with air conditioners (yet!), but you can improvise your own. How? At your next gas stop, fill your pockets and daypack with ice. You don't need much, and you can often score enough for free out of the soft-drink vending machine. The ice itself is cold of course, and as it melts, the water evaporates and takes heat with it. Works best with synthetic jackets. Alternatively, take along some of those soft, refreezeable ice packs used in coolers and put them close to your hide under your jacket.

HOT/COLD PACK

58 GEAR UP FOR RAIN

Water conducts body heat much, much faster than air of the same temperature. You already know this: stand around on a 32° F (0° C) day and you'll be a little chilly; fall into lake water that temperature and your life is in danger. Motorcyclists have an additional problem: wind chill. The faster you move, the colder the wind will feel, even if you're dry. With the right gear the battle's half won. Here are the basics that you'll need to stay warm and dry.

HELMET Make it a full-face model. Riding through rain in an open-face helmet is like getting sandblasted. To keep the faceshield from fogging, open the vents, use an anti-fog treatment on the shield, or ride with the shield cracked open.

OVERBOOTS Leather boots alone can do a good job for short rainstorms. Zip-up boots are the best (laces are leak points), the taller the better. Plenty of boots offer Gore-Tex liners to keep water out. For real downpours, thin, stretchy rubber overboots are best—they're compact and easy to carry, 100-percent waterproof, and provide a good grip on wet pavement.

RAINSUIT One-piece designs are convenient and offer fewer places for water to get in. Two-piece designs often fit better, but the pants-jacket junction is a weak point. Favorite solution? A two-piece suit with bib pants that come up high on the chest, held up by suspender straps. Get a suit big enough to fit over your other gear—rainsuits themselves don't offer enough abrasion protection.

GLOVES Pro tip: keep water out by overlapping your gloves and sleeves. Still, even the best waterproof gloves don't hold up well to the demands of motorcycle riding. Augment them by wearing surgical gloves underneath, or covering them in nylon shells (for snowboarding or mountaineering). For light rain and shorter rides, motocross gloves are great.

59 GET WIRED FOR WARMTH

Who says motorcycles don't have heaters? Sure they do—as long as you have an electrical system. With the right gear, you don't have to bundle up like the Michelin Man to keep ahead of Mother Nature.

WARM YOUR CORE Electric vests (A) provide the most bang for your buck—if you can keep your torso warm, the rest of your body will follow. Look for a garment thin enough to fit under your existing jacket. Wear the vest close to your skin, and layer over it.

HEAT YOUR HANDS Electric gloves may seem like a great idea, but the heating elements tend to break down after being flexed repeatedly. Try heated grips (B) instead. They fit over your current grips like little electric blankets. Even better, try replacement grips that are hard-wired into your bike's electrical system. These will let you ride with thinner gloves, for more dexterity and control.

TURN IT UP (AND DOWN) Whichever options you choose, make sure your system includes a rheostat (C)—it's like a volume control for electrical current. For more convenience, hard-wire a quick-connect plug between your battery and the vest—that lets you jump on, plug in, and take off with less hassle. Just remember to unplug it before you get off your bike!

60 KEEP DRY FOR LESS

Here are a few substitutions for regulation raingear that are easy on the wallet and will keep you dry—if not exactly fashionable.

GROCERY BAGS If your boots aren't all that waterproof, tuck them into a plastic shopping or grocery bag and secure firmly with tape. Keep them wrapped close to avoid scorching and melting on your exhaust. You can also slip them around your footwear to more easily pull on a pair of rainproof overboots.

GARBAGE BAGS A large enough liner makes an acceptable poncho, albeit with that less-than-flashy hobo look. Cut holes for your arms and your head, and you're set.

DISHWASHING GLOVES Stretchy, durable, and definitely waterproof, these can cover your hands nearly up to the elbow. You might look like you should be hard at work over a kitchen sink, but it definitely beats wet, frozen fingers. Warm, dry ride? You're soaking in it!

1. AERO HUMP Purely optional: helps streamline the rider in a full-tuck down the straightaway. Off the bike, it just makes you look like Quasimodo.

2. SPINE PROTECTOR Some riders prefer the convenience of a built-in spine protector, while others prefer a strap-on type worn under the suit.

3. ARMOR/PADDING This is the biggest breakthrough in suits— strategically placed padding and hard-plastic armor. A necessity in the elbows, knees, and shoulders; nice to have in the hips as well. European suits often carry CE certification.

4. FORWARD-SET SLEEVES The best racing leathers are cut to fit you on the bike. But, the design makes them comical and uncomfortable off the bike. Setting the sleeves about 19 degrees forward into the torso makes the suit fit better when you're reaching for the handlebars.

5. ZIPPERS Metal may seem like old tech, but it survives well in a crash. Have you ever seen what happens when a zipper fails at 130 mph? It's not a pretty sight.

6. CUSTOM LETTERING Purely optional, but if you're a professional, expect to have your name and major sponsors at least.

7. KNEE PUCKS Velcro patches on the knees let racers attach hard plastic pucks so they can drag their knees when hanging off in turns.

8. STRETCH PANELS Nylon or Kevlar stretch panels aren't the sign of a cheap suit—they help make it cooler and ensure a better fit. Look for them placed behind the knees, under the arms, and in the leg/groin inseam— areas where direct road abrasion is seldom an issue.

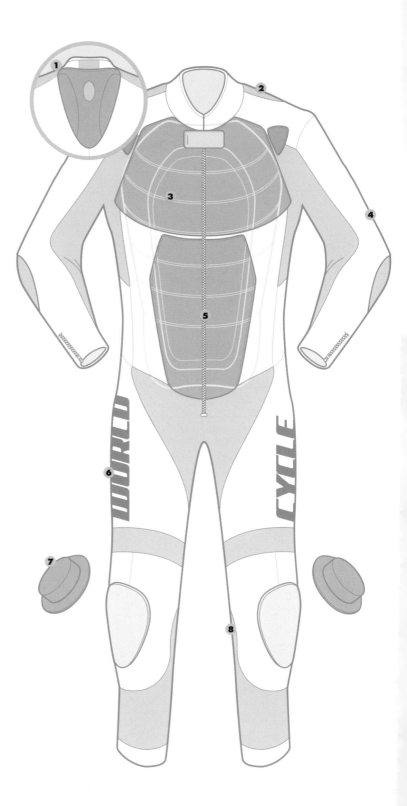

62 PICK YOUR BASIC DIRTBIKE GEAR

If leather is the road racer's best bet, nylon is the best stuff for off-road riders. Light, tough, and easy to get clean, it's also easy to find in just about every moto shop. The gear worn by most off-road racers will also serve the casual playbike rider or the weekend dual-sport enthusiast.

BOOTS Specialized motocross boots come up high on the leg and use buckles to close up tight. Normal construction-work or hiking boots aren't an adequate substitute—motocross boots offer superior shin and ankle protection, and their smoother soles won't grab if you need to put your foot down for balance in a turn. They also help keep mud and water out during stream crossings.

PANTS Look for a pair of riding pants that offer you high-quality stitching and a good fit. Synthetic leather patches on the inside of the knees cut down on wear and enhance grip. You should wear knee braces, so make sure the pants are big enough to fit over them. Do the pants go inside or outside the boots? That's a matter of fashion more than function.

JERSEY Nylon or polyester, pullover, long-sleeved. On a cold day, consider doubling up.

GLOVES Modern off-road gloves are made from synthetic leather and fabric, and feature some form of padding or hard-plastic protection over the backs of the knuckles. You definitely want this.

HELMET The large face port accommodates your goggles, while the long visor is able to deflect brush and shade your eyes.

63 THE INSIDE LINE
LE MANS

NUMBER OF TURNS: **11**

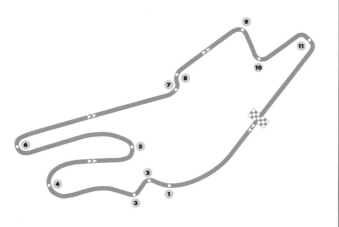

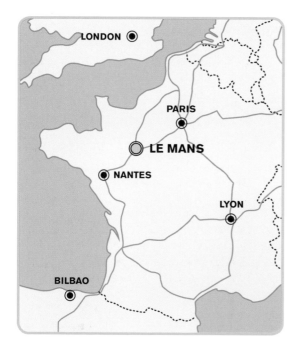

FAST FACTS

OFFICIAL NAME Bugatti Circuit des 24 Heures

LOCATION Pays de la Loire, France, south of Le Mans

TRACK LENGTH 2.564 mi (4.143 km)

DATE OPENED 1966

FAMOUS FEATURE Dunlop Bridge, between turns three and four. This tire-shaped arch is one of the most iconic pieces of track architecture/advertisement ever. Dunlop has put advertising on other footbridges, but this is the original.

TRIVIA Named after auto designer Ettore Bugatti, the Le Mans Bugatti Circuit is a subset of a much larger track, the Le Mans Circuit des 24 Heures (also called the Circuit de la Sarthe), which is used for auto endurance racing.

Although mostly purpose-built as a separate track, the Bugatti Circuit shares part of its length with the larger Le Mans Circuit, from the Ford Chicane at the end of the lap before the Raccordement turn, through the pit complex, the Dunlop Curve and Dunlop Chicane (a left-right dogleg added in 1987), and the straightaway leading under the Dunlop Bridge (before the La Chapelle turn).

This track is also used for the 24 Rollers, a 24-hour race with the participants on rollerskates.

64 PLAY DIRTY, STAY SAFE

Yes, your helmet, gloves, and jacket provide a measure of protection. But when you're out in the dirt, they're not enough to keep you safe and sound. Here are some additional protective essentials.

CHEST PROTECTOR Vented-plastic construction not only helps deflect rocks when your buddies roost you, but can add a degree of protection if you tip over or hit a wire strung across the road.

GOGGLES Goggles are necessary to protect your eyes from stones and dust. (No, your streetbike faceshield won't do the job.) In really dusty conditions, spread a little baby oil on your goggles' foam to help trap dust just like an air filter. If you wear eyeglasses, get a pair of goggles that fit over them, or consider a custom corrective-lens insert.

KIDNEY BELT Helps protect your internal organs from the jolts of off-road riding. Wide Velcro and elastic construction does the job; plastic armor over the kidney area adds impact protection.

OTHER ARMOR Elbow guards fit under a jacket, but are awkward if you're just riding in a jersey.

KNEE BRACES The best-designed braces will help prevent your getting a knee injury from twisting or overextension. At the very least, get a hard plastic padded kneecup to protect from impact.

65 GET THE (CAM) SHAFT

In almost every bike spec chart, you'll see something describing camshaft layout, and sometimes it looks like gibberish. SOHC, DOHC—what's it all mean?

First, the basics: virtually every four-stroke internal-combustion engine has a camshaft. Its job is to open and close the engine's intake and exhaust valves—like a person inhaling and exhaling. The cam can be in two locations: inboard or over-head.

Inboard cams (seen in Harley-Davidsons and old Triumph Twins) need to reach up to the valves with a system of pushrods and rocker arms, all of which reciprocate back and forth. That's a lot of metal thrashing around, and it means such engines can't rev as high, and consequently produce less power.

Overhead camshafts eliminate most of these extra parts by putting the cam(s) directly over the valves in the cylinder head. The vast majority of modern motorcycle engines and more and more automotive engines use this design.

SOHC stands for single over-head cam, and it means one shaft (via rockers) opens both the intake and exhaust valves. DOHC is double over-head cam, and means one shaft operates the intake valves while a second controls the exhausts.

DOHC designs allow the highest engine revs, and are typically seen in sportbikes. But they also often complicate valve-adjustment procedures.

SOHC designs allow high-speed engine operation, although not as high as DOHC. (The number of valves per cylinder and their individual weights influence this as well.) But an SOHC layout is often easier to service when it comes time for a valve adjustment.

Do you really need to know all of this just to ride?

Maybe not. But it'll sure help you seem like less of a doofus when you're talking to those salesman, or to the guy sitting next to you at a biker bar.

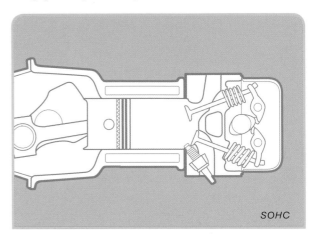

SOHC

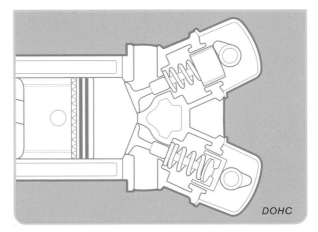

DOHC

66 DON'T MIX YOUR STROKES

Two-strokes and four-strokes are engine types. The "two" and "four" have nothing to do with the number of cylinders in an engine, but refer to how many times an engine's piston(s) travel during a complete power cycle. What's the bottom line? Basically, two-strokes are light, simple, and typically powerful, but pollution issues have reduced their numbers. They also require that you mix gasoline and oil together.

Four-strokes are much more like the engine in your car. They're heavier, but because of this, offer broader powerbands.

Today most motorcycle engines are four-strokes, while some scooter engines and small dirtbike engines are two-strokes. Either one will get the job done, but for the new rider, the four-stroke wins, if for no other reason than you'll have more choices.

67 GO FULL-AUTO

Over 90 percent of all cars sold in the United States have automatic transmissions, but few motorcycles do. That's changing now, especially with the rising popularity of "manumatic" (manual-automatic) transmissions, which you shift by simply pushing a button, instead of pulling in a clutch lever by hand and then pushing a shifter with your foot. Some motorcyclists resist them, saying they remove the joy of shifting from the ride. Not us. The current level of technology is very good and bound to get better. For urban commuters or casual riders, they're already a fine option. Here's what's out there now.

NO-SHIFT AUTOMATICS These transmissions are also known as CVTs (Continuously Variable Transmissions), are popular in scooters, and they're even simpler than the automatic in your car. There's no shift lever at all—not even for neutral or reverse. You just twist the throttle and go.

DUAL-CLUTCH MANUMATICS
Built with two clutches for odd and even gear sets, and allow the user to operate in automatic mode or shift manually. Advantages include a rugged internal design (compared with the conventional automatics in cars), genuine compression braking, and stall-proof operation. They can also offer excellent fuel economy. The biggest advantages are ease of use and convenience. You can also ride around with a cup of coffee or a giant cigar in your left hand (not advised).

CENTRIFUGAL-CLUTCH DESIGNS Not true automatics— you still need to shift them with your foot—but there's no handlebar-mounted clutch lever. Once popular on small motorcycles like the Honda Cub, now they're mostly found on all-terrain vehicles and some entry-level 50-70cc dirtbikes. Still, if you ever rent a scooter in Vietnam or Thailand, this is probably what you'll be riding.

68 SIZE IT UP

Confused? Don't be here are the basics.

- Beginners should choose by engine and chassis size first, and seldom need a machine larger than 500cc. They will also be well-served by a Single or a Twin, thanks to those bikes having user-friendly powerbands.

- Serious dirtbikes are almost always Singles. Big adventure-touring bikes (750cc or larger) are Twins or Triples. A four in the dirt is ill-advised.

- More cylinders equals a smoother ride, which is important for long trips.

69 GET SUSPENDED

The job of any suspension is to keep the bumps in the road or trail from upsetting the motorcycle's chassis, and to keep the tires in contact with the surface. Here are some terms you're likely to hear.

TRAVEL This is the measurement of how much a wheel moves up and down. Dirtbikes require lots of travel—up to 12 inches (30 cm) at both the front and rear—to deal with jumps, rocks, and ruts. Cruisers often have the least travel—as little as 3 inches (8 cm).

SPRING Most modern motorcycles use coil springs. The rear spring (or springs) is usually easy to see; the front springs are almost always concealed inside the fork tubes. The spring's strength is called spring weight; switching to a lighter or heavier weight can make your ride softer or stiffer.

RISING RATE Some suspensions, especially those using a single rear shock, get stiffer and stiffer the more the suspension compresses. That's called rising rate. On dirtbikes especially, this helps prevent bottoming over large bumps while still allowing for a plush ride over smaller ones.

PRELOAD Most motorcycle rear suspensions (and some front as well) push on the spring when the motorcycle is at rest—preloading it, which affects the ride height of the motorcycle, allowing it to carry widely varying loads. Increasing preload can be useful if you're carrying the extra weight of a passenger; racers use it to fine-tune a bike's attitude on the track.

BOTTOMING When a suspension deflects to its maximum travel, it's said to be bottomed out. If your bike bottoms regularly, you need a stiffer spring, a new shock, or to get your head out of the pasta at your local all-you-can-eat buffet.

UNSPRUNG WEIGHT The mass of your bike that isn't directly supported by the suspension springs: i.e., the wheels, tires, and brake discs. Less unsprung weight means your bike's wheels will better follow the contours of the road.

HARDTAIL A motorcycle with no rear suspension. Favored by chopper stylists for its purity of line; beloved by chiropractors and proctologists for providing a robust patient base.

70 GET TO THE BOTTOM OF WHEELBASE

Wheelbase is one of those things that seems obvious but . . . isn't. It's just the distance from the front wheel to the rear, right? Wrong.

Wheelbase is the distance from the point where the front wheel touches the ground to the point where the rear wheel touches the ground. You might visualize wheelbase more easily as the distance from the center of the front wheel to the center of the rear wheel.

Touring bikes and cruisers tend to have longer wheelbases, while sportbikes are much shorter. They are built this way because bikes with longer wheelbases tend to be more directionally stable, while those with shorter wheelbases tend to be more responsive to steering input. A dragster (or drag bike) is the perfect illustration: the extraordinarily long wheelbase helps keep it running in a straight line.

A long wheelbase makes a bike less wheelie-prone, and because the rider sits farther from each wheel, he gets a smoother ride. But for any given speed, a rider will need to lean a long-wheelbase bike further into a

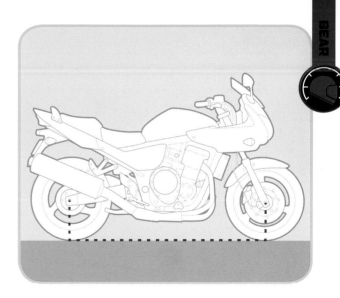

turn—another reason roadrace machines tend toward shorter wheelbases.

Adjusting your bike's chain may alter your wheelbase by up to an inch (2.5 cm) as well—something many riders won't notice.

71 UNDERSTAND RAKE AND TRAIL

Spec charts sometimes quote rake and trail numbers for a motorcycle chassis, but what does this mean? If you ask, you feel like you're getting sent on some sort of snipe hunt. Not to worry—we're here to help. And the concepts, while abstract, make perfect sense when you see them.

Rake (also called caster) is the angle of a motorcycle's steering head of the frame (A). Choppers have a lot of rake—their forks stick way out in front. Sportbikes have much less—their forks are closer to vertical. A typical sportbike might have a rake as steep as 25 degrees, while a chopper may be closer to 45 degrees. A touring bike is typically at around 29 degrees and a cruiser at 32.

More rake does two things: one, it makes the wheelbase longer, and two, it generally increases a motorcycle's trail.

Trail (B) is measured in distance (inches or millimeters) between the point of the front wheel's contact with the ground and a line drawn through the axis of the steering head.

Under normal operation, this contact point is always some distance behind the projected line—somewhere between 2 and 4 inches (5–10 cm). Think of it as how far the contact patch trails behind the steering axis. Too much trail makes a motorcycle difficult to turn; too little makes it unstable.

Comparing the rake and trail numbers for different motorcycles

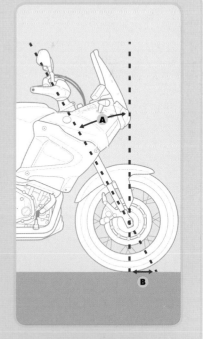

may give you some idea of how they're going to handle, even if you've never ridden them.

72 READ A DYNO CHART

A dyno chart is a two-dimensional representation of an engine's horsepower and torque over the engine's speed range, as measured by a device called a dynamometer. Most dynamometers either connect to the bike's countershaft sprocket, or use a roller that bears against the rear tire (sometimes called chassis dynamometers).

Torque is a moment of force, acting at a distance, trying to rotate something. When you're trying to twist the cap off a jar of pickles, you're applying torque, whether the cap gives way or not—no movement is involved.

Horsepower is a measurement of actual work done in a given time. It was originally stated as the force needed to move 550 pounds one foot in one second, or 33,000 pounds one foot in one minute. *Cycle World*'s dyno charts are calibrated in horsepower and pounds/feet of torque; countries using the metric system use kilowatts or PS rather than horsepower and newton-meters for torque. While the units of measure change, the fundamentals remain the same: you're trying to use

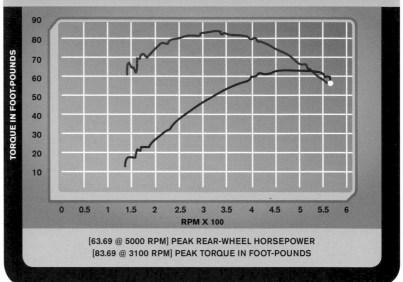

2011 HARLEY-DAVIDSON BLACKLINE FXS

TORQUE IN FOOT-POUNDS

RPM X 100

[63.69 @ 5000 RPM] PEAK REAR-WHEEL HORSEPOWER
[83.69 @ 3100 RPM] PEAK TORQUE IN FOOT-POUNDS

these lines on a chart to understand an engine's output.

Power = force x distance ÷ time. In any measurement of distance and time, like a bike's quarter-mile (400 m) times and top speeds, horsepower is going to be the determining factor.

But we don't ride our bikes at peak power or peak torque all of the time. What we need to do is look at the shape of a bike's horsepower and torque curves, and

that's where a dyno chart is invaluable. To quote *Cycle World*'s own Paul Dean: "Flat torque curves and wide powerbands make for great street motors; steep torque curves and narrow powerbands are usually best suited for racing."

Or, just shade in the areas under a bike's torque and power curves with pencil. The more total shaded real estate under them, the more likely you'll enjoy the ride.

73 GET ON THE (POWER) BAND WAGON

Dyno charts show how much torque your engine puts out at a given rpm. That curve keeps increasing before reaching maximum, then shows diminishing returns. The highest area of the curve, wide or narrow, is where the engine works most efficiently—it's called a powerband for that reason.

Your engine provides the same power, and the same actual powerband, no matter what gear you're in. The transmission influences how it is expressed to the rider. At your engine's lowest gear, the transmission provides the highest mechanical advantage, and thus

the widest apparent powerband. That's good for acceleration—race performance, riding uphill, and getting out of trouble. But at higher gears, you don't need much torque to keep moving, as Newton's first law will tell you. The apparent powerbands may seem narrower, but the higher gears will make your bike happier and less frantic at higher speeds.

When you're shopping for a bike, consider not just the engine's horsepower, but also the transmission that influences the powerband. It's all about striking a balance between power and user-friendliness.

MOTEGI

NUMBER OF TURNS: **14**

FAST FACTS

OFFICIAL NAME Twin Ring Motegi

LOCATION Haga District, Tochigi Prefecture, Japan, east of Motegi

TRACK LENGTH 2.983 mi (4.801 km)

DATE OPENED 1997

FAMOUS FEATURE Motegi's unique twin-track layout means that the road course (the one used for motorcycle racing) crosses under the oval course twice: once between turns 4 and 5, and again between turns 11 and 12.

TRIVIA Motegi gets its name from the two ("twin") track sets—the oval Super Speedway and the twisting Road Course—and the circular "ring" layout.

The Super Speedway, an American-style 1.5-mile (2.4-km) oval, has been used by the Indy Car series, while the Road Course is European in styling, and used much more often. Several major racing events take place at Motegi, including the MFJ Superbike race and MotoGP.

The two tracks can run separate events concurrently; better still, by opening roadways between turns 2 and 13, and 12 and 3, the Road Course can also be divided into two smaller tracks for junior events—an 11-turn East Road Course, and a 6-turn West Road Course.

Aside from its real-world fandom, Motegi has featured in a number of racing video games, and was part of the opening credits for the Japanese TV show *Kamen Rider Agito*.

75 TRIANGULATE YOURSELF

What's the first thing riders do when they walk into a dealership or a bike show? Swing a leg over the saddle, sit down, and reach for the handlebar. Then they usually issue an insightful pronouncement along the lines of "I'm in love," "this sucks," or something in between. In other words, they've done a complete road test in ten seconds!

What our erstwhile experts have just experienced is the rider triangle—next to seat height and flashy paint job, it's probably the most influential criteria of any motorcycle purchase.

The triangle is nothing more than the three points where your carcass makes contact with the machine: your hands (on the bar), your feet (on the footpegs) and your posterior (on the seat).

There's no industry standard for giving the triangle a value, but the next time you sit on a bike, pay particular attention to these three relationships and not

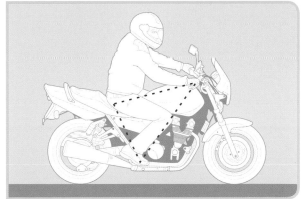

just an overall feel. And most important, remember this: Motorcycles are dynamic vehicles, designed to work in motion. What feels comfortable sitting on a dealer's floor doesn't necessarily work when a bike's going down the highway at 60 mph (96 kph)—if it did, we'd all be riding two-wheeled Naugahyde recliners with built-in drink holders.

RIDING

YOU CAN BUY A PIANO, BUT IT DOESN'T MAKE YOU A MUSICIAN.

In the same way, merely owning a motorcycle, helmet and gloves hardly makes you into a proficient rider.

Motorcyclists have a tough job of it too: In a car or an airplane you can have an instructor sit next to you. Motorcycles? So often instead you get something more along the lines of, "Here are the keys. Good luck."

Riding well is not just about climbing on and holding the handlebars. It involves all your senses, both hands, and both feet. It's about the way you sit on the bike, and how you move your body. It's about learning how to read the road or trail surface, or the flow of traffic. Windy, rainy, or hot or cold, you'll be in very intimate contact with the elements. And while those variables are some of the reasons riding is such a challenge, they also contribute immensely to its rewards.

We'll try to show you a few tips in this chapter, but your learning certainly shouldn't stop here. Don't be shy about asking other riders how they handle various situations. Think about taking a special riding school—track days for sportbikes, and dirt-skills-specific schools for dirtbikes. Riding well doesn't just mean riding fast—it means riding safely, and riding aware. The best riders are almost always the smoothest; speed—if you're after it—is a natural result of that efficiency.

76 HAVE A BIKER FILM FESTIVAL

Hollywood loves bikes as much as it loves flashy pyrotechnics, complicated romances, and blondes with extensive cosmetic surgery. So it should be no surprise that Tinseltown has produced some epic motorbike movies and shows. When it's too cold to ride, or your engine is in pieces on the shop floor, put on one of these classics, kick back, and enjoy the next best thing.

THE WILD ONE (1953) Marlon Brando and Lee Marvin. Triumph and Harley. Turned off a generation and put the hook into another.

EASY RIDER (1960) Nothing says the '60s, experimental cinema, and choppers like this classic.

THE GREAT ESCAPE (1963) Steve McQueen (Bud Ekins, actually) and that epic jump for freedom—the bike is the perfect metaphor. Even a crash can be cool!

HELLS ANGELS ON WHEELS (1967, with Jack Nicholson) One of many painfully camp bikesploitation flicks from the '60s.

THEN CAME BRONSON (American TV series, 1969–1970) One man goes looking for the meaning of life on a Harley-Davidson Sportster.

ON ANY SUNDAY (1971) Bruce Brown's epic probably did more to put an entire generation on two wheels than anything else. To this day it'll bring a tear to your eye and make you want to go riding.

ELECTRA GLIDE IN BLUE (1973) One of the few mainstream movies ever named for a bike, it follows the travails of a groovy yet doomed motorcycle cop (and his Harley Electra Glide, in Arizona Highway Patrol blue, of course).

MAD MAX (1979) In future post-apocalyptic Australia, a highway patrolman (played by then-unknown Mel Gibson) defends civilization from rampaging biker gangs.

V-FOUR VICTORY (1983) One lap around the Isle of Man with the legendary Joey Dunlop. Even though it's getting a little long in the tooth, streetbike riders and road racers will reach for a strong drink after watching it. Whatta rush.

FASTER (2003) A peek behind the curtain of MotoGP life. Even non-enthusiasts will appreciate the drama between Valentino Rossi and Max Biaggi.

77 READ UP ON RIDING

Crack open one of these books and enjoy writings and reflections on riding, racing and track culture, biker lifestyle, understanding your bike, and much more.

HELL'S ANGELS
Hunter S. Thompson, 1966
The original Gonzo journalist spent a year with America's most famous outlaw biker gang.

OGRI
Paul Sample, 1970s to present
British cartoonist Sample documents the adventures of Ogri, a scruffy biker with a heart of gold.

ZEN AND THE ART OF MOTORCYCLE MAINTENANCE
Robert Pirsig, 1974
Part philosophical musings, part road diary, all 1970s groovy.

JUPITER'S TRAVELS
Ted Simon, 1979
The story of an epic four-year journey around the world by bike.

A TWIST OF THE WRIST
Keith Code, 1983
This book may be 30 years old, but the basic riding hints still hold true.

BIKES OF BURDEN
Hans Kemp, 2005
Dutch photographer Kemp shoots beautiful photos of the developing world's working bikes.

MOTO MANIA
Holger Aue, 2012
These German-language comics are widely beloved for their tales of a group of wacky bikers.

MOTOCOURSE
MotoGP, annual
The annual grand prix and Superbike yearbook is packed with amazing photos and insider facts.

LONG WAY ROUND/LONG WAY DOWN (Television documentary series, 2004/2007) Ewan McGregor and Charley Boorman go on the adventure-bike ride(s) of a lifetime.

WORLD'S FASTEST INDIAN (2005) Anthony Hopkins stars in a biopic of Kiwi motorcycle legend Burt Munro. The story of a 69-year-old racer and his highly modified 47-year-old Indian, seeking one last world speed record.

DUST TO GLORY (2005) A cinematic celebration of the epic Baja 1000 race.

78 PLAY 10 CLASSIC MOTORCYCLE TUNES

Purists want to hear nothing more than the sound of their engines. For everyone else, these great songs will come in at a close second. Crank them up and hit the road.

HARLEY-DAVIDSON *(French)*
—*Brigitte Bardot* (1968)

MOTORCYCLE SONG ("I DON'T WANT A PICKLE")
—*Arlo Guthrie* (1972)

BORN TO BE WILD
—*Steppenwolf* (1969)

LITTLE HONDA
—*The Hondells* (1964)

LEADER OF THE PACK
—*The Shangri-Las* (1964)

1952 VINCENT BLACK LIGHTNING
—*Richard Thompson* (1991)

JOHNNY VALENTINE
—*Andy Anderson* (1958)

HARLEY-DAVIDSON BLUES
—*Canned Heat* (1972)

ROLL ME AWAY
—*Bob Seger* (1983)

BLACK DENIM TROUSERS
—*Vaughn Monroe* (1955)

79 BREAK IN AN ENGINE

From "ride it like you stole it" to "you can ruin your engine in the first hour if you're not careful," you'll hear more superstition and voodoo around engine break-in protocol than about virtually any other aspect of motorcycle ownership.

Most riders want their engine to have a long life, produce good power, and not burn oil. Here's what to do to make sure that happens.

MIX IT UP Avoid operating it at droning, constant rpm for the first several hundred miles or kilometers. Speed up, slow down, repeat—this exercise creates both positive and negative pressure in the combustion chamber and especially on the rings. The alternating forces help create good ring seal, which in turn boosts power and cuts down on oil consumption.

EASE INTO REVS Don't over-rev the engine, but don't under-rev it either. Taking it up to 50 percent of redline for the first 50 miles (80 km), and then up to 75 percent for the next several hundred is a good rule of thumb. Practice this in turn with the alternate on/off power and load technique we've discussed.

KEEP IT UP Never neglect the need for routine maintenance. Many bikes call for an initial inspection after 600 miles (965 km): adjusting the chain, setting the valves, changing the oil. Do it—especially the oil and filter. Oil isn't like wine or scotch—it doesn't get better with age. In those first few hours of operation, your engine is producing tiny metal shavings as the parts wear in, and all that metal ends up in your oil and filter. Pull the plug and get that junk out of there.

81 PERFORM A PRE-RIDE CHECK

Pilots perform a walk-around (a visual and mechanical inspection of the aircraft) every time they fly. You should as well—it's called a pre-ride check, it'll take just a minute, and it might save your life. Here's what to look for.

☐ **TIRES** Check visually first, looking for excessive damage, wear, or nails in treads or sidewalls; check pressure with a gauge at least weekly.

☐ **RIMS** Especially on dirtbikes and dual-sports, inspect the spokes to make sure none are broken. Run a wrench or screwdriver over the spokes—this will emit a tone, and a loose spoke will sound different.

☐ **LEAKS** Your bike shouldn't be leaking oil, coolant, fuel, or brake fluid.

☐ **THROTTLE** It should operate smoothly, without binding, and fully close under its own power.

☐ **BRAKES** Pull the brake lever and depress the pedal to check that the brakes are operating as they should.

☐ **LIGHTS** Make sure the brake, taillight, headlight, and indicators work right.

☐ **ENGINE OIL** Check the oil level and add more if necessary.

☐ **FUEL LEVEL** Obviously.

☐ **DRIVE CHAIN** Check condition, tension, and lubrication.

☐ **CLUTCH** Check for smooth operation.

☐ **CABLES** Check for loose control cables.

☐ **NUTS AND BOLTS** See if anything has vibrated loose or fallen off, especially before and after dirtbike rides. Give a light tug with a wrench on any known problem nuts and bolts, especially the ones located in the exhaust system.

80 LEARN FROM EVERY RIDE

The first key to learning is to do something different. If you normally ride city streets, try riding in the canyons. Or in the dirt. Or in another country.

And even that five-day-a-week commute is an opportunity to hone your skills. On Monday, practice your braking. Tuesdays, look farther ahead. Wednesdays, concentrate on your footwork, weighting the pegs in turns. Thursdays, practice smoothness. Fridays, countersteering. And on the weekend, put it all together.

An athlete does pushups and situps not to become pushup champion, but to become more fit overall. Think of your riding the same way.

82 BECOME A BETTER RIDER IN 12 STEPS

PAY ATTENTION Thoughts drifting as you ride? Park the bike, get a cup of coffee and get your mind right.

RIDE A DIRTBIKE Nothing teaches you about traction and body positioning like a dirtbike. You'll also learn what to do when you encounter water or sand on paved roads.

RIDE BEHIND A BETTER RIDER Think you're good? Riding with someone better will show you just how much you can still learn.

COMPETE Nobody wants to finish last. Competition at any level makes you focus and try harder, even if you never make it to the podium.

LOOK FARTHER When we get lazy or tired, we look only a short distance in front of the bike. Lift your chin and look ahead. In turns, look where you want to go: through the turn, not just into the entrance.

SIT RIGHT Motorcycles are dynamic vehicles; your body position makes a tremendous difference in how they respond. Riding like a couch potato doesn't help.

ADJUST YOUR CONTROLS Always check your controls, handlebars, and footpegs.

CLEAN AND MAINTAIN YOUR RIDE As you clean your bike, you can spot problems. And doing your own maintenance makes you more aware of your machine's overall condition.

RIDE IN THE RAIN Riding well in the rain makes you focus on traction, lean angle, steering input, braking, and overall smoothness.

RIDE ANOTHER BIKE It's easy to get complacent when riding the same bike daily. A new machine makes you sharpen your focus and keeps you learning.

BE SMOOTH Pick a day of the week and forget about everything else but being smooth. It'll make you anticipate the road or trail and all of your inputs, and that builds awareness.

BRAKE HARD Don't wait for a panic stop to practice this one. In a safe area, practice hard stops using both the front and rear brakes.

83 KNOW YOUR TRANSMISSION

The best way to understand how your motorcycle's transmission works is to ride a bicycle. Why? Because on a bicycle, you're the engine, and you feel how the load on the engine changes as you shift gears.

Motorcycle transmissions (the most common manual-shift kind) use pairs of gears moving laterally on a pair of shafts to change the ratios between the engine and the rear wheel. Pushing the foot-shift lever pushes or pulls these gear pairs into or out of engagement. Here are some of the principal parts, and what they do.

PRIMARY DRIVE Power from the engine's crankshaft flows into the engine through these gears or chain.

CLUTCH Couples or uncouples engine power to input shaft.

SHIFT LEVER Used to change gears.

SHIFT DRUM Converts the up-and-down motion of the gear shifter to the shift fork's horizontal motion.

SHIFT FORK Moves gear pairs into and out of engagement horizontally on shafts.

INPUT SHAFT Power flows through this shaft to a selected gear pair and then out through the countershaft.

GEARS Multiply force from the engine.

DOGS Gear pairs slide laterally on their shaft, and the dogs connect adjacent gear pairs.

OUTPUT OR COUNTERSHAFT The power-out shaft.

FINAL-DRIVE Connects the transmission to the rear wheel. Usually a chain, but can also be a driveshaft.

84 SHIFT WITHOUT THE CLUTCH

Sacrilege you say? Maybe if you're driving your Aunt Averna's econobox or your boss's Ferrari. But not with modern sportbikes and dirtbikes. Here's how it's done.

Upshifting is easiest, and it gets easier the higher the gear pairings are. So if you want to practice, start with fifth-to-sixth, and then fourth-to-fifth. Because of the wide ratio jump from first to second, use the clutch for that shift, but after that it's fair game. It's also easier at higher rpm.

You'll want to pre-load the shift lever a little by slipping your toe under and applying a bit of pressure. When you reach your shift point, back off the throttle with a flick of your wrist while snapping the shifter up. Once the shifter moves up, quickly re-open the throttle.

Once you've mastered upshifting, you can downshift the same way. This is rare on streetbikes, but useful on a dirtbike. Again, start at higher rpm and the upper gears, and avoid the 2–1 downshift.

85 KNOW YOUR BIKE'S LIMITS

If your bike doesn't have a tachometer, how do you know when to shift? Virtually all modern motorcycles feature rev limiters, so you'll probably never over-rev your engine so long as you're in gear. But running your bike up to redline for each shift is a bad idea.

UPSHIFTING For the best fuel economy, shift early and often, operating at small throttle openings. Pay attention to how many rpm your bike drops between each shift. As long as your next upshift doesn't drop the rpm in the next gear below idle, you'll be fine, although upshifting won't produce much power. For the most power and fastest times (and correspondingly poor economy), you'll want to upshift at your bike's horsepower peak.

DOWNSHIFTING There are two reasons to downshift—to slow your bike, or to adjust the engine's rpm to make more power. The first, slowing, is inefficient—that's why you have brakes, and brake pads are less expensive to replace than rings, bearings, and pistons. The proper technique? For an upcoming curve, use your brakes to slow in advance of the turn, anticipating what gear you'll need to use to exit the turn. As you're slowing, downshift the bike, releasing the clutch as you finish braking.

Sometimes it pays not to shift at all—like on a long uphill or downhill in the dirt. Bottom line? In the words of *Cycle World*'s Kevin Cameron, "When the bike quits lunging forward, it's time to shift."

86 IMPROVISE A CRUISE CONTROL

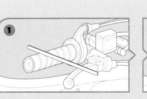
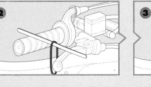

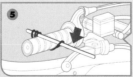

You're droning through the Russian steppes, on a road so straight you can see the curvature of the earth. And your wrist is killing you. What to do? With nothing more than a simple rubber band and a pencil or a popsicle stick, relief is on the way!

STEP 1 Place the stick over the throttle grip so that it's lying on top of your front-brake lever.

STEP 2 Loop one end of the rubber band over the front portion of the stick as shown.

STEP 3 Loop the other end of the rubber band over the rear portion of the stick, pulling it tight. Adjust tension with more wraps as needed.

STEP 4 Twist the throttle to the desired opening.

STEP 5 Holding the throttle in position, push the stick/pencil down so it contacts the top of the brake lever, then release your grip.

We won't fully recommend using this, but your wrist will thank you.

JEREZ

NUMBER OF TURNS: **13**

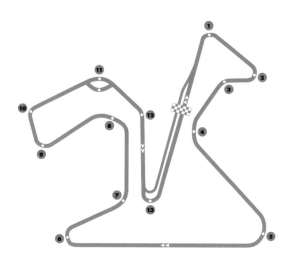

FAST FACTS

OFFICIAL NAME Circuito de Jerez

LOCATION Andalucia, Spain, northeast of Jerez de la Frontera

TRACK LENGTH 2.751 mi (4.428 km)

DATE OPENED 1985

FAMOUS FEATURE Lorenzo Curve (Turn #13), named in May 2013 after Spanish MotoGP champion Jorge Lorenzo, who won first place after a near-disastrous botched overtake by second placer Marc Marquez.

TRIVIA Built in a region that's renowned for its sherry production, this track hosted the first international motorcycle event in Spain, as well as a variety of auto racing events and testing. Its remote location hampers spectator attendance (and Formula One events are now being held in Barcelona), but the track's stands can seat up to 125,000 viewers.

Jerez's colorful history has included incidents on and off the track, including a temporary ban from Grand Prix hosting after the mayor of Jerez presented a trophy that was supposed to be handed out by a representative from the Daimler-Benz corporation instead.

Its engaging twists and turns have challenged auto racers as well as motorcyclists; the Senna Curve (Turn #11, named after famed F-1 racer Ayrton Senna) was altered to include a chicane after the 1990 career-ending—and near-fatal—crash of another driver, Martin Donnelly.

88 DON'T DISREGARD THE DOWNSHIFT

The primary reason you downshift is to keep the engine in its powerband for the given speed and situation. A second, less intuitive, reason is to utilize the engine's compression braking. With the throttle closed, the engine applies a steady braking force to the rear wheel, which is very useful on long downhills, especially off-road. When driving a car, you downshift to keep from burning up the brakes or boiling the brake fluid. On a bike, it's about maintaining traction and control.

89 COUNTERSTEER CORRECTLY

Every rider knows that you lean when your turn. Yet few understand a critical aspect of this—countersteering.

Countersteering is the technique you consciously or unconsciously apply to initiate that lean. In short, you steer left to lean right, and vice versa. In order to fully understand the theory, you need to get your head around camber thrust, roll angle, and centripetal force. But to ride you only need to understand the practice.

To really get a feel for it, get going down a straight piece of road at a moderate speed—anything over 10 mph (16 kph). Now, still holding the handlebar, open both your hands so only your palms are in contact and your fingers point straight up—so you can only push the bar, not pull. Now push with your right hand, and see what happens.

You'll experience a momentary dip to the left, and then the bike will bank slightly to the right. Combine countersteering with a quick weight shift to the inside footpeg, and *voilà*—your bike responds instantly and goes where you want.

Why is it so important to understand what's happening? It can, quite literally, be a matter of life and death. After all, in a car, when we need to turn right to avoid an accident, we yank the wheel to the right. Doing that same thing on a bike does just the opposite, so that instinct can be deadly.

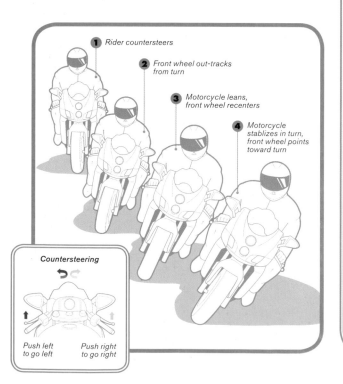

1 Rider countersteers

2 Front wheel out-tracks from turn

3 Motorcycle leans, front wheel recenters

4 Motorcycle stablizes in turn, front wheel points toward turn

Countersteering

Push left to go left   Push right to go right

90 DON'T GET (TANK) SLAPPED

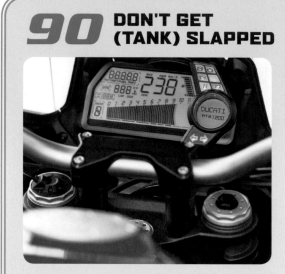

Also known as the death wobble, the speed shimmy, or, for the more technically minded, the undamped second-order positive feedback mechanism, the tankslapper is a force to be reckoned with. It's a rapid back-and-forth oscillation of the handlebar, often increasing in force and amplitude. The small ones can be either entertaining or terrifying; the large ones inevitably will leave you looking for a soft place to land.

The baby tankslapper cycles back and forth two or three times and then goes away. A big one grows faster and more intense until either you crash or it yanks the bar right out of your hands, and then you crash.

What causes it? A whole variety of contributing factors: tire stiffness, forward weight transfer, road surface, and chassis stiffness. Wheelie your bike long enough for the front wheel to quit turning, land hard, and you'll often conjure one up. The most common causes are exiting a bumpy corner or a sudden weight transfer.

What should you do? First, don't let go. Second, stop doing whatever it was that brought it on. Of course, this is easier said than done, but usually you should slide back on the seat and take some of the weight off the front end with the throttle.

And, of course, the best method is to fit a steering damper before the fact—which is why you'll seldom see a race bike without one.

91 MASTER TRAIL-BRAKING

Brakes aren't just for slowing down or stopping—proper brake use also can help you turn as well as settling your bike's chassis.

Traditional riding instruction says do all your braking with the bike straight up and down—before you turn. This technique certainly is safe, but it's not the only way. Trail-braking is a technique where you stay on the brakes through the turn entrance, perhaps even all the way to the apex. You brake less and less as the apex grows closer, releasing the brakes as you accelerate out of the turn. Why? Racers like it because it's faster. It also makes it easier to tighten the radius towards the end of the turn if you need to avoid an unseen problem.

Most of the time you'll be using both your front and rear brakes. But a second technique involves lightly dragging the rear brake while you're on the gas. The idea here isn't to slow down, but to settle the bike's chassis and to help it stand up on acceleration.

The secret with either technique is smoothness—easy on, easy off. And both are skills every rider should practice and master.

92 HIT THE (ENGINE) BRAKES

Your motorcycle's engine obviously gets you up to speed, but you can also use it to slow down. When you need to decelerate—coming to a stop, going into a turn, or on a long downhill that may roast your brake pads—your engine can save a bit of wear and tear.

By rolling off the throttle while still in gear, the engine's compression does a good job of slowing down the bike. Downshifting increases that effect—and also prepares you to accelerate again after slowing or stopping.

Your engine is a robust, high-performance piece of work; it can be used to slow the bike as long as you do so judiciously and safely: Don't engine-brake too quickly, or downshift through gears too fast, or from high engine rpm. And don't be afraid to use the front and rear brakes as well, to give you greater braking power and finesse.

93 BE A GOOD PASSENGER

Most of the responsibility for the ride falls to the pilot, but as a passenger, you can help to ensure a good experience. Here's how.

DRESS FOR SUCCESS Wear what a smart rider wears: Long pants, sturdy over-the-ankle shoes, a long-sleeved jacket. Borrow a good-fitting helmet if the rider doesn't have one for you, and bring gloves that fit.

FIND YOUR FOOTING Almost every bike will have a set of fold-down passenger footpegs— if their location isn't obvious, ask the rider. Once you're on the bike, keep your feet on the pegs, even at stops. Also, watch for the exhaust pipes. If the bike's been running for a bit, they'll be hot enough to give you a bad burn.

GET ON FROM THE LEFT SIDE It's just like mounting a horse. Let the rider get on first, so he can hold the bike stable before you climb on.

HANG ON Ask if they prefer that you hug them from behind, place your hands on their hips, hang onto handrails or seat straps, or place one hand in front of you and one hand behind.

LEAN WITH THE RIDER Motorcycles lean when they turn. If you lean the wrong way, you'll annoy the rider at best, and throw him or her off balance at worst. If the bike is turning right, look over the rider's right shoulder; for left turns, make it the left shoulder. When in doubt, keep your helmet in line with the rider's and you'll naturally follow him.

DON'T BE A HEADBANGER Anticipate when the rider will brake. When they do, your body will want to shift forward. Try to keep your helmet from banging into theirs. It's not dangerous, but it is annoying. You can support yourself by placing your hands on the fuel tank.

SPEAK UP If you're uncomfortable, then say something, A frightened passenger tenses up and makes the rider uncomfortable. The bike becomes more difficult to handle, too. The best compliment a rider can pay to any passenger is to tell her he didn't even know she was there.

THE INSIDE LINE
ASSEN

NUMBER OF TURNS: **17**

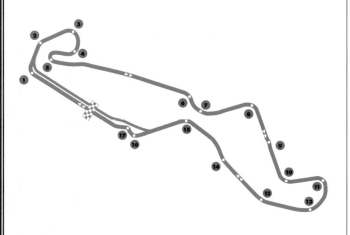

FAST FACTS

OFFICIAL NAME TT Circuit Assen

LOCATION Drenthe province, Netherlands, southwest of Assen

TRACK LENGTH 2.830 mi (4.555 km)

DATE OPENED 1925

FAMOUS FEATURE Assen's most famous feature is its fans—every year hundreds of thousands turn up and stay for a week. The track itself is surrounded by rolling, grassy banking, offering excellent viewing.

TRIVIA Although famed for nearly 80 years as a motorcycle track and the host of various World Championship events including MotoGP, Assen has been around almost as long as bikes and bike racing, with its original 17.7-mile (28.4-km) track getting its start back in 1925 with the Dutch Tourist Trophy race (the source of the "TT" in the track's full name).

A more formalized track of 4.8 miles (7.7 km) was built near that original brick-paved road in 1955, and it included banked curves, although by now those banks have been altered for safety issues, and the track itself was shortened in 2006, down to the current 2.8 mile (4.6 kilometer) length.

Assen is a challenging, heart-racing combination of tight technical curves and long speedy straightaways. But no matter the alterations and redesigns, this track's finish line has never been moved, and its many racers and spectators continue to be hailed by a bevy of brolly-bearing beauties.

95 TAKE THEM FOR A RIDE

Plenty of people are happy to tell anyone who will listen why riding is a bad idea. Most of them mean well, a few have an anti-bike agenda, and some are just plain ignorant. The easiest way to fight back? Offer a lot of rides to friends and family members.

You're not trying to get them hooked on bikes and turn them into riders—although that may happen, too. Just think of yourself as an ambassador. Even if that person never gets a license or buys a bike, they'll be more likely to look out for riders when they're driving, or to support a kid or significant other who wants a bike. Show them how much fun riding can be—get them outdoors and let them feel the wind and smell the trees. Show them what you already know—that bikes are all about freedom and fun.

96 MAKE A GREAT FIRST IMPRESSION

You want to make this fun for your passenger, right? Here are a few things you can do. First, make sure your bike's set up right. Plenty of air in the tires? More preload in the rear shock? Then, familiarize yourself with state laws in your area for carrying a passenger. Make sure he or she is dressed correctly and has a helmet (provide one if you can). Pick a ride that's fun but not too long.

Next, before you start, talk through every step—how to get on the bike, where to sit, what to hang on to, how to lean with you. Start off slow, and keep it smooth—no sudden starts, stops, changes of direction. Pick a smooth line and watch for bumps. Minimize lean. I've found that leaning the bike, especially at speed, freaks a passenger out more than anything else. Slower, wider turns minimize lean angle.

Take breaks so your passenger has some time to decompress, and take the opportunity to ask if he or she is comfortable. You'll feel if your passenger is anxious long before you hear it.

97 STAY DRY

Backpacking and mountaineering shops offer a variety of waterproofing treatments for leather and textile garments. Even if a jacket isn't totally waterproofed, the treatments make it easier to keep clean. Gore-Tex garments require special treatment; an outdoor shop is your best source for supplies.

98 RIDE SAFELY WITH JUNIOR

When is a child old enough to go for a ride? It's really less a matter of age and more about size and strength. Junior needs to be able to hold on securely and put his or her feet on the footpegs—you may need to improvise some peg extensions or blocks. And depending on your girth and the child's arm length, holding on around your waist may not be an option. A belt for you with handles the child can grip is a better option if your machine lacks handholds that are kid-friendly. Here are some other things to consider.

☐ Check all local and state laws and guidelines. Some regions restrict the age of a child passenger, or have other rules. This information should be easily available online; if not, call your local department of motor vehicles or other similar agency.

☐ Never carry a child in front of you.

☐ Make sure the child wears the same level of protective clothing as any other rider, especially a helmet and eye protection.

☐ Keep the rides short and fun. If a child falls asleep, you may not notice until he falls off.

☐ Choose a bike with a passenger backrest if possible.

☐ Make sure the child is mature enough to understand and obey instructions.

☐ Make sure the child is enjoying the ride. If you frighten him now with excessive speed or scary lean angles, he may dislike bikes forever.

☐ Provide positive feedback—take photos, tell them how well they did, ask if they had fun.

99 ENCOURAGE KIDS TO RIDE

Kids are the future of motorcycling. Get them started early, and you're ensuring the future of the sport. Better still, riding is good, clean fun.

Riding a motorcycle is all about personal responsibility, and the sooner a kid learns about that concept, the happier he or she will be.

If you have a streetbike, put them on the passenger seat and take them for a ride. If they're old enough, getting them on their own dirtbike is even better.

And you know what? Someday when you're in the old-folks' home, that same kid may show up to visit you. Or better yet, spring you from that place for a couple of hours and take you for a ride. Ain't payback grand?

100 SPLIT LANES THE RIGHT WAY

Lane splitting, lane sharing, traffic filtering, white-lining—whatever you call the practice, it's one of the huge advantages motorcycles offer over cars in traffic. Basically, it's about riding between lanes of slow or stopped traffic. It's legal in most of Europe and much of Asia. In the United States, it's legal only in California (and we can only hope some other states will eventually get a clue). Here's how to do it safely.

BE AWARE Consider the total environment where you're splitting. Lanes too narrow? If you can't fit, don't split. Don't split next to large trucks or other high vehicles—the danger of being knocked under their wheels is too great. As you roll up on a car, take a second to see if the driver is on the phone or texting.

BE SMART Split lanes only if traffic is moving slower than 30 miles per hour (48 kph). You won't have much room to maneuver, so time is your primary cushion. And higher speeds mean you cover more ground, and consequently have less time to react and brake.

PICK A LANE Typically, it is safer to split between the fast lane and the next-fastest. Look ahead, but not too far ahead. The car that's going to get you is the one next to you, or two or three cars up in front.

DON'T SPEED Never ride more than 10 miles per hour (16 kph) faster than the moving traffic. The greater the speed differential, the less time you have to identify and react to a hazard. Consider running your bike a gear lower than normal to take advantage of instant compression braking, and more responsive acceleration if necessary.

AVOID EXITS You've all seen a distracted driver spot his exit at the last minute and swerve over four lanes of traffic—you don't want to be in his way.

STAY SOLO Don't split lanes when there's another motorcycle rider doing so between adjacent lanes. Sometimes, when drivers see a bike moving their way, they move over as a courtesy. If they see the other bike first, they may move over into your space.

BE READY Always cover your (front) brake lever and (rear) brake pedal when splitting.

BE NICE If someone moves over to give you room, it's OK to give him a courtesy wave. If someone doesn't move over, it's not OK to make an obscene gesture. Who knows what he's going to do to the next biker he sees if *you* make him angry?

101 PLAY SAFELY IN TRAFFIC

Think road racing is dangerous? Those guys have it easy compared to your average urban commuter. The following tips can keep you alive.

CHOOSE YOUR ROUTE Look for a route that moves well and gives you room to maneuver.

MIND THE GUNK The crud on city streets can compromise your traction and ability to corner and stop. It's worst in the center of a lane, just before intersections, or if it hasn't rained recently.

LOOK AROUND Don't just gaze in front of you; look ahead and around. Use your mirrors, but don't trust them alone.

PLAN YOUR ESCAPE What if that car comes into your lane, or something falls off that truck ahead of you? Where are you going to go? Always look for a way out.

KEEP MOVING Don't pull up so close to a car that you can't maneuver; if you're sitting still, you're a sitting duck.

STAND OUT Wear bright, reflective colors, use a headlight modulator (if legal in your area), and use your horn if you have to.

AVOID BLIND SPOTS If you can't see the driver's face in his mirrors, he can't see you, and that puts you in danger. Leave that blind spot ASAP.

KEEP CONTROL Keep your fingers on the front brake and clutch levers (and the horn button), and your foot over the rear brake.

BEWARE OF INTERSECTIONS Most motorcycle accidents involve a car violating the rider's right of way, especially turning left in front of him. And intersections are where people turn.

DON'T BLOCK EXITS Riding between a car and a freeway exit is asking for trouble.

102 COMMUTE SMART

A bike is a great way to get to work in most places. Keep a few things in mind to keep the experience good.

Dress for the fall, not the ride. Always wear all your protective equipment. Carry work clothes in a backpack, or wear a one-piece oversuit on top of them. Bring your rain gear, too, or leave a spare rainsuit at work.

Keep everything you need to commute in one bag. When it's all in one place, you're less likely to leave something behind.

Finally, secure your bike at work. If you thought your job was bad, just imagine clocking out and finding your ride stolen. Leave a big lock there for daily use.

103 AVOID TARGET FIXATION

"Look where you want to go." Even a beginning rider course should teach you that, and it's sound advice no matter how much experience you gain. The bike is going to go where you're looking. If there's a pothole or debris in front of you, or a car pulls out, or an animal runs into your path, don't look directly at it—look for a way out, where you want to go.

Two corollaries: Look through the turn, not just at the apex. And second, don't look in front of you; look ahead of you. Flat-track riders call that shortness of vision "riding the front wheel." You'll never be safe if you're not looking far enough ahead.

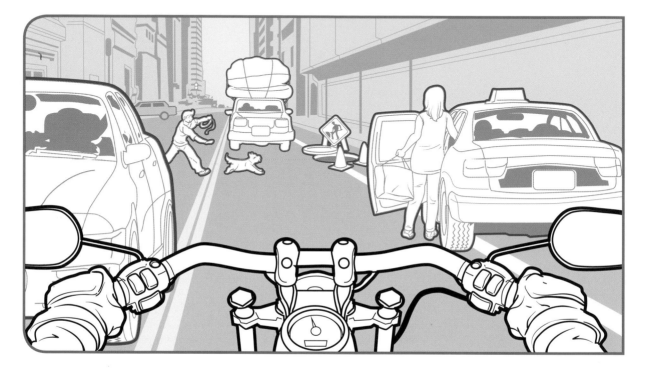

104 USE YOUR RADAR, RIDER

In countless numbers of action-packed war flicks from World War II up to the modern age, you've seen the sweep-and-ping of the submarine sonar as it picks out enemy boats and torpedoes, or the same kind of display with aircraft on a radar station's console. Your bike may not come equipped with surface-to-surface missiles, but you can still apply the same concept while you're in the saddle to enhance your safety on the road.

The basic principle is to keep your eyes moving. Just like avoiding target fixation, look where you want to go, and look for a way out of potential (or clear and present) danger. But just like sonar or radar, once you're done surveying your immediate area, start another sweep.

Your eyes move faster than almost any other part of your body, and you can quickly take in the details of the road and any potential obstacles in a literal blink of an eye. Sweep your gaze over your field of vision near to you, then farther away, then farther still. Keep objects in mind, but don't fixate on them, and start your sweep again.

A good rule of thumb is to do a full sweep of your field of vision every five to 15 seconds. Ping!

105 READ THE RADIUS

Increasing radius, decreasing radius, constant radius—sounds like a geometry class. Pay attention to this course; if you don't understand how a turn is built, you'll end up with more than just a bad grade. If a turn curves around at the same rate the whole way through, it has a constant radius. You adjust your speed at the entry, and then you accelerate at the exit. Simple.

If the turn starts out sharp and then opens up wide, that's called an increasing radius, and it's an even more forgiving turn.

But what if a turn tightens in on itself? Lots of freeway offramps and plenty of mountain roads do so; this turn is a decreasing radius, and it's what you really need to watch out for. You'll need to lean more and more if you get into one of these too fast, and that can push you to the edge of the road or over the centerline. With a decreasing-radius turn, you will have to enter more slowly than normal, lean more, or ride a slightly wider line and apply throttle only when the remaining corner is fully seen. On unfamiliar roads, assume every turn is a decreasing radius.

106 READ THE CROWN

Paved roads are rarely flat; they usually slope in one direction to help water drain or to help a vehicle hold the road surface. The most common type of construction is the crown—a road higher in the center than the edges.

Since you lean a bike over when you turn, it's important to pay attention to the crown. On right turns, the crown works for you, but on left turns it works against you. (This presumes that you ride on the right; in the UK, Japan and countries where you ride on the left, the opposite holds true.) If you drift over onto the crown, your machine loses its cornering clearance very quickly. And sometimes the crown won't be in the center of the road at all.

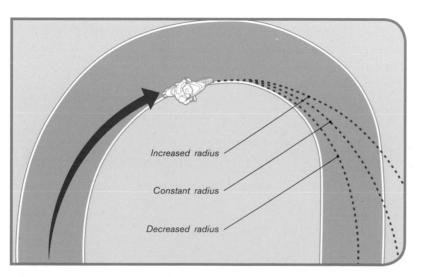

Increased radius

Constant radius

Decreased radius

107 FOIL BIKE THIEVES

There are few things worse than coming out of your home in the morning keys in hand, ready to ride and seeing . . . nothing. Motorcycle theft is all too common, but you can thwart those evil bastards. Here's how, in six easy steps.

KEEP IT OUT OF SIGHT If a thief can't see your bike, he can't decide to steal it. Parking your machine in a secure garage or shed, especially at night, is choice number one. Well, choice number two, really. A bank vault would be even better.

KEEP IT IN SIGHT On the road and need to stop for lunch? Park your bike by the restaurant window and sit right next to it. Or how about paying someone to watch it for you? Darkness is the bike thief's friend, so park in a well-lit area.

BE A KILLJOY Something as simple as a hidden kill switch can stop a bad guy from hot-wiring your ride. Even pulling a plug wire can stop the casual thief, or at least buy you time.

MAKE SOME NOISE Invest in an alarm, ideally one that also kills the ignition while it alerts you.

BOX IT IN A single bike sitting in a wide-open parking lot is just calling out to some bad guy to take it. But that same motorcycle wedged into a small, cramped gap between a wall and a house gives them much less room to work.

LOCK IT UP Well, duh. Of course you're going to lock it. But are you going to lock it up right? The next set of tips will tell you how.

108 PICK A LOCK

If you want to keep your bike, you need to get aggressive when it comes to security. You should always use more than one method: Your handlebar lock, a disc lock, and a chain secured by a U lock are a good combination that's still portable. Keep locks and chains off the ground to deny thieves leverage, and consider an alarm and/or a kill switch in addition to active locking devices.

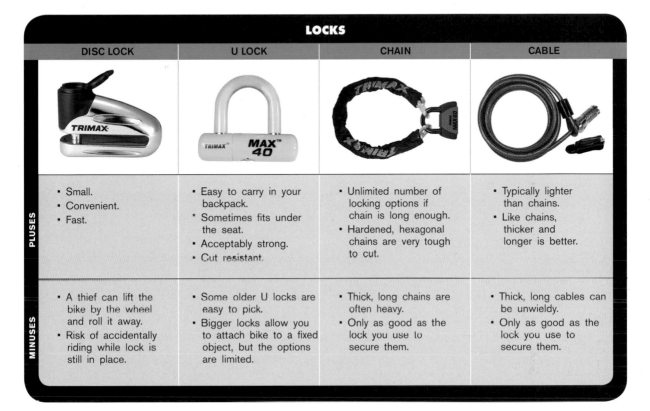

LOCKS			
DISC LOCK	**U LOCK**	**CHAIN**	**CABLE**
PLUSES • Small. • Convenient. • Fast.	• Easy to carry in your backpack. * Sometimes fits under the seat. • Acceptably strong. • Cut resistant.	• Unlimited number of locking options if chain is long enough. • Hardened, hexagonal chains are very tough to cut.	• Typically lighter than chains. • Like chains, thicker and longer is better.
MINUSES • A thief can lift the bike by the wheel and roll it away. • Risk of accidentally riding while lock is still in place.	• Some older U locks are easy to pick. • Bigger locks allow you to attach bike to a fixed object, but the options are limited.	• Thick, long chains are often heavy. • Only as good as the lock you use to secure them.	• Thick, long cables can be unwieldy. • Only as good as the lock you use to secure them.

109 LOCK IT OR LOSE IT

If you don't lock it up right, that lock may be worth less than the oil spot on the pavement that tells you your baby's long gone.

DOUBLE DIP Always use two locks. A big lock and an asymmetric, hardened, cut-resistant chain is the best, backed up by a U lock and/or a disc lock that can fit tightly around a wheel.

ANCHORS AWEIGH You need to lock your bike to something, otherwise the thieves will just pick it up or drag it off. Even if the bike is parked in your garage, you need a solid anchor.

WEAKEST LINK Chain your bike to a stop sign, and you may come back to find both sign and bike have done a vanishing act. Chain it to a steel stoplight post and you're looking at better odds.

SLACKERS LOSERS Leave your chain or lock slack enough to reach the ground, and you might as well leave the keys in it. The ground means leverage: Get your lock up high and you gain an advantage.

THE INSIDE LINE

PHILLIP ISLAND

NUMBER OF TURNS: **12**

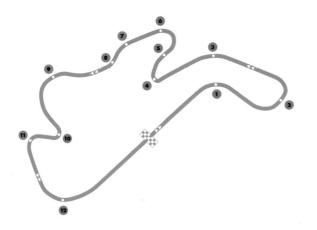

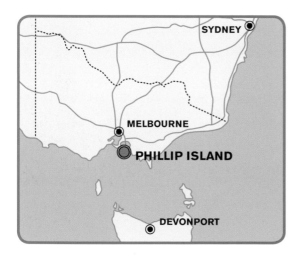

FAST FACTS

OFFICIAL NAME Phillip Island Grand Prix Circuit

LOCATION Victoria, Australia, south of Melbourne

TRACK LENGTH 2.762 mi (4.445 km)

DATE OPENED 1956

FAMOUS FEATURE Stoner Corner, the circuit's third turn, so named after Australian MotoGP champion Casey Stoner. The five-time-consecutive Grand Prix winner has described it as his favorite turn.

TRIVIA 1928 saw the beginning of Aussie motor racing on a tiny island on the southern coast of the country, when the Australian Grand Prix (originally known as the 100 Miles Road Race) took place on the island's local roads. The creation of an actual circuit track on the south edge of the island began in 1951, with the modern course's grand opening meet in 1956.

The track has been closed multiple times for repairs and alterations, it continues to operate today. It has been called "the mecca of Australian motorsport," hosting events such as the Superbike World Championship and Australian MotoGP.

Phillip Island also offers visitors a wide range of 4- and 5-star-rated accommodations, and a garden and animal enclosure to allow visitors to get a glimpse of a host of native Australian critters.

111 PARK YOUR STREETBIKE

When parking your bike on the street, roll it into the parking space backward, so the rear tire touches the curb. Leave your bike in gear so it doesn't roll. Doing so is especially important if you must park it with the front wheel facing downhill.

Park defensively. It's better to be in the center of a parking spot than at one end where a car may try to squeeze in and knock your bike over. Share a space with other bikes if possible. There's power in numbers, and it conserves parking resources. Consider putting it on the sidewalk, but be aware that you might get a citation for that.

If you have to park on a hill, try to keep the sidestand on the downhill side. Try to park with your rear wheel facing downhill—it makes pulling out easier, and keeps the bike from rolling off the sidestand and tipping over.

If you're parking on a soft surface (dirt, grass, gravel) or brutally hot asphalt, put something under the sidestand to increase its footprint. A scrap of wood, a crushed soda can, a flat rock, a square of scrap metal all work—even something like a thick magazine folded in half.

In a public garage, utilize unused spaces where a car can't fit—behind pillars in parking garages, in wasted spaces next to elevators, etc. You'll leave a parking spot open for a car, and doing so will also keep cars from trying to encroach on your space.

112 GET A ROOM

If you're traveling way (way) off the beaten track, you might actually be able to roll the bike right into your ground-floor hotel room, a common strategy when riding in Latin America (just remember to tip the maid if you leave an oil spot on the carpet).

113 RIDE IN THE COLD

In very cold weather your suspension oil may thicken, and your bike may ride harsher; your tires might also offer a little less grip on the pavement. These things are worth being aware of, but they don't really affect your ability to ride.

All of that said, unless it's actively snowing or you're trying to keep traction on an icy road, riding in the cold doesn't present any special problems for the way your bike handles—rather, your main concern is keeping yourself warm and comfortable.

A cold rider is going to have less coordination and longer reaction times. Motorcyclists make their own windchill, too. Winds of 60–70 miles per hour (95–110 kph) would make the top of the evening news, but on a bike, you experience that every day. So you need to remember three important things.

KEEP THE WIND OUT This means wearing windproof clothing (leather, textile) that seals tightly around your wrists, neck, lower legs, and waist. Boots and long gloves that overlap your pant legs and sleeves are a must. A scarf or neck gaiter can seal up your throat area.

KEEP THE WARMTH IN Several thin layers of insulation work better than thick ones. Even some folded newspaper shoved inside the chest of your jacket can make a noticeable difference in your comfort. Gloves need to be thicker on the back of your hands than on the palms.

GET WARMER Electric vests, seats, and handgrips can keep you warm even if your other clothing is marginal. And there's always that old biker favorite: a cup of hot coffee or tea to stoke the fires within.

114

SURVIVE A CROSSWIND

Few things upset riders as much as riding in a crosswind that pushes them around in a lane. Short of staying home or panicking every time it happens, here's what to do.

HOLD YOUR SPEED It's tempting to slow down when a gust hits, but that reduces your bike's stability. If you get hit by a gust, keep the throttle steady. That said, in windy conditions you should definitely slow down a bit, just not right after a gust hits you.

CROWD THE SIDE OF THE ROAD If the wind is blowing from right to left, crowd the right side of the road. You'll seldom overcorrect into the wind, but you'll have more lane to work with if the wind does move you.

HANG OFF INTO THE WIND Shift your body lower and into the wind to compensate. Hunching over also reduces the sail effect your body presents.

READ THE WIND Look for blowing trees, grass, or dust up ahead so a gust doesn't catch you unaware.

COUNTERSTEER Don't let the wind bully you; push back instead.

RELAX Don't tense up. Relaxing a little will actually help you react more easily.

Storseisundbrua

115 PLAY IN THE SNOW

Riding in snow is a lot like riding in the rain, at least until the snow really starts to build up. And while rain dampens every road surface, the real danger with snow is ice: It forms in corners where water runs off and then refreezes. It also forms much faster on bridges, where the air blows under and over the road surface. What to do?

GET KNOBBIES In Scandinavian countries, you can buy special studded motorcycle tires. Short of that, a dirtbike with knobbies will work better than most streetbikes. If you're stuck and just need to ride a short distance, you can sometimes rig up ersatz tire chains by wrapping rope or bungee cords around your rear tire—just make sure they clear the chain and swingarm.

FOLLOW THE TRACKS Staying in the tracks other vehicles put down helps—but only if they're fresh. If they're old, they'll ice up; you may be better off riding in the fresh snow next to them. Use more rear brake than front—this is normally the opposite of what a street rider would do, but riding in the snow is more like riding in the dirt.

WATCH THE LEVER In really deep snow, the stuff can upshift your bike when it presses up against the shift lever. You may have to ride with your foot on the lever to keep it down. When the snow gets much deeper than six inches (15 cm), it may be time to trade in for a snowmobile.

116 GET YOUR BIKE WET

We've talked elsewhere about how to stay dry on a bike. Now we're going to talk about how to ride more safely when the road is wet.

Your biggest issue is reduced traction. Painted lines, manhole covers, and metal bridge gratings are real danger zones. Puddles may seem benign, but they can hide deep, sharp-edged potholes. If you see standing water on the road, pay attention.

Gentle control inputs are the key. You needn't ride significantly slower in the rain, but you won't be able to lean as far, or as suddenly. Easy on and off the throttle; ditto for the brakes. Take conservative lines—this is no time to dive for the apex. Try to be smooth, like you're giving your grandmother a nice ride on the back. Keep your brakes dry—this means you'll have to drag them lightly every 3 or 4 miles (5–6 km), in order to heat them up and drive the water out.

It's smart to short-shift the bike (shift earlier to keep the engine revs lower) on the street, but do just the opposite (let the bike rev higher) on the freeway. Short-shifting helps keep the wheel from spinning at low speeds and lessens the torque multiplication at the rear wheel so the bike doesn't step out on paint stripes or manholes. Letting it rev higher on the freeway lets you use compression braking to gently slow the bike without depending on sudden brake inputs.

Finally, wear a full-face helmet. At speed, even small raindrops feel like bullets.

117 ACCESSORIZE FOR THE RAIN

Two items can make a big difference in comfort and safety. The first is the "Biker Squeegee," which fits over your thumb and helps you keep your faceshield clean. The second is an anti-fog treatment for your faceshield or goggles—if you can't see, you can't ride.

118 BEAT THE HEAT

Planning to ride across Death Valley in July? Most modern bikes are pretty tolerant of hot weather, as long as you keep them moving so there's airflow over the radiator or cooling fins. Riders are a different issue, but there's plenty you can do to stay cool.

First, wear textile clothing instead of leather. You can wet it down, and the evaporative cooling from the windstream can keep you from cooking in your own juices. Even better, pack some ice into your jacket's pockets—it will lower your temperature, and as the ice melts, it wets down the rest of your garments. If you do wear leather, look for a jacket that features zip-open vents or perforated leather panels.

No matter how hot it is, keep covered up. A crash is just as likely when it's hot as when it's cold. Plus, long sleeves prevent the sunburn and windburn the desert can dish out, as well as slowing your body's sweating processes, to help keep you from dehydrating. And bring a hat—when you remove your helmet you'll still need to keep your head cool.

119 SURVIVE IN THE DESERT

A breakdown in the desert is no joke, and it's a real possibility for off-road or adventure riders. So what to do if you end up staring at a broken bike and a cactus? Of course, you should be riding with a friend who can pack you out as a passenger or tow your bike. On your own? You'd better get busy.

Heat, cold, and water are your main concerns, along with rescue. If it's the middle of the day, seek out organic shade (trees, brush, rock overhangs). No cover? Use your tarp, bike cover, space blanket, trash bag, or tent fly to create a small shaded area.

At night, the desert loses heat quickly. Your bike provides lots of ways to start a fire—gas from the tank, oil from the engine, a spark from the plug or the battery. You can burn your seat, a tube, or a tire to make a smoky signal fire if there's no wood or brush. Your bike's mirrors, horn, and headlight are all potential signaling devices.

As for water: DON'T drink the coolant from your radiator. The best way to carry water on a dirtbike is probably a hydration pack, the biggest you can find.

Stay with the bike. If you must hike out, wait until the cool of the evening. You should be carrying sandals or comfortable walking shoes with you; if not, the inner booties from some motocross boots provide protection but are a lot more comfortable to walk in than the boots themselves.

Your helmet will keep you warm at night, but it's a lousy hat during the day. Take a brimmed boonie-style hat along with you, or make one from a T-shirt.

120 CHOOSE YOUR COLORS

Ravens live in the desert, but they have black feathers. Polar bears lives in snow and ice, but they have white fur. Lighter colors should be cooler than darker colors, so what gives?

It's less about color, and more about how your clothes fit. Loose fitting, dark garments (such as a raven's fluffed-up plumage, or a Bedouin's loose, flowing caftan) are actually cooler than loose-fitting white clothes. If the garment fits tight against your skin, though, the opposite is true. So keep your T-shirts and helmet white, and your riding suit dark.

121 TREAD LIGHTLY

Riding responsibly off road means caring about your environment. It's the right thing to do. And if you don't, you'll soon find your riding area shut down and out of bounds. You can be a responsible rider by adhering to these guidelines.

BE RESPECTFUL Travel only on designated roads and trails or in permitted areas. Respect the rights of others, including private property owners and campers. Keep speeds low around crowds and in camping areas. If crossing private property, be sure to ask permission from the landowner(s), and leave gates as you find them.

MAINTAIN CONTROL On slick trails, moderate the throttle and minimize wheelspin. Ride over, not around, obstacles to avoid widening the trail. Yield the right of way to those passing you or traveling uphill, and give way to mountain bikers, hikers and people on horseback.

KEEP NOISE DOWN Less sound equals more ground: Make sure your bike has a quiet exhaust system and a spark arrestor. Avoid spooking livestock and wildlife you encounter, and be sure to keep your distance.

TAKE CARE Avoid sensitive areas such as meadows, lakeshores, wetlands, and streams. Leave the area better than you found it: Properly dispose of waste (and pick up litter left by others) and minimize the use of fire. Help to avoid the spread of invasive species, and restore degraded areas. Consider joining a local environmental organization.

122 KICK UP SOME DUST

The first rule for riding in dust: Don't ride faster than you can see. When you're out with a group, you can either stay close to the rider in front of you so his dust doesn't get a chance to rise (which only works if there are two of you on a wide trail) or ride at 30- to 60-second intervals, so the dust has time to settle. Standing up on the pegs can also help you see farther and over the dust.

Inhaling dust is bad for your lungs. A damp bandana over your nose and mouth helps. Even better: a dust mask from a hardware store, or a surgeon's mask.

Service your air filter after long dusty rides—if it gets too dirty, your bike will lose power and may ultimately suffer engine damage.

123 RIDE OVER A LOG

So, there's a fallen tree across your trail. Unless It's a sequoia or a redwood (in which case it's better to go around), it's time to rock some off-road skills.

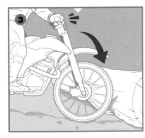

STEP 1 Approach at a right angle, if possible.

STEP 2 Stand up on the pegs.

STEP 3 Just before your front wheel contacts the log, shift your body weight forward and/or tap the front brake to compress the fork.

STEP 4 As the wheel touches the log, rock your body weight backward, tug up on the handlebar, and open the throttle sharply.

STEP 5 Stay on the gas until the rear wheel climbs over the log.

STEP 6 If you get the front wheel over the log but not the rear, either stay on the gas or stop and drag or lift the rear wheel over.

124 TRY A TRIALS BIKE

If you're looking for a great way to improve your off-road riding skills, check out a trials bike. What is trials riding? It's about negotiating highly technical obstacles without putting your foot down. It's a great way to learn to read terrain, improve your balance, and find out what your bike can do.

Pro-level trials bikes are specialized machines with minimal scats and tiny fuel tanks. Not ready to invest in one yourself? Sign up for a school or visit a club in your area. You can even trials-ride on your own standard dirtbike. You won't be able to match the performance of a specialized trials machine, but the next time you need to traverse a trail with a terrifyingly steep dropoff on one side, you'll be glad you have the skills.

125 DUSTPROOF YOUR GOGGLES

Off-road bikes use foam air filters impregnated with oil to stop dirt from entering the engine. You can use the same trick with your goggles. Just take a little baby oil and put it on the foam goggle vents. They'll trap the dust, and can be washed out with a little soap and water when the ride's over.

126 RIDE IN THE MUD

Off-road riding demands some adjustments to the environment, your gear, and your skillset too. With these tips, you can avoid getting bogged down.

In the mud, you need to conserve momentum. Keep the bike as upright as possible and never slow to a stop. Don't be afraid of wheelspin as long as you're still moving—your rear tire may spinning at 35 mph (56 kph) when the bike is only moving at a crawl, but hey, if you're still mobile, that's all that counts.

Short-shift your bike to run it in a higher gear. Your riding position will probably be neutral or a little farther back, and you'll probably sit down more than when riding in sand. To slow down, don't use your brakes, or just use the rear.

Look for the high, dry (or drier) line. Mud riding is all about finding and using traction. Stay out of ruts, and maintain your balance on the bike.

Mud riding uses a lot of gas and power. Even when it's soaking wet out, your bike can easily overheat in deep, thick mud, so watch your engine temperature. Just like when riding in sand, look as far ahead as you can, and stay on the gas.

127 PREP YOUR BIKE FOR MUD RIDING

Taking your dirtbike into the mud is fun, but the cleanup is murder. Still, you can keep your bike running clean even in the dirtiest places.

Run duct tape beneath your fenders, airbox, and other spots where mud sticks. Coat undersurfaces with non-stick cooking spray or WD-40. Use it on your chain; consider running the chain looser, too.

Stretch pantyhose over your radiator guards or oil cooler. You can also put them over the fenders.

Pack coarse, open-cell foam into gaps between the skidplate and engine, or between the brake lever and shift lever, and zip-tie it in place.

Reduce the tires' air pressure a bit in order to get a better grip in deep mud.

Make sure you safety-wire your grips on.

And after the ride, clean your bike *thoroughly*.

128 RIDE IN SAND

Before you even begin, lower your bike's tire pressure, especially on the rear tire. Depending on your specific bike and tire, this may even be as low as 12 psi (0.83 bar). Remove excess weight on the bike if you can—it makes riding easier, and picking the bike up easier still.

THROTTLE Sand respects confidence, aggression, and speed. Stop and you'll dig in. Don't fear wheelspin as long as you're making forward progress. It's tempting to let off the throttle, but sudden transitions are a bad idea here. Keep your revs up. As for brakes, you won't need them at all in deep sand. If you do brake, do it early, and gently. Get back on the gas as soon as you can.

BODY POSITIONING Unweight the front end as much as you can. That means lean back and keep your butt down, like you're trying to sit on the bike's taillight; you want to keep the front from digging in and to let it skim over the top of the sand.

YOUR LINE Front end starting to wander? Let it. With enough engine speed and bike speed, you can control the machine's direction with the weight of your feet on the pegs. The wagging handlebar can be unnerving at first, but you'll be fine.

Most important? Don't give up. If you're still moving, you're not stuck. When in doubt, and especially if you're getting tired, react with more assertiveness. If you do have to stop, wait for a patch of solid ground or a section with only light sand—getting restarted from here will be easier.

129 TIE 4 ESSENTIAL KNOTS

Some situations may require more specialized knots, but with the four pictured here, you'll be able to tow a bike, pitch your tent, secure a ruptured pannier, or strap your buddy's unconscious body to the saddle and get him back to civilization.

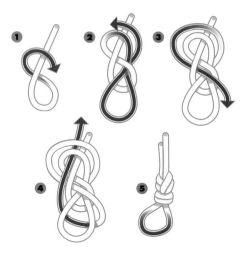

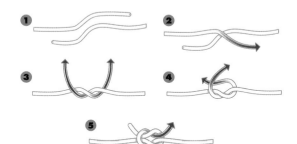

SQUARE KNOT

WHAT IT DOES Joins the ends of a rope.
KNOT NOTES While weak, unstable, and easily untied (sometimes unintentionally), the square knot is still a sound starting point, and an essential first-aid knot. It's more reliable if you back up the loose ends with an overhand knot.

FIGURE 8

WHAT IT DOES Multiple uses.
KNOT NOTES Slower to tie but versatile. Tie it in a bight of rope for a loop that won't slip; thread the rope back through the loop for a noose that cinches tight; weave one Figure 8 into another to make a great bend for joining two lines.

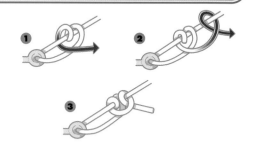

BOWLINE

WHAT IT DOES Makes a tight loop that will not slip.
KNOT NOTES One of the world's great knots. Essential for rescue. Secure, yet since it unties easily after holding a load, it's a good choice for towing.

TAUT-LINE HITCH

WHAT IT DOES Makes a loop that slips, but only when you want it to.
KNOT NOTES You can slide it where you want and it stays put, or tighten a tentline without retying the knot. Perfect for making a clothesline to dry soaked riding gear. Add more turns for more power.

130 SPEND THE NIGHT OUTDOORS

Run out of gas, stamina, or luck? Here you are after dark, out in the open. Now what?

We'll assume using your cell phone to call for help is not in the cards. So the first thing you need to consider is your immediate safety—get your bike out of the road or trail, and yourself as well.

CHOOSE YOUR SPOT You'll stay warmer if you avoid the top of a hill or the bottom of a valley. Also, south-facing hillsides (in the northern hemisphere) hold heat longer after dark. If rain is coming, find shelter quickly—a rocky overhang or bridge overpass is a great choice.

STAY PUT Unless you're on a familiar paved road, hiking out after dark is usually a poor choice. Light and fire can bring help to you. If you've dressed smart, you'll probably be warm enough. Keep your helmet and gloves on. Riding with a passenger? Maybe it's time to share body heat.

BE VISIBLE If you plan to stay awake or want to attract attention, a fire may be appropriate. Your bike's headlight is another way to get spotted, but your battery will run down fast. Using a taillight or turnsignal bulb will give you a lot more time.

TAKE SHELTER The bike itself may offer a windbreak, but some form of natural shelter is probably better. You'll want to be insulated from the ground; removing your bike's seat and sitting on it is a good solution.

131 START A FIRE 3 WAYS

If you're out in the boonies long enough, you'll eventually need some way of keeping warm, cooking food, or signaling for help. Just don't start a brushfire.

MATCHES The best are the weatherproof lifeboat matches from camping stores. We prefer the NATO wind/water matches; they burn so long and hot you could probably use them to weld a cracked crankcase.

LIGHTERS The disposable butane models are found everywhere, from gas stations to grocery stores, and are cheap to boot.

SPARKERS A ferrocerium or magnesium alloy tool lasts for thousands of strikes and works in the snow and rain.

Don't be shy about using the fuel from your bike's tank as an accelerant. You can also set fire to a piece of inner-tube rubber to coax wet wood into flame. The same goes for the glue from your tire-patch kit. Follow up on these flammables with tinder and firewood, and you're set.

132 BE A NIGHT RIDER

Riding at night offers two challenges: seeing and being seen. Bright lights, reflective clothing and helmet graphics, and even additional lights on your bike or person are the key. Bright colors aid conspicuity by day, but don't help much after sunset. A reflective vest is a good solution, as are reflective strips attached to a daypack, or as a graphics kit for many sportbikes. Flash your brake light to attract attention, and brake early to give ample warning to drivers behind you.

Your headlight needs to be in good order, and you may want to upgrade to a brighter bulb. But you also need a clean, scratch-free faceshield; ditto for your headlight lens. Consider adding auxiliary riding lights or fog lights if your electrical system can handle them.

You may have a fast motorcycle, but only short-range headlights—don't over-ride them. And be particularly aware of wildlife at night—deer and other animals are most active at dusk and dawn, and often dart out into the road.

Use other vehicles' lights to your advantage—that truck ahead of you is illuminating a lot of road, and what he sees you can see—if you place yourself in the right spot and bother to look.

Remember, if you have to brake hard at night, the front end of your bike will dive, and consequently the headlight will dip too. Be ready to sudeenly see less until you release the brakes—all the more reason to brake early and gently.

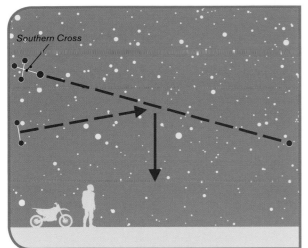

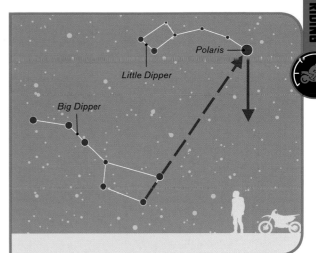

133 NAVIGATE BY THE STARS

You thought you'd be home by dark. Then you had to repair that flat, and then you took that wrong turn. What to do? If you're without a GPS or compass, look to the sky. You just need to learn two constellations. In the Northern Hemisphere, you need to recognize Polaris, the North Star; in the Southern Hemisphere, the Southern Cross. With either of these, you can identify north (or south) and keep yourself on track.

To find Polaris, first look for the Big Dipper, then trace a line upward between the two stars at the end of its "cup," and you'll find the North Star—the last star in the Little Dipper. Meanwhile, in the Southern

Hemisphere, look for the Southern Cross, and trace a line downward through its long axis. Find the two bright "pointer stars" near the Southern Cross, and draw a T with the stars as its top bar. The intersection between the bottom of the T and the line from the Southern Cross, will point you south.

If it's too overcast to see the stars, wait for moonrise. Many people don't realize this, but the moon always rises in the east, which can help you locate yourself. If it's so overcast you can't see the stars or the moon, get ready to stop, shiver through the night, and ride out in the morning.

134 NAVIGATE WITHOUT A COMPASS

Every trail rider should carry a compass at all times. But you should save money, eat right, and get enough exercise, too—but how many of us do all that? It's stunning to realize how many riders forget that the sun rises in the east and sets in the west—if there's enough light to see by, there's probably enough to navigate by. But here's a neat trick to give you a more precise fix: the sun-and-watch method.

In the north temperate zone: Take your wristwatch and point the hour hand toward the sun. A line drawn midway between the hour hand and the 12 on the watch face will point north/south. (If you're on daylight saving time, the north-south line is found between the hour hand and the 1.)

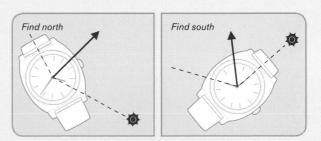

Find north

Find south

In the southern temperate zone, you need a different method: Point the 12 on the watch face toward the sun, and halfway between the 12 and the hour hand is the north/south line (on daylight savings time it's halfway between the hour hand and the 1 on the clock face.

Got a digital wristwatch? You can still make the method work if you draw a clock face on the ground.

135
CARRY SPARE GAS

Lots of MX bikes only hold enough fuel for a half-hour moto. So what to do if you're out trail riding? The first solution is to get a bigger tank. Can't find one for your machine? Here are some options.

CAMPING GAS BOTTLES These containers hold up to one quart (1 liter), are rugged and easy to stow in a backpack, and seal well. Downside: not very much fuel.

TWO-LITER SODA BOTTLES Twice the capacity, half the durability—if that. Better than nothing, and readily available.

BLEACH BOTTLES Fill a basic 1-gallon (3.8-liter) bottle with fuel, and slip your belt (or backpack strap) through the handle to secure it. If the gasket in the cap is Styrofoam, replace it with a disc of rubber cut from an old innertube.

As soon as you burn through the first gallon (3.8 liters) in your tank, dump the bottle in—you'll minimize the time you have to carry its weight.

As for other, softer containers (like your hydration pack), don't even think about it. Note that carrying any extra fuel outside of your gas tank comes with a certain risk of self-immolation. Ride with the appropriate caution.

136
RIDE WASHBOARD

Washboard (or corrugated) roads occur from vehicular traffic and the harmonics of suspension oscillation. And anyone who's ridden them knows they can be so bad that you chip a tooth, see double, or get hopped clean off the road itself if you ride them wrong. Want to float across them like a pro? Here's how.

DEFLATE YOURSELF First, air down your tires—you can go as low as 12 psi (0.83 bar). Stand up on the pegs, or put at least an inch (2.5 cm) of air between your butt and the seat. Look as far ahead as you can while you ride, and vary your speed. Depending on the depth and frequency of the washboard ripples, you'll find a sweet spot.

GO FAST A little counterintuitively, riding faster is often much smoother and offers more control than riding slower. Think of it as tuning a guitar, with twisting the throttle as twisting the tension key—you need to vary your speed until you find the right harmonic.

137
FILTER DIRTY GAS

Beggars can't be choosers, especially when the sun's setting, your bike is running on fumes, and the only gas available is sitting in a questionable roadside steel drum.

Poorly stored gas generally has three issues—rust, dirt, and water. None of those things will do your engine any good, especially if your bike uses fuel injection. But there's hope: a piece of chamois (the split skin of sheep, used for drying cars after a wash). For decades, bush pilots have strained aviation fuel through a square of chamois to filter those troublemakers, and it will work for your bike too. Be sure you get real leather chamois, not a synthetic look-alike.

Another tool—especially if you know your fuel supply is questionable—is a fine nylon-mesh screen to fit into your bike's gas-cap opening. These are usually for fuel-injected motocross bikes, but you can adapt them to other machines. They won't stop water, but will catch most sand and rust.

138 GET IN A RUT

Riding ruts is a lot like riding sand, but with one big difference. Sand riding is almost always on flat terrain, whereas ruts can be uphill, downhill, or flat.

Motocrossers use ruts as mini berms, but they can be trouble for casual riders. Controlling the front wheel is key. Stand on the pegs and get your weight over the middle of the bike or slightly over the rear wheel—this is easier uphill and on flats than downhill. Look ahead, not at the front wheel. Try to stay out of the rut. If the rear wheel drops in, stay on the gas, control your

direction with the front wheel, and ride out.

If the front wheel drops in, use the side knobs on your tire to control your direction. Steer in the direction your bike wants to fall, and the side knobs will grab the rut and help right you. Stay on the gas and ride it out. If both wheels are in the same rut, you can either ride it out, or try to loft the front out of the rut and get the rear to follow.

If your wheels end up in different ruts, it's best to stop and drag the rear into the same rut as the front.

139 RIDE FLAT TRACK

Flat-track riding combines the best of a track race and dirtbike riding.

THE SHORT VERSION
Gas it and turn left.

THE LONG VERSION
Flat track looks like a no-brainer; in reality it's one of the most valuable riding skills any dirtbike or streetbike rider can master. World champion road racers like Nicky Hayden, Kenny Roberts, and Colin Edwards all credit flat track for giving them the edge they need to win on pavement. Both Roberts and Edwards set up flat-track training facilities to share their secrets with other riders. Here are Edwards' Twelve Commandments.

1. Look where you want to go.

2. Smooth inputs are key—slow on the gas, and gentle braking.

3. Minimize the time between brakes and throttle, which leads to finding neutral throttle. Crack the gas open before you're completely off-brake.

4. Throttle control keeps the chassis steady! Off-throttle to pinned is one smooth motion. Neutral is okay after opening the throttle; rolling off is not.

5. Elbows out for maximum control, and grip the throttle like a screwdriver, not a club.

6. Scoot forward in the turns, sit atop the bike, and hang that inside leg off for balance.

7. Compress the fork with the brakes and your weight to steepen rake and make the bike want to turn. In the dirt, use both brakes in every corner.

8. Push the bike down and keep your spine perpendicular and shoulders parallel to the ground; you're sitting on top of the leaned-over bike. (Body position in the dirt doesn't translate to road racing.)

9. Weight that outside footpeg!

10. Slow down to go fast.

11. Relax. You can't feel your bike if your body is ultra-tense.

12. Watch your tire pressures, but keep a closer eye on your opponents' tire pressures.

140 RIDE IN SWAMPS

Swamp riding is less about technique than preparation. And the best preparation you can have is probably to get an ATV or a personal watercraft. But if you are going to ride through a swamp, try to stick to the high ground wherever possible. Most dirtbikes have sealed ignitions, high exhausts, and sealed spark plugs, but their weak link is the airbox—if your engine sucks in water, it will stop running *right now*.

Seal all of your airbox with duct tape, leaving only a small snorkel-type opening at the top. Even if your engine power is reduced, it's better than having *no* power because of a drowned engine. If your bike has a carburetor, you'll need to run the carb vent hoses up higher too—under the top of the gas tank is a good spot. If the vent lines are submerged for too long, your bike will starve for fuel.

Keep your momentum up, keep the bike running in a lower gear (more rpm) than normal, and try to stay balanced on the footpegs. And if you see an alligator, it's time to pack up and head home.

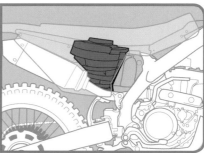

141 ROCK AND ROLL

Rock gardens and dry streambeds are often challenging, but they don't have to be. Of course, the size of the rocks makes all the difference.

SCOPE IT OUT First, stop and check out the section and your line. Pay particular attention to your entry and exit points.

KNOW YOUR LIMITS Be aware of your bike's ground clearance. If you get halfway and high-center on a rock, you'll be stopped cold. But if you know your machine has good clearance, you won't have to pass up an easy line due to a big rock.

STICK TO THE BASICS Pay attention to throttle control, balanced body position over the footpegs, and directing the bike where you want to go. Stand up in a neutral position with your knees bent and your chin up, looking at your exit. Keep the balls of your feet on the pegs. Keep your momentum up, and stay on the gas.

GET UNSTUCK If you do get stuck, try rolling the bike back as far as you can. Doing so lets you get your feet back on the pegs and regain your momentum for your next attempt. If you fall over, don't put your hand out to cushion your fall—it's a great way to break a wrist or a shoulder. If you know you're headed for a rocky section, you'll probably want to run higher air pressure in your tires to avoid pinch flats or bending a rim.

142   GET THE HOLESHOT

Ever been to a motocross race? The riders line up 20 or more abreast, all waiting for the start gate to drop. At the end of the starting straightaway there's only room for one rider at the first turn—and whoever gets there first gets the holeshot. Scoring the holeshot requires three things: clutch control, throttle control, and body positioning.

CLUTCH Your left hand has two jobs—to hold the grip and release the clutch. Use your index and middle fingers on the lever; grip the bar end with your ring and little fingers. Put the transmission in second gear. Let the clutch out almost to engagement. If the bike creeps forward, hold it back with the front brake.

THROTTLE While waiting to take off, hold the throttle at a high idle. At the starter's signal or when the gate drops, release the clutch and roll on the throttle at the same time. Once you've launched, hold the throttle open; if the bike wants to wheelie, slip the clutch only enough to control the front-end lift.

BODY Stand with both feet on the ground, your elbows out, and your body well forward on the bike. Point the bike directly into the first corner. Look ahead to the first turn and watch for the gate drop with your peripheral vision. As the gate drops, lean forward into the bar pad to keep the front end on the ground.

143 STAND UP FOR YOURSELF

Over and over and over in this section of the book you've heard us tell you to stand up on the footpegs when riding. A motorcycle set up for proper control will have the footpegs pretty close to directly under your hips—dirtbikes are probably the best example, and cruisers with their pegs set way out in front probably the worst.

Think of all the active sports you've ever tried—tennis, baseball, soccer, even golf—being balanced on your feet is the first fundamental you learn. Same with riding a motorcycle. Along with your butt and hands, your feet are crucial points of contact with and control of the bike.

Standing up on the pegs turns you into a dynamic part of your bike rather than just dead weight. It makes you an active part of the suspension. Off-road, it lets you see farther and above the dust.

For long distances, standing with your legs fully extended and your knees locked is the least fatiguing. In short sections, you can still "stand" even though there may only be an inch (2.5 cm) of air between your butt and the saddle. But compared to someone sitting down, you'll have more control.

When in doubt, or when you're tired, try these three things: stand up, give the bike more gas, and look farther ahead. Those are your three get-out-of-jail-free cards.

144 THE INSIDE LINE
DAYTONA

NUMBER OF TURNS: **12**

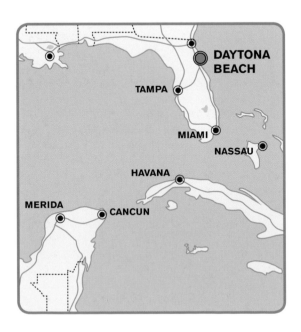

FAST FACTS

OFFICIAL NAME Daytona International Speedway

LOCATION Florida, United States, in Daytona Beach

TRACK LENGTH 2.950 mi (4.748 km)

DATE OPENED 1959

FAMOUS FEATURE The High Banks. Daytona's banking sets it apart. Tilting up at 31 degrees, it's nearly impossible to walk on and allows very high corner speeds.

TRIVIA Home to a huge number of both auto and motorcycle racing events (as well as part of Daytona's yearly Bike Week), the speedway's tri-oval track also hosts a slightly shorter bike course with twists and turns for AMA Superbike, MotoGP, and several other races. In addition to the Moto-Course's many events, Daytona also holds shorter flat-track races for dirtbikes.

Despite many injuries and fatalities over the years (including the notorious 2001 death of NASCAR racer Dale Earnhardt), the Speedway continues to live up to its name, with its fastest motorcycle lap set in the 2007 AMA Superbike races, by Suzuki team racer Ben Spies, with a blinding 1-minute-and-37.546 second record.

Daytona provides access packages to a "fan deck" to watch teams in their garages as they prepare for races, and a "party porch" which combines amusement park-style attractions and concessions with a view of the track.

145 HAVE A BLAST AT BIKE WEEK

Motorcyclists got it right a long time ago. While most the Northern Hemisphere is freezing, bikers have been heading to Daytona Beach, Florida, every March for racing, riding, and partying since 1937.

RIDE THERE It's all about bikes. Lots of people drive or fly in, but the best way to take part is to ride there. If you can't, at least rent a bike while you're in town.

GET TO THE RACES Bike Week got its start because of racing, and the Daytona International Speedway still hosts an epic event every year.

SEE THE FLAT TRACK The Daytona flat-track race is an underappreciated event, and as such is a real gem. It's always held at night, so spend an evening in the stands and watch these talented riders do their thing.

CHECK OUT THE NEW BIKES All of the major manufacturers show off their new bikes outside the Speedway; some also offer demo rides. Bring a license and a helmet. Sign up early—the lines will be long but it'll be worth it.

CHECK OUT THE CUSTOM BIKES Park on a street corner and watch the world go by, or check out the many custom-bike contests sponsored all around town.

BRING HOME A SOUVENIR Prove you were there. You can't walk more than a block on Main Street without finding another T-shirt shop. Or get a tattoo.

CHECK OUT MAIN STREET It's a little ways from the track, but a world of difference. It's loud and crowded, traffic is a nightmare, you'll have to wait in line for your food—and you'll love every minute of it. Spend at least one entire afternoon and evening here.

EAT GATOR TAIL Hey, Daytona is in the south, and the south is all about food. Alligator tail, hush puppies, crawdads—it's all part of the experience.

WATCH COLESLAW WRESTLING Coleslaw will never taste the same after you witness this tradition.

FOLLOW THE ACTION Every year there's one place that draws all the cool sportbikes and customs. Impromptu street races have been known to occur. Location may change year to year—think flash-mob.

SEE THE BIKE DEMOLITION DERBY Surreal. Gotta see it at least once.

BRING BAIL MONEY If it doesn't happen to you, it's going to happen to a friend.

146 BLEND IN AT STURGIS

Sturgis is a little town in the Black Hills of South Dakota. About 6,000 people live there, but for a week every summer, up to ten times that many people show up on their bikes. It's an experience you need to see to understand. And even then, you'll have trouble getting your head around all of it.

RIDE THERE Nothing gives you that grizzled, wind-burned look like riding a motorcycle across the United States in an open-face helmet. Men should swear off shaving for a couple of days too. Even better, do all that *and* ride there on a Harley. Or a Boss Hoss. Sturgis is all about living large.

NO TRAILERS Only racebikes and dirtbikes belong on trailers—everything else is meant to be ridden. Trailering a bike to Sturgis is like a cowboy carrying his horse on his back.

SPORT A TATTOO But not a new one. The best kind is one you got 20 years ago in the Navy or the Marine Corps. Can't go wrong with something associated with Harleys. Bonus points if it bears the name of a former partner you haven't seen in years.

TOTE A MACHINE GUN Interstate transportation of automatic weapons is a sticky subject, so do your research. But at least you can shoot one here.

CAMP Spend at least one Sturgis weekend sleeping at a campground—that is, if you can call that time between dusk and dawn sleep, when you're going to be hearing music, burnouts, and fights all night long.

GET VIP TICKETS A whole host of bands play at Sturgis every year. Some of them you can see for free, but why not go whole-hog and get up close to your favorite heavy-metal artists?

EAT A BUFFALO BURGER Or an Indian taco. Sturgis is a big food event, and there's a great deal of Native American heritage here. Embrace it, along with some tasty barbecue fare.

STYLE IT UP Black leather. And fringe. And big silver-and-turquoise jewelry. And halter tops. And boots, cowboy or otherwise. This is one place nobody's going to make fun of you for wearing fringed chaps.

147 MAKE SOME SPARKS

Nothing says hooligan like a big ol' stream of sparks flying off your centerstand as you tear down the highway at night. People in cars are going to think it's the end of the world. Do it in front of the cops and you'll get in trouble faster than if you'd mooned the police chief's wife. And nothing is as much fun.

It's easy. Just get going at a nice rate of speed, 30–60 mph (48–96 kph). Keep the bike vertical, without leaning left or right. Then take your left boot heel, put it on your centerstand tang, and press down, hard! A huge stream of sparks will fly behind you, and you'll laugh like a maniac inside your helmet. Do it enough and you'll grind the entire stand into uselessness and discover the high cost of replacing it. Which will be totally worth it.

148 BURN OUT THE DAY

The simple burnout is pretty safe and easy to do, but you will destroy your back tire, so consider whether there's a more eloquent and less expensive way of saying, "Screw you, I'm outta here." Doing your burnout down a painted road stripe will be a little easier on your tire and produce more smoke.

STEP 1 Start in second gear, standing firmly on the ground. Pull in the front brake and the clutch all the way.

STEP 2 Ease the throttle to about 7000–8000 rpm, keeping the brake and clutch levers in.

STEP 3 Release the clutch, keeping the front brake fully engaged. The back tire will start to spin in place. The more throttle you provide, the more smoke you'll make.

STEP 4 Pull in the clutch, ease off the throttle, and ride off in a super-cool, carcinogenic cloud of tire dust and smoke.

149 MAKE YOUR BIKE BACKFIRE

Being tailgated by some brain-dead idiot who's texting and driving? Here's a sure way to get his or her attention.

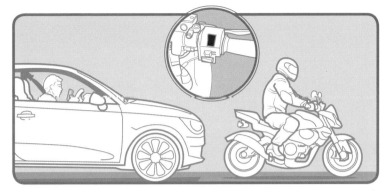

STEP 1 Flick off your bike's kill switch. Not the ignition key, but the switch mounted on the right handgrip, which stops the spark to your bike's ignition. Be aware that your bike will slow suddenly at this time.

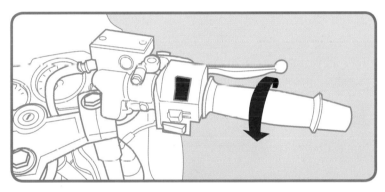

STEP 2 Hold the throttle wide open for two or three seconds. Opening the throttle with the bike in gear keeps the engine pumping gas and air into the exhaust and muffler system.

STEP 3 Flick the kill switch back to "run." This reintroduces hot gasses into the muffler, and all the gas vapor in there ignites. The trick only works with bikes that are carbureted. And if you do it enough, you'll probably reduce your muffler to junk status.

150

DRINK AND RIDE?

In one word: Don't. In two words: Don't. Ever.

About half of the motorcycle deaths in the United States involve a rider who was drinking. A staggering 70 percent of ALL motorcycle accidents involve riders who have had a drink.

It's bad enough out there with all those distracted drivers eating hot dogs, texting, putting on makeup, and generally driving like a bunch of half-trained monkeys even on their best days. On the weekends, probably half of them have been drinking, too. Having a drink yourself on top of all that is just plain stupid.

Riding a motorcycle well is demanding. Most military pilots follow the 12 hours bottle-to-throttle rule. You should, too. And if you're on a date, it can make for a great excuse to spend the night.

151 POP A WHEELIE

There are three kinds of wheelie: the intentional, the unintentional, and the intentional gone bad. Here's how to do it right. Best bike to learn on? Someone else's, preferably a dirtbike. And wear all of the protective gear that you possibly can.

THE POWER WHEELIE Perfect for beginners. Sit back on the bike. Take off in first gear. When you're moving and the clutch is out, open the throttle quickly until the front comes up. Repeat this, trying to get the front end lighter and ride the wheelie farther. You'll learn throttle control and get used to the idea.

THE CLUTCH WHEELIE Start the same way that you would for the power wheelie, sitting back on the bike. Take off in first gear. When you're moving, pull the clutch in enough so that it slips. Rev the engine and let the clutch out until the front wheel lofts. Repeat until you can ride this wheelie farther.

Wheelie gone wrong? If the bike's starting to loop out, stab the rear brake and the front end will drop back down. It's always easier to wheelie with the bike pointed uphill. Sometimes, a small bump in the road or trail can help you loft the front wheel.

152 DO A STOPPIE

This is the wheelie's evil twin, sometimes called a nose wheelie. The first two steps (what bike to learn on, what to wear) are the same as for a wheelie, although a streetbike with a powerful front disc brake and a sticky front tire will work better.

Approach a flat, smooth area (parking lot, runway) and ride in at 30–45 mph (48–72 kph). Lean forward and get your weight over the handlebar. A sportbike with a low bar is the best choice.

As you reach the area you've targeted, smoothly and quickly squeeze the front-brake lever until the

fork is compressed. Then squeeze harder while tranferring your weight forward until the rear wheel begins to rise off the pavement.

Remember: You're not trying to stop the bike, just get the rear wheel to come up. Once you can do that, increase your pressure and weight transfer until you can bring the rear wheel higher and higher.

Start out small. If a stoppie goes bad, all you can do is release the front brake, but there's a good chance it's all over. On the other hand, if it does go bad, you've mastered the endo.

153 PASS IN A TURN

Overtaking another bike in a turn can be tricky. Here's how to do it right.

STEP 1 Let the other bike know you're there—be sure he or she has spotted you before you make your next move.

STEP 2 Pass on the outside. This means a longer, wider line, but it's safer. The key is to accelerate well before you're parallel to the other rider.

STEP 3 Understand your line. The other rider may be on your ideal line, so you'll have to come in wider and maybe exit wider as well. Never count on the other rider holding his or her line—they'll almost never close it up, but may run wider. If they do, they'll push you wider, too, so be ready for it.

STEP 4 Plan to overtake the other rider before or at the apex—that'll give you far more control on the exit. If you've carried more speed into the corner for the pass, you should easily out-accelerate the other rider from the apex to the exit.

154 PICK THE PERFECT LINE

When motorcyclists talk about "line," they don't mean something you use for fishing. They're talking about the exact path their bike travels over a road or track. Each line has three parts: the entry, the apex, and the exit, and a line is usually described as having an early or late apex. In addition to the illustration here, a great way to visualize line is to visit a racetrack and look at the darker area on the track surface, where the bikes have laid down rubber from their tires.

Most new riders begin their turns too soon and go into an early apex, which forces them to run wide on the exit. Entering the turn wider and waiting later to make the apex may seem counterintuitive, but it's usually both safer and faster. You can see farther through the turn, and at the turn's exit you'll find you have much more road to work with.

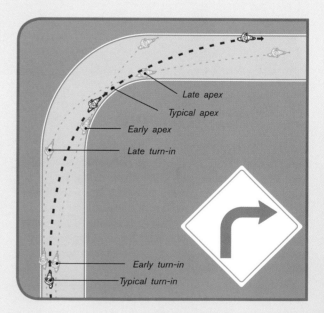

Late apex
Typical apex
Early apex
Late turn-in
Early turn-in
Typical turn-in

155 PASS A CAR SAFELY

Ride often enough and you'll come to view moving cars as dangerous, rolling roadblocks. Motorcyclists have two great advantages over automobiles—acceleration and maneuverability. Smart riders use both to their best interests.

BE DECISIVE The key to proper overtaking is to execute the maneuver as quickly as is safe. When ahead of or behind the car, you're relatively safe, but when you're beside the other vehicle you're vulnerable and have fewer collision-avoidance options. Don't speed up when you've pulled beside the car; instead, make the decision to pass, indicate, and then begin to accelerate while you're still far behind the vehicle. Downshifting allows your bike to accelerate faster, but you don't want to have to upshift in the middle of your pass. Choose a gear that's low enough for aggressive engine response but that still lets you finish the pass.

BE AWARE Avoid passing in intersections, and be extra careful in areas with lots of driveways or side roads on the passing side. Why? If the car wanders into your lane, runs wide, or decides to change lanes or pull into a driveway, you need to have a way out already in mind. When you begin your pass, look for an escape route if the car changes direction.

BE CAREFUL Watch the driver's mirrors and front wheels—these often hint at a turn a split second before the driver changes lanes. Be particularly careful if the driver seems distracted by things like texting or talking on the phone, eating, or other non-driving activities.

156 TAKE AN OBJECT LESSON

As riders, we've had to deal with some crazy items in the road, including a canoe, a flock of sheep, aluminum extension ladders, and 4,000 sausages. And that was just last week!

If you hit (some of) this kind of stuff in a car, you usually run over it. On a bike, you fall over. So don't hit it. Which means don't fixate on a target—instead of looking at that television set in the middle of the

highway, look for a way around it. Use your motorcycle's maneuverability to avoid that junk. And don't presume that because something looks harmless, it's safe to run over it and keep rolling. That's car-think, and you're a rider, not a driver.

As a corollary, don't follow behind vehicles with unsecured loads—when stuff starts flying and rolling off, it'll have your name on it.

158 RIDE ROUGH ROADS

Maybe there's some magical place where all the roads are as smooth as a putting green and the traction's perfect in every corner. If you find it, let us know; wherever we ride the pavement looks like the aftermath of a WWII bombing raid. The best strategy with any of these problems is avoidance.

POTHOLES These pits can do real damage to your tires and rims, and put you on your head, too. If you have to hit one, at least make sure your bike is straight up and down, as opposed to leaning over in a corner. If there's a pothole right in your line while cornering, stand the bike up, cross over the pothole, and then lean your bike over again and complete your turn. Stand up on the pegs dirtbike style, too—you don't need full leg extension, but at least get your backside just barely off the seat.

ROAD SEALER Those black snakes slithering across the road are tar strips sealing up cracks. Adjust your line to miss them if you can. You want to avoid hitting them with your front wheel—crossing them with your rear isn't as bad. Downhills will be worse than uphills because of the weight on the front end. If the front does tuck, the sealer usually isn't very wide, so you still have a chance to save it.

PAINT Wet road-marker paint can be a real hazard. As with potholes, try to cross paint stripes with less lean angle than normal.

157 SWERVE SAFELY

One word: countersteering (see item #89).

Also, avoid target fixation. Look past the problem to your exit point. A safe swerve is made up of two parts: avoiding the object, and then recovering from the swerve to continue your path of travel. You can get some practice in a parking lot, using a small, soft object (like a paper coffee cup) as a pylon. Head for it, look past it, and countersteer around it. When you're on the road you won't have much time to react, so you need to ingrain this skill as an automatic response.

159 NEVER BUY A BIKE YOU CAN'T LIFT

In a world of hoary motorcycle clichés, this one deserves a place of honor. And yes, like many clichés of course it's true to some degree. You never want to be in the situation of having dropped your bike and being literally unable to get back into action. But here's the tricky part: You can probably lift a lot more bike than you think, using the techniques on the next page. If you're a person with some reasonable upper and lower body strength and you're not riding a bike that's as big as a barge, you'll probably be fine. Not sure? Find someone with a bike about the weight you're interested in, and ask if you can practice. Picking it up, that is, not laying it down.

160 RESTART ON A HILL

You've stalled on an uphill slope—what now? Don't panic; it happens. Just hold the bike up with your left foot, and use your right foot to apply the rear brake to stop the bike from rolling backward; you can also put both feet on the ground and hold the bike with the front-brake lever. Now, it's time to get it started again.

First, forget about finding neutral. Just pull in the clutch and start the bike in gear. Begin letting the clutch out before you release either brake. You'll feel the front suspension begin to compress—let it. As the engine begins to load, slowly release the brake while giving the bike plenty of gas. Get your feet back on the pegs as soon as you can.

Alternatively, you can just roll the bike back down the hill and restart at the bottom or while the bike is headed down. Both are easier if you can turn the bike around, and then go downhill nose first, which isn't usually an option on the street, but on the dirt it can be the easiest way to get the job done. Just be sure to lean into the hill while you're turning, or you may take a wicked fall. It may even be easier to get off the bike entirely and stand between the bike and the hill.

161 GET BACK ON THE (IRON) HORSE

You've come to an unceremonious halt, and either fallen off your ride or dismounted in a hurry. First, make sure you're okay. If you're in one piece, the next order of business is to get your ride up on its wheels again.

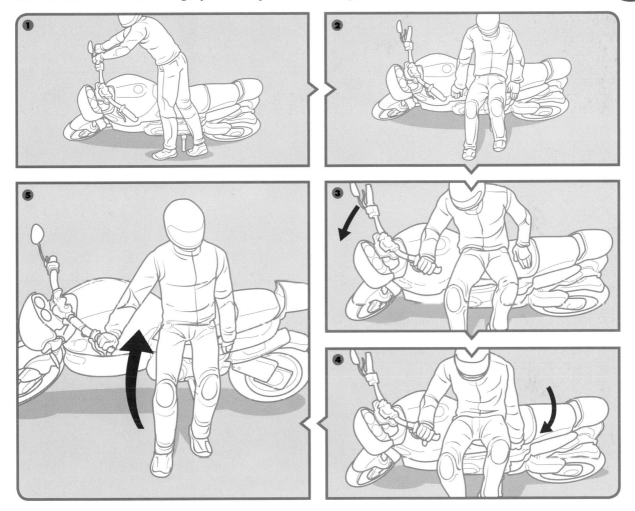

STEP 1 Kill the ignition, and make sure the bike is in gear. Turn the handlebar in the direction of the fall—if the bike's on its left side, turn the bar to the left. If it's on its right side, lower the sidestand.

STEP 2 Back up to the bike with your butt in the middle of the seat.

STEP 3 Squat down and reach for the handlebar. Hold the grip on the low side of the bike—if the bike's on its left side, take hold of the left grip with your right hand.

STEP 4 Use your other hand to hold the frame or other sturdy part of the machine under or behind the seat, as low as you can get it.

STEP 5 Place your feet close together. Lift your chin and look up (this will help straighten your back to prevent injury). Now, push with your legs and your butt. Slowly take tiny steps back and walk the bike up. Once it's vertical, take care not to push it over.

Practice on a small dirtbike first. If there's anyone else available to help, by all means ask!

162 SURVIVE A CRASH

No two motorcycle crashes are alike, but if you do kiss the pavement, knowing how to fall can make a big difference. Most important? The right gear (a jacket, boots, gloves and a helmet at the bare minimum). Back protector? Elbow and knee armor? Full leathers? You'll wish you had all of them in a crash.

Your first imperative is to get clear of the bike. Famous last words: "I can save it!" It's admirable that riders don't want to give up, but once the bike touches the ground, it's time to let go. Get a hand or a limb trapped between a sliding bike and the pavement and you're looking at a serious injury.

Keep your hands up if at all possible. It isn't always (see the unlucky rider below), but do your best. If you're sliding, get onto your back and get your feet forward as soon as you can. Don't get up until you've come to a full stop. This may sound funny—how could anyone make that mistake?—but racers do it all the time. They think they're stopped, but they're not. They try to stand up and go flying.

Once you've stopped, get out of traffic as soon as possible, too. Logic dictates that you shouldn't move until you know nothing's broken, but you really don't want to be lying in the road and get run over.

163 HANDLE AN EMERGENCY

Maybe you've hit the ground. Maybe it's a friend who's fallen. But there's a rider down, and it's bad. The obvious action is to call 911. The best answer is to take some formal training before the incident—something that concentrates on trauma, the most likely form of injury a motorcyclist will encounter. Your local Red Cross is a great place to start, as are the local fire department and hospital ER; they can direct you to first-responder or EMT courses. In the meantime, you need a plan, and you'll need to execute it quickly. Remember the following, and it's imperative that you execute this plan in the following order: S-R-ABC-S.

SAFETY First, your own; next, the victim's. Accidents happen in dangerous places. Stopping to help is noble, but don't hit by another vehicle because you're too focused on helping the victim. Be sure basic safety is under control, then call 911 pronto.

RESCUE Don't move a victim unnecessarily. But what if the person is in a place where he or she needs to be moved to prevent additional injury? Dragging someone out of a burning house is a no-brainer.

AIRWAY Make sure the patient's airway is clear. You can do this even if they're wearing a full-face helmet.

BREATHING The patient needs to be breathing. If not, consider beginning CPR.

CIRCULATION Look for two things here—a heartbeat, and any life-threatening blood loss. Relatively minor blood loss can look terrifying, but may not be life threatening at all. Learn how to assess the difference.

SPINAL Don't remove a patient's helmet unless you absolutely must—you might worsen any neck injuries.

Use the resources you have available to you. Are there lots of bystanders? Put them to work directing traffic, calling emergency services, and so on. Take charge of the accident scene, and be sure nobody else gets hurt.

The first hour after an injury is most critical to helping treat critical injuries. If help is slow in coming, you'll at least have done as much as you can in those first 60 minutes. If there are multiple victims, it's time for triage. Assess their injuries quickly and prioritize treatment accordingly.

164 UNDERSTAND STOPPING DISTANCE

Every basic driving course tells you there are two components to how long—and how far—it takes you to stop: reaction time and braking time. But motorcyclists need to know more.

A good sportbike can outbrake many cars, but not all motorcycles are equal in that regard. And more and more bikes offer ABS (anti-lock braking systems), a real benefit for most riders.

As speed increases, stopping distance increases a seemingly disproportionate amount. For example, let's say you're going 20 mph (32 kph), and it takes you 20 feet (6 m) to stop. Now let's triple your speed to 60 mph (97 kph). Tripling the stopping distance isn't accurate—in reality, you'll need more than 180 feet (55 m) to stop.

Of course the best way to know exactly how much road you'll need is to go out and practice—carefully.

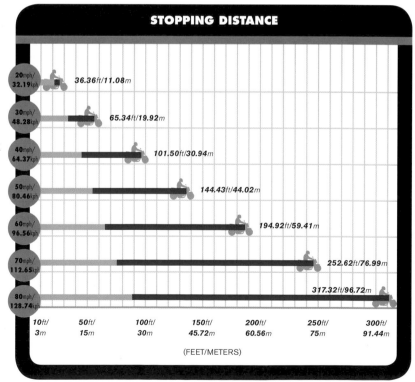

STOPPING DISTANCE

Speed	Distance
20mph/ 32.19kph	36.36ft/11.08m
30mph/ 48.28kph	65.34ft/19.92m
40mph/ 64.37kph	101.50ft/30.94m
50mph/ 80.46kph	144.43ft/44.02m
60mph/ 96.56kph	194.92ft/59.41m
70mph/ 112.65kph	252.62ft/76.99m
80mph/ 128.74kph	317.32ft/96.72m

10ft/3m 50ft/15m 100ft/30m 150ft/45.72m 200ft/60.56m 250ft/75m 300ft/91.44m

(FEET/METERS)

165 MAKE AN EMERGENCY STOP

Despite your best efforts, you're boxed in, and there's no escape route. It's time to hit the brakes. You've just learned the math on reaction time and braking time, but in real life, riders need to know more. Here's how to stop safely and swiftly.

1. Get the bike straight up and down you can't stop hard if you're leaned over.

2. Use both the front and rear brakes, hard. Up to 75 percent of your braking power is up front—if you only use the rear, you greatly increase your stopping distance..

3. Shift your weight as far back as you can. You'll need to slide your butt back on the seat and push hard on the handlebar to keep from sliding forward.

4. If the rear wheel locks, let it. Research shows that in a panic situation, riders who release a locked-up rear wheel will also release the front-brake lever, increasing stopping distance. Practice will show you that you can still control a bike with a locked rear wheel—learning on a dirtbike is a great help.

5. Pull in the clutch lever right at the start. Don't worry about using engine compression braking and downshifting in this scenario. If this is a real panic stop, you need to keep things simple and eliminate those variables.

166 HANDLE A SKID

In a car, you're taught to steer into a skid. On a bike, things are considerably more complicated. If your rear wheel starts to skid when you brake, the easiest solution is just to release the rear brake. But if you can't do that, here are some things to remember.

KEEP YOUR EYES UP Watch the horizon and where you want to go. The bike's natural tendency is to follow the front wheel. If the rear is loose, but the front still has steering authority and is pointed in the correct direction, you're in good shape.

SHIFT YOUR WEIGHT Putting more weight on the rear wheel may reduce the skid. Sliding forward, on the other hand, will probably give you more control by putting more weight on the front wheel—the one that's doing the steering, and not skidding.

GET ON THE FOOTPEGS Here sportbike, enduro, and dirtbike riders are at a big advantage because footpeg placement lets them "post" as on a horse—stand or weight the pegs to relieve the dead load on the chassis. You don't have to be fully standing, but getting the balls of your feet on the footpegs will give you and your bike better balance.

167 UNDERSTAND ANTI-LOCK

Most bikes differ from cars in that they have separate front and rear brakes, while most cars' brakes function as one. In addition, motorcycles use different front and rear tires; weight shift is also a major part of a motorbike's stopping performance. Anti-lock brake systems for bikes and cars face different challenges.

Anti-lock braking systems (ABS) are relatively new for bikes. There's no one standard system. But all ABS work in a similar way: they compare front- and rear-wheel rotation speeds, and if one wheel is locking up under braking (skidding), ABS momentarily releases braking force to that wheel and then re-applies it. The best systems do this about 24 times a second—much faster than any human.

Many also automatically apply both brakes, linking the front and rear. Your rear-brake pedal still (mostly) controls the rear brake, but applies some front brake as well; ditto for the front-brake lever.

ABS helps you stop faster because it helps to eliminate skidding, though it will do nothing for increased stopping distances on wet roads or ice. But since most riders tip over if they lock a wheel, anti-lock brakes are a real benefit. They're usually more costly, add weight and complexity to a bike, and some riders resent the perceived loss of control.

168 DON'T GO TOO LOW

Imagine leaning through a turn and simply falling down on the low side of the bike—that's how the lowside crash gets its name. You may slide a bit, but since it's a short fall, your bones usually stay intact. The bike is also in front of the rider—good news, because otherwise it might slide over you.

Most riders think lowsides come from leaning over too far, but it's usually a loss of traction on slick roads, or caused by too much braking when leaned over. It can also happen if you tuck the front end with too much steering effort.

169 DON'T GET HIGH

A "highside" happens when the rear wheel loses traction, then regains it suddenly. Watch enough roadrace videos and you'll see exactly what goes on—and it's never pretty. When that big rear tire slips and grabs, it's enough to launch a rider right out of the seat, pitching him or her so high their feet end up higher than their head. A really bad highside flips the bike horizontal, a couple of feet above the pavement.

Most streetbike riders highside because they run a bike out of cornering clearance, lift the rear tire, and then a bump in the road causes the rear tire to regain traction. Or the rear tire spins under acceleration, the bike starts to slide, the rider closes the throttle suddenly, traction returns, and they go airborne.

How to avoid this? Once it starts, the highside is over in a split second. If the bike is leaned over and the rear wheel starts to slide, don't chop the throttle; it's better to lowside than have the bike hook up now.

170

RIDE THE GLOBE OF DEATH

If your loved ones think that all motorcycles are dangerous, just take them to watch someone ride the Globe of Death—they'll never give you a hard time about your 20-minute commute again. But what if you did actually end up locked inside this giant steel-mesh hamster ball? How do you ride around inside this thing without turning it into a giant spherical cheese grater—where you end up as the cheese?

GET THE RIGHT BIKE Most Globe of Death riders use 100cc dirtbikes. Whatever you do, don't get conned into trying this on your own machine.

PICK THE RIGHT SPEED The globe is all about keeping a consistent speed. At first, try out some small circles, working your way up to full horizontal loops, and then full vertical loops.

USE PERIPHERAL VISION Veteran globe riders will tell you they concentrate on one point—like the head of the swimsuit-clad model in the center of the globe—and watch everything else out of the corners of their eyes.

WORK WITH OTHER RIDERS The only thing crazier than riding in the globe by yourself is riding in it with another bike or two. If you do, visualize yourself on a merry-go-round, always keeping the other rider (or riders) the same distance from you.

171

PREPARE FOR A TRACK DAY

The street is no place to practice advanced sportbike riding skills— that's why you head for the track. Track days and race days both happen on the same pavement, but a track day is about improving your riding, not beating the other guy.

BIKE If your bike isn't in top condition, you're wasting time at the track. Pay close attention to the tires, suspension, and drivechain. Do all the work before you go off to the track. Normal maintenance aside, most tracks will require specific bike prep—taping over or removing mirrors and lights, safety wiring oil drain bolts and filters, and replacing radiator coolant with distilled water. Check with the track beforehand for further instructions.

RIDER Visiting the track as a spectator is a great idea; attending the riders' meeting is a must. Getting your mind right (a track day isn't a race day) is a huge step forward. If you can, arrange a lap of the track in a car with you as an observer. You can also find video "virtual laps" of some of the bigger tracks in video games and get familiar with them at home.

GEAR Most tracks require you to wear one-piece racing leathers (or a two-piece leather suit that zips together), a helmet, boots, and gloves. A back protector is a good idea, too. For short breaks you'll probably just unzip your leathers, but on longer breaks, a pair of shorts and sandals are welcome. If you don't own leathers, you may be able to borrow or rent a pair from a track school.

172
PACK FOR THE TRACK

Ideally, you'll go to a track day with a friend who's familiar with the drill, but just in case, here are some pointers.

TRANSPORT Save riding the bike for the track. You can team up with friends to save money on renting a truck, trailer, or van.

COMFORT Bring a pop-up canopy for shade, and some folding chairs. You're going to be here for the next eight hours. You'll also want a cooler with water and snacks. Don't eat too much, but do eat something, and stay hydrated.

TOOLS & PARTS You shouldn't be making major setup changes or repairs at the track, but you'll need the basics to remove bodywork (for inspection) and make adjustments to the chain, chassis, control, and suspension. Extra brake and clutch levers let you keep riding after a minor tipover, too. While you really should have your tires sorted before you head to the track, if you want to test other tires, have them pre-mounted on a set of spare rims.

OTHER ESSENTIALS Bring about 10 gallons (38 liters) of fuel, a funnel and a fire extinguisher. The 10- or 20-liter bottles are best. You'll need a swingarm stand at the minimum; a front-end stand that holds the bike by the steering head is also a good idea. And don't count on electricity in the pits. Bring your own generator (get a quiet one), as well as gas for it and a spare plug. Finally, don't forget to pack a notebook. You'll want to keep track of all what worked and what didn't.

173 DON'T BE THAT GUY

Remember, you're here to learn, not to be the fastest guy on the track. Guys who try to race you on track day are jerks—don't be one of them. Even if you're slow, nobody will laugh at you as long as you're riding safely.

A common complaint about new riders is their failure to enter and exit the track correctly. When entering the track, follow the course marshal's directions. If you're going to exit the track, or suddenly need to slow, ride with your left hand off the bar and held up, and/or your right foot off the peg and held out. If you're heading to the pit, signal first, then slow down.

Definitely the number-one complaint is that new riders, out of misplaced courtesy, try to move over to give an overtaking rider room. Don't—just stay on the line you've been using. Unless you're actively trying to block someone, all the burden of passing safely lies with the overtaking rider. You should also remember to leave room when passing. This isn't a race, so there's no need to pass in a corner. Pass on the straights, and leave six feet (2 m) of room—most tracks are plenty wide enough.

Stay focused. The track is going to be a demanding and intimidating place. Getting tired? It's time to take a break.

174 KNOW YOUR FLAGS

While you're on the track, conditions are bound to change, due to human error, environment, or just plain bad luck. Keep an eye out for these signals to ensure a safe track day run.

FLAGS		WHAT IT MEANS
GREEN		Track is open for full-speed riding.
YELLOW		Caution; usually shown if there's a problem on the track. If the flag is waving, slow down and be vigilant.
RED		Stop. Usually you finish your lap, but at greatly reduced speed; check red-flag protocol for your track.
PASSING		You're about to be overtaken. Hold your line, but be prepared.
DEBRIS		Warns of oil or other debris on the track.
MEATBALL		Signal given to an individual rider. Pull into the pits.
WHITE		In racing, one lap to go. Crossed white and green flags (often rolled) means session is halfway done.
BLACK		Go to the pits immediately. Either you did something bad or there's a serious mechanical problem.

175 TAPE YOUR HANDS

Many dirt riders and some road racers tape their hands to avoid blisters when riding. Clean, good-fitting gloves are the first place to start, but with a roll of half- and one-inch (1- and 2.5-cm) medical adhesive tape, you can prevent almost any blister. Just follow this step-by-step guide.

STEP 1 Make sure your hands are clean and completely dry.

STEP 2 Cut moleskin patches to cover up any areas where you have blistered in the past—usually the top of the palm where the fingers join the hand, but sometimes the inside of the thumb as well. When in doubt, make the moleskin about twice the size of your last blister.

STEP 3 Cut a piece of tape 6 inches (15 cm) long; apply as shown. Repeat in any area where you get blisters.

STEP 4 Using the 1-inch (2.5 cm) wide tape, wrap a strip as

shown, starting at the back of your hand and wrapping it over the palm. Press the tape down smooth and tight. Use two layers of tape.

STEP 5 Flex your hands. You want the tape tight,

but not so tight that it restricts your hand movement. Don't use so much that you can't put on your gloves.

STEP 6 Dust talcum powder lightly on your hands or inside your gloves, to help you slide your hands into the gloves without balling up the tape. It will also help reduce blisters by keeping your hands drier and cutting down on chafing.

176 WARM UP YOUR TIRES

Motorcycle tires aren't just rubber—they're actually a chemically complex combination of materials designed to work best at specific temperatures. What temperatures? Typically around 165° F (74° C). Not exactly a cool breeze. So how do you get them to be that hot?

There are two ways to do it: by using tire warmers, or by working the tires. The warmers are simple—think of them as custom electric blankets for your tires. Watch any Superbike or MotoGP race on television and you'll see them on the bikes before they go out on the track—that way the racers get hot tires ready to go from lap one.

Not on the track? Then you'll have to do it old-school—by working the tire. Ride far and fast enough and the tire will come up to temperature naturally. But you can speed up the process with a series of progressively harder accelerations and stops. In the old days, riders used to swerve side-to-side as well, but testing has proven this to be ineffective.

Cycle World's Nick Ienatsch has a great approach: Ride on cold tires as you'd ride in the rain—be smooth, use authority, and make the most of your large inputs with the bike straight up and down—or close to it.

177 LAUNCH AT THE DRAGSTRIP

The standing quarter-mile (400 m) is the measure by which all serious streetbike engines are judged. A great time depends on a great launch. How to pull it off?

First, set your tire pressure right. Warm up your rear tire with a burnout: Hold the front brake tight, slip the clutch and spin the rear wheel. You'll usually want to start out in first gear. Bring the engine up to peak torque—usually between 4500 and 9000 rpm.

Let the clutch out quickly while increasing engine speed. Rev up fast enough and the bike will start to wheelie; shift your weight over the front end to help keep the front wheel down. A bit of of wheelie is fine, and better than not giving the bike enough gas. But if the bike jumps up, you get wheel loft, not distance.

Another technique is to hold the engine rpm just below redline. Control your traction and speed with the clutch until the first upshift. The clutch will hate you, but the stopwatch will love it.

178 MAKE A PIT STOP

Endurance racers and Baja riders both need to make pit stops in competition. A fast road racing pit stop (two tires, full tank of gas) can be right around ten seconds; a dirtbike pit can take a minute or more.

KNOW WHERE YOUR PIT IS There's no shifting into reverse on a course if you blow past your pit.

BE CALM You shouldn't be in too great a hurry. Don't get tunnel vision—take in the big picture, especially if there are other riders pitting at the same time.

PUT IT IN NEUTRAL Coast into the pit. For a fuel-only stop, idle the engine; for tires, shut it down.

SIT BACK The fuel man will come in from your left. Stay on your bike but take your left hand off the bar, lean back, and give him enough room to work. While you're waiting, you can use that time to take a drink of water, polish your faceshield or change goggles, and get a brief race report.

EXIT UNDER CONTROL Off-road, you don't want to roost your crew, so get well clear of the pit before you dial up the gas. On a paved track, accelerate smoothly out of the pit, obeying the pit speed limit.

PRACTICE You and your crew both need to practice your pit technique. Smoothness counts!

179 DRAG A KNEE

Nothing defines the modern road-race style like dragging your inside knee through turns. (Pro tip: racing leathers with hard plastic knee pucks are a must.) This is less about your knee and more about your whole body. Keep your inside foot firmly planted on the peg through the turn—you want to weight the chassis hard. Now slide your butt as far off the inside of the seat as you can while sticking your knee down and out, and moving your torso forward.

You'll find that for a given speed and turn radius, you won't have to lean the bike over as far. Rather than concentrating on leaning and then getting your knee down, do the opposite: assume the position, and then gradually increase your turn radius (go in deeper), your speed, and your lean angle. Touchdown!

180 GET THE HANG OF IT

Motorcycles stop faster and accelerate harder when they're straight up and down, because that's when the tires put the most footprint to the road surface. Suspension components also work best in the pure vertical plane—leaning the bike over puts side loads on them, encouraging binding and frame flex.

But we need to lean bikes over in order to turn. What can we do about it?

Hanging off on the inside of the turn reduces the amount we need to lean a bike for a given speed and turn radius. In each illustration below, you can see three red circles: one represents the center of gravity (CG) for the bike, one for the rider, and the

third the combination of the two. There's little you can do about your bike's CG, but by hanging off you can move *your* CG (and thus the combined CG) lower and farther into the turn, and that means the bike won't have to lean over as much. In return, you'll have a greater tire footprint and better suspension compliance.

If you hang off far enough to actually touch your knee to the ground, you can also use your leg as stabilizing support to help hold the bike up in the turn. Naturally, this is an advanced technique only for racers, but even everyday riders can benefit from hanging off in turns, especially in the rain or on poor pavement.

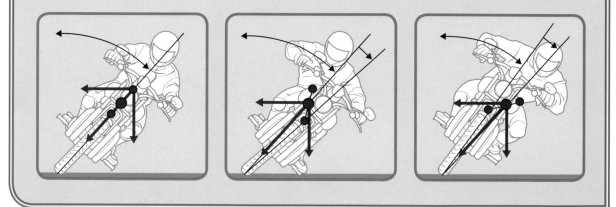

181 GET DOWN TO THE ELBOW

Wars escalate—what starts out as a little border dispute ends up a giant international confrontation. Same with racing: Mike Hailwood dragged holes in the outsides of his boots when he leaned his bike over in turns. Kenny Roberts and Jarno Saarinen dragged their knees. And now Marc Marquez, pictured here, drags his elbows. We have to wonder what's next—dragging your helmet?

When you combine such a body-to-the-inside style with the amazing grip of today's tires, there is no longer room under the machine for the classic knee-on-the-pavement position. Instead, you see today's riders packaging themselves along the bike. The inside knee is up against the bike, and the elbow is very close to the ground. All this is done to keep from having to lean the machine over any more than absolutely necessary. Today, big lean angle numbers, like 63 to 64 degrees, are common.

Many have noted that Marquez's bike is not leaned over as far as some. The reason is that his body is far off the inside to hold the bike more upright. And when he is ready to accelerate, he pushes the machine more upright very rapidly, putting it "on the carcass" instead of on the very edge.

182   GET A DATE WITH AN UMBRELLA GIRL

You see them standing around at all the road races: those tall, pneumatically enhanced women in short skirts. Their job? Ostensibly it's to hold the umbrella that shades riders while they're on the starting grid. Sure it is. So how do you get a date with one of these trackside beauties?

BE A WINNER Everybody loves the smell of success. But tragically, even superstars soon discover that the umbrella girl sometimes knows nothing about your sport, and maybe didn't even watch the race. Bummer.

BE RICH Everyone follows the money in racing. Big wallet? Step right this way, sir.

BE FAMOUS Not just road racer famous—you'd better be movie-star famous.

ASK THEM Hey, just because they look superhuman doesn't mean they're not people, too. Just be prepared: every other single guy at the track has the same idea. Pickup lines? She's heard them all. Maybe you should do something radical like develop a personality.

183 WATCH A RACE

Lots of people look at races; few truly know how to watch them. Even fewer know how to do so like Yoichi Oguma, at one time the head of HRC, Honda's racing department. He would tell his staff never to attend a race without the "Three Sacred Treasures" of racing—camera, stopwatch, and binoculars—to turn them from passive viewers into active observers.

The camera can photograph bikes for later analysis. The stopwatch can time gaps between riders, or how fast they are going through specific turns. Binoculars can vastly increase the area you can critically observe.

Divide your day into three parts. First, spend time in the pits seeing the bikes and crews up close. Walk past the tire-changing area and check out what the riders are using. Next, choose a turn and watch at least one full session to see how riders and bikes work in that part of the course. Last, get to a vantage point to watch the final races, and see at least half of the track with binoculars. To those three treasures, add a fourth: a notebook, to record what you see.

Pay attention to how late a rider brakes, the line he takes through the turn, where he hits the apex, and how soon he gets on the gas. Watch his racecraft—how he deals with riders close by, especially setting them up for a pass. Look for what's invisible—how far back drafting is effective on the long straights. Put it all together and you'll get much greater appreciation and understanding of the event than just watching the bikes go round.

184 SNEAK INTO THE PITS

There are two kinds of people at the track: The unwashed masses in the grandstands, and the royalty roaming the pits. (Maybe the racers are the real royalty, but at least the washed masses get into the pits.) The easiest way in is with a pass—but you need cash or a genuine reason, neither of which you have if you're reading this. What to do?

FORGERY Snag a pass and scan or copy it somehow. Forgery used to be easier, but increased security measures (holograms, reflective ink, RFID chips) have upped the difficulty. Still worth a try.

DRESS THE PART Get a team shirt. This is easier than ever, since many teams sell them to bring in a little extra cash. It doesn't even have to be a current team shirt, or from your favorite team—track security are paid by the hour and aren't enthusiasts. Props like a tire cart, a rim, or at least a clipboard and a radio help.

DOUBLE DOWN Someone gets a legitimate pit pass. That person walks into the pits, heads over to an unwatched section of the fence, and throws the pass over to you. Repeat until your whole crew is inside. But, if they catch you, everyone gets kicked out, and the pass gets confiscated.

PIT PASS

185 BECOME A RACE MECHANIC

What could be better than exposing yourself to all sorts of poisonous chemicals, working insane hours, sleeping in bedbug-infested hotels while you're out criss-crossing the country in the back of a clapped-out box van, and existing on a steady diet of soda and lukewarm hotdogs?

Sound like your dream job? Welcome to the realities of being a race mechanic.

Racing is hard work, but there's nothing like it. And working as a top-line race mechanic will open doors for the rest of your life.

Lots of race mechanics are former racers who worked on their own bikes and found they had more talent behind a wrench than behind the handlebars.

Plus, racers relate well to tuners and mechanics who once raced themselves.

Formal training is another option. Race teams typically recruit top graduates from schools like the Motorcycle Mechanics Institute. Nationality doesn't matter—no matter what language you speak, if you have the technical skills you'll find work.

Working at a dealership that sponsors racers is a natural way to get started, as is an apprenticeship with one of the bigger teams. Plenty of mechanics and technicians got their start chasing down parts or standing over the solvent tank with a brush. And while you're doing all of that, make sure your bike always finishes, and usually wins.

186 LOVE LIFE AS A TEST RIDER

Want to make your living riding new bikes and writing about them? Hey, that's what the *Cycle World* staff does, and that's what I did at the late, great *Cycle* magazine. And I won't lie to you—it was the best job I've ever had, bar none. But being a test rider demands a set of skills, and not just those you use in the saddle.

WRITING Like your mom said, stay in school, study English or journalism, read as much quality writing as you can, and get published—even if it's just a blog. You need writing skills for this gig.

RIDING Expose yourself to every aspect of motorcycling—road bikes, touring bikes, sportbikes, motocross, etc. Since you probably can't afford all of these yourself, working at a dealership may be a way in. But try to ride as many different machines as you can—you'll be doing that for a living, if you're lucky. Racing in any form is a huge help; the more extensive your racing resume, the better.

WRENCHING Working in the service shop of a dealership is a great way to get some hands-on experience. So is working for a race team. Even just doing your own maintenance is a start, and formal training (see item #185 on becoming a race mechanic) is a big bonus. And don't discount the time-honored method of just buying a basket case and spending the summer putting it back together and making it run.

187 RIDE ON A TIGHTROPE

Ever wonder what the art of tightrope walking is called? Funambulism. (Knew those years spent in grad school as an English major would pay off.) So what do you call someone who wants to ride across a tightrope or highwire on a motorcycle, other than nuts? Actually, it's relatively simple—there's the hairball method, and the sure-fire method.

HAIRBALL Find a suitable tightrope or highwire. Remove your bike's tires—riding the rims will center the wheels on the wire. Now, get a ginormous pole and hold it across the handlebars, left to right. The longer and heavier the pole, the better; the pole helps to distribute mass away from the pivot point, thereby increasing the moment of inertia. As is so important in any sort of riding, you should look up to the end of the wire, not just in front of the wheel. Gas it and go. *Bon chance, mes amis.*

SURE-FIRE Find a suitable wire and remove your bike's tires as in the hairball method. Now, construct a vertical strut that attaches solidly to your bike's chassis. The longer it hangs down the better. At the bottom, attach as much weight as you can. Think of

this as a giant pendulum. The longer the strut, the less weight you'll need. The super-uber-foolproof method is to have a weight greater than the combined weight of motorcycle and rider hanging below you—there's no way you can flip.

188 PACK FOR A TRIP

Backpackers and motorcyclists soon learn that, as with so many things in life, less is more. The same goes double when it comes to packing for a trip. Some folks buy giant touring bikes, load them to tire-bursting capacity, and then hook up a trailer for good measure. Minimalists will take along a credit card, cell phone, and toothbrush, and probably cut half the handle off the last item. As for the rest of us, here's what we've discovered works for most journeys.

GET YOUR PRIORITIES STRAIGHT The bike comes first. Bring a small kit with a set of tools and some maintenance materials.

PACK RIGHT When you're shopping for luggage, buy small—it'll force you to pack light. Backpacks are the most versatile. Also, consider luggage designed for motorcycles, such as saddlebags or tank bags; they'll take the load off you and put it on the bike instead. When you do start actually packing, don't just throw

stuff in. Instead, put everything on the floor before you pack—then put half of it back. You may want to bring that stuff, but you don't need to.

PACK LIGHT Choose multitasking items. The pocket multi-tool (such as the iconic Leatherman) is a perfect example. Your bike cover might double as a ground cloth if you're camping, or your hammock might double as a bike cover. If you want to ride all the great back roads to that MotoGP race across the country, but you want to keep your bike light and nimble, then you can ship your clothes to the hotel via UPS, FedEx, or some other service. And remember, nothing is as compact or as versatile as cash.

SECURE IT ALL Bungee cords are your friends here. Motorcycles shake and move, and their loads compress and shift. The elastic in bungee cords compensates; rope can't. If it moves and it shouldn't, use zip ties or duct tape. If it's not moving and it should, use WD-40.

189 GET A DRIVER'S ATTENTION

Texting, phone calls, narcolepsy, general ineptitude—automobile drivers may not be deliberately trying to kill you, but they can do a fine job of it without trying. Your defense? First, get as far away from them as possible—especially their blind spots. Second, be conspicuous. In other words, let them know you're around.

SOUND Loud pipes? Some riders think they save lives. Not us—we've had too many idiots wake us up in the middle of the night blasting around on their loud ego enhancers. But loud horns? Big fan—we like them loud enough to have physical recoil.

CLOTHING Two words—bright colors. Especially your helmet. A bright construction-worker-style vest is an adequate substitute if you can't stomach a fluorescent pink jacket.

LIGHTS Blinking lights are best. A pulsating headlight may be legal in your area. And you can find bright blinking clip-on LEDs at any corner bicycle shop.

REFLECTIVITY The better riding suits and jackets incorporate large reflective areas. For helmets, you can apply reflective stickers. And that construction worker's vest will often have reflective patches, too.

MOVEMENT As predators, humans are hard-wired to spot movement. Droning along at the same speed as the cars around you makes you invisible. Moving in your lane, speeding up and slowing down and (best of all) passing the cars makes you more visible.

MIRRORS Don't presume a driver ever checks his or her mirrors, but position yourself where they'll see you if they *do* look.

190 FIND A GREAT ROAD

My father thought Interstate 5 was the eighth wonder of the world: smooth, flat, wide, straight, well-policed by the Highway Patrol, and an absolutely mind-numbing monument to the modern highway. With great affection he called it the Superslab, and he droned along every bit of its 1,381-mile (2,223-km) length over and over with a smile on his face.

Most motorcyclists would consider this a slow and painful form of lobotomy. The best motorcycle roads are the opposite of I-5, or whatever the equivalent is wherever you live. Bike roads are twisty, picturesque, don't have much traffic, gain and lose elevation, and take you to a pleasant destination.

The old-school way of finding a good road is still a paper map. See big, fat straight lines? Avoid those like the plague. Look for the little, thin, squiggly lines that wind around next to those big arteries, or that snake along through uncharted lands.

Once a rider finds a road like this, he'll usually share it with other like-minded souls. Get plugged in to one of the social networks for motorcyclists, or one of the forums on a motorcycle website. New to riding or new to an area? Your local dealership might be full of riders who'll share one of their favorite stretches of road—they may even organize monthly rides.

191 RIDE IN A GROUP

Want to be the Leader of the Pack, or at least a member? Keep these tips in mind and you'll be on your way to being a respectable participant in a group ride.

BE ON TIME AND BE READY If the group has to wait, then your ride may be over before it begins. Be there on time with a full tank and an empty bladder.

HAVE A PLAN Who's the group leader? Who's the navigator? Who's riding sweep? Does everyone have a list of everyone's cell phone numbers? Where will you stop for gas? What do you do if someone gets a flat? Who has the tools? The first-aid gear? Does everyone know the route? What to do if you're split up at a red light? Do you all wait, slow down, or keep going?

RIDE THE PACE Group rides are a social commitment. If you can't keep up, drop out. If the group rides too slowly for your taste, ride with someone else. If you're a laggard or a speed demon, the ride will be miserable for you and the others too. Don't tailgate, either—no one likes a rider crawling up their tailpipe.

RIDE STAGGERED OR SINGLE-FILE On winding canyon roads, single-file riding is the smartest way. In town or on the highway, a staggered formation gives everyone room to maneuver. Riding side-by-side looks cool, but it's nowhere near as safe.

DON'T DAWDLE At gas or bathroom stops, get in and out quickly. Don't remove your helmet. Stay with your bike. Line up single-file at the pump, fill up, and roll your bike clear to let the next rider in.

SIGNAL YOUR INTENT If you're going to slow down or change lanes, let the other riders around you know what you're going to do.

CLOSE UP THE GROUP A number-one annoyance. Maintain some distance from the riders around you, but too much is as bad (and more common) than too little. A two-second rule—neither faster or slower—is probably right for most riding. In the dirt, riders string out on 30-second intervals to let the dust settle. When you come to a fork in the trail, wait until you can let the rider behind you know which trail to ride down.

IF A RIDER GOES DOWN Park your bike safely out of the road, and don't stand around in the middle of the road yourself. You don't want to get hurt, too.

192 CLEAN YOUR FACESHIELD

If your helmet's faceshield is doing its job, it's going to collect all sorts of bugs, oil, road tar, and more. Keeping it clean is critical. Clean it wrong and you'll scratch it and make matters worse.

STEP 1 First, remove the shield if you can. Lots of riders alternate between a clear shield for night riding and a tinted shield during the day. If so, store the unused shield in a soft bag or sleeve to protect it from scratches.

STEP 2 Always, always wash the shield under clean running water, and use the mildest soap you can—dishwashing liquid usually works fine. If there's no water available, at least use a spray bottle of shield cleaner. Never, ever, wipe a shield clean when it's dry.

STEP 3 Try to use nothing but your fingers when you're removing bugs and road grime. If you really need to use something else, make sure it's a clean microfiber cloth. Soaking tough, baked-on gunk in warm water for a couple of minutes is better than a hard scrubbing.

STEP 4 If you have to scrub, be sure to use small, circular motions.

STEP 5 Blot the shield dry with clean paper towels or a clean microfiber towel.

193 EAT WHILE YOU RIDE

Time was, you used to have to stop every hour or so because a bike shook so much. Now they're so smooth you can ride until you're out of gas. Hunger's bound to set in. No burger stand in sight? No problem. (Note: This is one of the few times an open-face helmet is the hands-down choice.)

ENERGY BARS These things might even be healthy. While they're usually nothing more than glorified candy bars, they pack well and are readily available—the modern grab-and-go food.

BEEF JERKY The standby of college students, backpackers, and recently divorced husbands for decades. Keeps forever, so you can leave it in your leather jacket where it's always handy.

BURRITOS This is an act of culinary daredevilism that's only for the experts. Try not to choose a burrito or wrap that's overstuffed. Insider hint: The bite-and-suck method of consumption seems to work best.

HARD CANDY Things like M&M's are a natural fit, like biker food pellets. The larger peanut-sized version is easier to handle with gloves.

194 EAT ROADKILL

If you're going to be one with the road, why not eat something that's *already* one with the road? In some places, larger roadkills (deer, elk, moose) are collected by police and distributed to food banks or other institutions. Montana recently enacted what's known as the "you kill it, you grill it" law. In some states, residents can even join a waiting list to chow down on large animals that get whacked on the highway. On a motorcycle, you have a good view of what's available. Why not take advantage of those nice, one-meal critters like squirrels or possums. (A whole moose? That thing weighs more than you and your bike put together.)

If it's truly flattened—aka road pizza—skip it. You want a critter that's been clipped (preferably in the head) by a bumper or front wheel. Still warm and pliable? Primo. Flies or maggots? Pass. But if it has fleas, that's a good sign that it's still fresh. And no matter how fresh it might seem, cook it thoroughly. And use plenty of hot sauce.

195 BE A TWO-WHEEL CHEF

There are more than 800,000 restaurants in the United States—about one eatery for every 12 motorcyclists. It's easy to find a place to eat on the road. Still, everyone loves cookouts. Why not kill two birds with one stone and cook while you ride?

The basic idea is to securely wrap your meal, and use the heat generated by your bike to cook it. Double-wrap it or risk losing dinner and having to clean BBQ sauce off your engine. Tin foil, chef's tongs, and wire to secure your dinner are key. Be sure to keep it away from air intakes and throttle linkage. Liquid-cooled bikes give more regulated heat (but watch out for the engine fan).

Another hot chef tip—the fins on an air-cooled bike provide a professional-looking grill finish.

196 PICK A RECIPE FOR THE ROAD

Now you know how to cook on your engine . . . what should you cook? Here are a few ideas.

	BIKER BEANS	CAMSHAFT HOBOES	TACOS/BURRITOS/FLAUTAS	MRES
PREP	Tear the paper label off a can of pork and beans. Punch a small hole in the can so the pressure doesn't build up and the can doesn't explode.	Chop up some veggies and lay out on heavy-duty foil. Add pieces of hamburger, chicken, beef, or fresh roadkill. Season with salt, pepper, and ketchup.	Make these in advance just as you would at home, wrap them in foil, and keep them in a plastic bag until you're getting hungry.	"Meals, Ready to Eat" in Militarese. Loaded with calories, a long shelf life, and a choice of entrées; sold at gun shows and camping stores.
COOKING	With a worm-drive hose clamp, fasten the can to your exhaust header's downpipe. 15 minutes at half throttle ought to do it!	Wrap tightly, and tie to a DOHC engine between the intake and exhaust cams. Rotate after 10 minutes; cook another 10 or so. Eat!	Toss them on the head, tuck behind the radiator, or wedge next to your muffler. About 10 miles (16 km) later they'll be nice and toasty.	Throw one on the cylinder of an air-cooled BMW twin, or tuck it up in the V of an old Moto Guzzi.

197 RIDE OVER BRIDGES

There are three reasons motorcyclists need to be extra aware when riding over bridges: Wind, ice, and steel decking. Bridges pose a double wind hazard: they're usually spanning some gap (river, canyon, valley) that's probably a wind conduit. But worse, since the wind blows both under and over a bridge, it will likely be much worse than the normal roadbed where the wind is only blowing above. Adjust your speed and position yourself in the lane accordingly.

In cool weather a bridge (and some tunnels) will ice over much faster than a blacktop road. And ice will put a bike down sooner than just about anything else. Go slow, and keep your eyes open. If you do hit ice, just try to relax and don't make any sudden control inputs. If it's a small patch, you may be over it before the bike slides too much. But if the bike hooks up suddenly, get ready for a tankslapper (see item #90).

Steel decking plates can be tremendously slippery, especially if they're wet and/or oily. Try to ride in the clean area where car tires have cleaned off most of the surface—riding in the center of the lane where all the oil drips are is a huge mistake.

198

CROSS RAILROAD TRACKS

Railroad tracks can be intimidating to new riders, and even experienced riders need to treat them with respect. But crossing them is easy if you know how. Most important: Attack them from a perpendicular angle—cross them at 90 degrees to the way they run, or as close as you can to that. This may mean you need to swerve in your lane, cross the tracks, and then swerve back.

Stay on the gas while you cross them. Better still, slow before the tracks, and then gas it as you cross. Why? You'll lighten the front end so you maintain more steering authority, and the tracks won't grab the front wheel.

Finally, weight the pegs. You don't have to stand upright, but lifting your butt an inch (2.5 cm) above the seat turns your legs into a live part of the bike's suspension, and pushes your weight/contact point lower into the chassis (where the pegs join the frame). Keep a firm grip on the handlebar and look ahead. Congrats! You're safely on the other side.

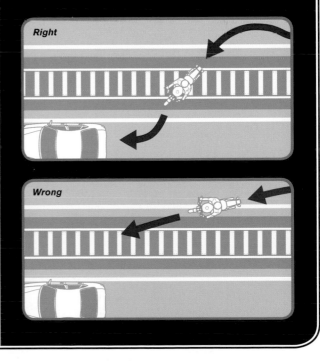

Right

Wrong

199 RIDE WITH A SIDECAR

When it comes to riding with a sidecar, forget all you've learned about riding a motorcycle—or almost all of it. When you hook a sidecar to a bike (and we're talking about traditional sidecar rigs here), the bike is transformed into a whole other animal.

Unless you're in the UK, Japan, or New Zealand, your sidecar will most likely be mounted on the right side of the bike. When you speed up, the combo will tend to turn in the direction of the sidecar; when slowing down, it will want to turn away.

Most sidecars have (or should have) a separate brake for the sidecar wheel linked to the rear brake of the motorcycle. Applying the rear brake will want to make the rig stop in a straight line—great if you're going straight, but maybe not so hot if you're trying to stop in a turn. Get your braking done in a straight line, whenever possible.

Within thirty seconds of your first ride, you'll find that you can't lean your traditional sidecar in a turn as with a bike. Forget countersteering, but do lean in the direction of the turn, as you would on a normal bike.

Sidecars handle best with weight in the chair. If you don't have a passenger, put as much weight as you can in the sidecar, and set it as low as you possibly can. About 50–100 lbs (23–45 kg) is good—that's about the weight of a couple of big bags of dog food. The worst thing you can do is ride with an empty chair and a passenger behind you.

Lifting the sidecar wheel in turns, known as "flying the chair" is an advanced technique that looks spectacular—as long as it's intentional. To practice, find a large, empty parking lot and ride some figure eights, starting out slow and gradually increasing your speed until the chair lifts. You'll immediately notice that you're now riding a large, unbalanced motorcycle that responds like a traditional bike.

200 ALIGN YOUR SIDECAR

Thinking about building your own sidecar, or just want to understand what's going on with these monsters? A few subtle differences make a huge change in the way the machine handles compared to a "normal" bike. The bike is leaned out a few degrees as a counter to the sidecar's mass. The front also toes in a few degrees more than the rear, to reduce wear on the rear tire. Most factory combos come pre-aligned, to reduce the headache.

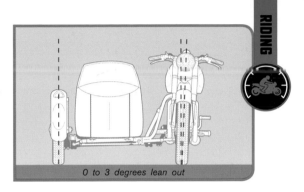

0 to 3 degrees lean out

201 TOW A TRAILER

Who says you can't take it with you? If you've jammed your saddlebags to the bursting point and still need to pack more gear, there's only one way to go: a trailer. They're popular accessories for long-distance touring riders, especially if they're travelling two-up and camping, but you should keep a few hints in mind.

USE ENOUGH BIKE It makes no sense to try to pull a giant trailer with a Vespa. Pick a bike that has enough power for the job—1000cc or more.

FILL YOUR TIRES The trailer puts additional load on both bike tires, especially the rear. Inflate them properly, on the upper end of your bike's GVWR.

HITCH IT RIGHT Your bike needs to lean into turns, but the trailer doesn't lean. You'll need a hitch that lets the trailer both turn and swivel—think about how a U-joint works.

FIND YOUR PLACE Trailers are almost always wider than a bike, so you'll need to ride closer to the center of the lane than you would without a

trailer. You'll also be riding closer to the center-of-the-lane oil slick you'll find on most roads, so exercise caution.

STOP THAT THING Trailers increase a bike's weight and stopping distance. They also want to overrun the bike when stopping unless equipped with their own separate trailer brakes. Ride with caution, brake early, and allow yourself plenty of stopping room.

FIND PARKING Your motorcycle-and-trailer rig is much longer than your bike alone, so you need to scout out an appropriate parking spot. Fine one that will let you pull straight out when leaving. Bikes are agile; towing trailers, not so much.

202 TAKE THE TOP 10 RIDES

Everyone has their favorite rides, but this list of locales is hard to beat.

ALPS AND DOLOMITES Hairpin turns, gorgeous vistas, and great food make this entire region a no-brainer. The great mountain passes of the Tyrol region have no equal.

CHILE/PATAGONIA The west side of South America is a world unto itself. Wherever mountains tumble down to the ocean like this, the roads twist and turn—a rider's dream!

RIO AND REGION The ride between Rio and Sao Paulo is an amazing 900-plus miles (1,450 km) from the coast through the mountains.

CÔTE D'AZUR The famed French Riviera, on the Mediterranean's north edge, offers beautiful scenery, great roads, and wonderful food.

ROME AND ITS ENVIRONS The Roman road system is one of the best in the world. Also, you get rugged topography and legendary cuisine.

CAPE TOWN TO JO-BURG South Africa is one of the easiest destinations on the big continent, and this ride is one of the best. You'll see it all—ocean, grasslands, and mountains.

AUSTRALIA'S EAST COAST From Melbourne to New South Wales to Queensland, this Pacific-coast route means surfing and easy cruising along with more demanding twisties.

SOUTHERN NORWAY This underappreciated motorcycle destination offers lots of gorgeous and challenging terrain, easily enough for two weeks' worth of riding.

NEW ZEALAND A rider's paradise thanks to the roads and terrain—and people. Christchurch to Auckland makes for a grand trip.

CALIFORNIA'S PACIFIC COAST The ride from San Francisco to Malibu is best, and you can stop for the MotoGP races at Laguna Seca.

203

LEARN COMMON RIDER HAND SIGNALS

Riding in a group? Everyone needs to know these common signals so you can communicate clearly and efficiently with each other. Need to give that rude driver a signal he or she will understand? There's always the extended middle finger.

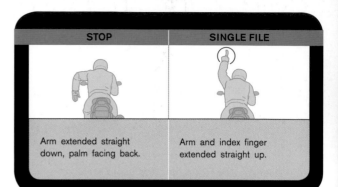

STOP	SINGLE FILE
Arm extended straight down, palm facing back.	Arm and index finger extended straight up.

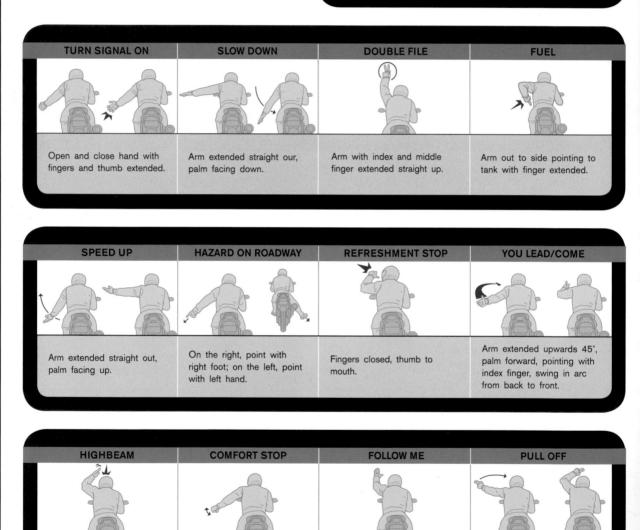

TURN SIGNAL ON	SLOW DOWN	DOUBLE FILE	FUEL
Open and close hand with fingers and thumb extended.	Arm extended straight our, palm facing down.	Arm with index and middle finger extended straight up.	Arm out to side pointing to tank with finger extended.

SPEED UP	HAZARD ON ROADWAY	REFRESHMENT STOP	YOU LEAD/COME
Arm extended straight out, palm facing up.	On the right, point with right foot; on the left, point with left hand.	Fingers closed, thumb to mouth.	Arm extended upwards 45°, palm forward, pointing with index finger, swing in arc from back to front.

HIGHBEAM	COMFORT STOP	FOLLOW ME	PULL OFF
Tap on top of helmet with open palm down.	Forearm extended, fist clenched, with short up-and-down motion.	Arm extended straight up from shoulder, palm forward.	Arm positioned as for right turn, forearm swung toward shoulder.

204 RIDE AROUND THE WORLD

Who hasn't looked at a motorcycle, and thought how much fun it would be to chuck it all and ride around the world? Plenty of people have: just check out accounts like Helge Pedersen's *Ten Years on Two Wheels* or Ted Simon's classic *Jupiter's Travels*. You can do it, too—if you want it bad enough.

Much of the world—at least the interesting parts—hasn't been paved (yet), so you'll be riding on dirt roads. You don't need a full-on motocross bike, but a single-cylinder of at least 650cc like the timeless Kawasaki KLR650, or a twin like the KTM990, BMW 1150 or 1200 GS are all proven choices. The great German aircraft designer Kurt Tank outlined four key attributes necessary for military equipment: It needs to be simple, robust, reliable, and easy to maintain. The same guidelines apply to your round-the-world bike.

It's easy to overload your bike, so do like Pedersen recommends and fit your bike with small panniers.

Nature (and your panniers) abhors a vacuum, and you'll end up filling whatever you have. Almost all serious round-the-world riders choose some sort of aluminum-box pannier for the winning combination of security, capacity, and weather resistance. A tank bag and a cargo rack give you additional storage room, but remember, you're just going to the next place where you can buy gas, not to the moon.

Bring a change of clothes, everything you need to repair multiple flat tires, GPS and paper maps, and paperwork: passport, driver's license/permits, visas, registration, proof of ownership, and Carnet de Passage en Douane (a temporary bike import document).

As for the cost . . . well, how much do you have? $20,000 is probably a good working budget for gas, freight, and the basics, and of course the price goes up from there. Best currencies to bring? The US dollar and the Euro; in Africa you can add the British pound, too.

205 NEGOTIATE ROUNDABOUTS

The first time I ever rode in Rome, it was at night, in the pouring rain, and I was following a local who rode like a madman. I had no idea where I was going, didn't know our hotel's name, and if I lost him, I was finished. So I stood up on the pegs, pinned the throttle, and rode the way I'd ride a motocross bike. When in Rome . . .

When negotiating any roundabout, traffic circle, or developing-world intersection, just dive in and go for it. Use your bike's advantages to their fullest: maneuverability and acceleration. If you overshoot the turn, keep going and try again.

This is no place for the timid; ride with conviction. Hand signals and blinkers are often ignored; the only escape is to ride faster than whatever is trying to run you over. Don't stop or slow down. It's like being in an avalanche—keep moving, stay on top, and you'll be fine!

206

CARRY A LIVE PIG

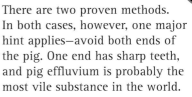

There are two proven methods. In both cases, however, one major hint applies—avoid both ends of the pig. One end has sharp teeth, and pig effluvium is probably the most vile substance in the world.

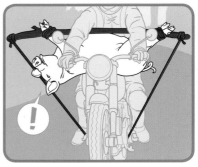

POLE METHOD Tie the pig to a bamboo pole, cannibal style (with the forefeet and hind feet tied together, and with the pole slid through the gap between the legs and the feet). Secure pole crosswise over the bike's chassis. This idea works best if you keep the pig in the step-through area between the seat and the handlebar.

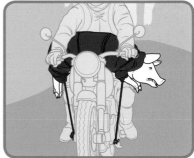

WRAP METHOD Wrap the pig in something (a blanket, fish net, or chain-link fence section). Tie securely. Lay pig on lap, and tie each end to a footpeg. Alternately, you can lay the trussed pig on the seat, and sit on top of it.

207 RIDE IN EUROPE

For an entire generation, riding a motorcycle in Europe has been a dream holiday. In recent years, with the advent of the European Union, it has become easier than ever. No visas or passport checks between countries, no (or much less) changing currency every day or two—the euro experience is easier than ever.

You can bring your own bike, or buy one there—BMW, Ducati, Moto Guzzi, Triumph, Aprilia, and KTM are the major European brands. But you can also rent a bike. Easiest of all is to hook up with a tour company (Edelweiss Bike Travel and Beach's Motorcycle

Adventures are two of our favorites). In terms of dream rides, most riders head for the Alps, running through France, Austria, Italy, and Switzerland.

If you've never visited Europe, be aware that laws and driving/riding styles vary tremendously from country to country. Germans are serious, fast, precise, and professional, and will expect no less from you. Spain is mad for anything with two wheels. In Italy, the laws are often more like guidelines. But wherever you ride, motorcycles tend to be more of a rarity in Europe, and their riders take their sport seriously.

208 KNOW YOUR DOCUMENTS

You know how all those war movies have the uniformed officer with a clipped accent asking for your papers? It won't be quite like that, but you should be sure you have everything in order.

INTERNATIONAL DRIVER'S LICENSE Most European countries will honor your home driver's license (as long as it has a motorcycle endorsement), but it never hurts to also have an international driver's license. Your local motor vehicles department or automobile club can usually arrange one.

INSURANCE You may be able to take care of a policy through your insurance company back home. If you're with a tour, they'll probably handle everything. Frequent travelers could join a local auto club, like Germany's ADAC, which offers comprehensive insurance packages, including medical transportation.

HIGHWAY TAX Note that in some countries (especially Switzerland) you'll need to purchase a "vignette," a small decal to show that you've paid to use the country's highway system. You can purchase them in advance or at the border in the customs office.

209 RIDE LIKE A NATIVE

Riders from elsewhere need to learn to read European road signs in advance. You'll be riding fast, and some won't be immediately intuitive. You'll reduce your risk of getting confused or lost if you study up in advance.

In Europe, lane etiquette means staying in the right lane unless you're passing. Pay attention to your mirrors. Respect car drivers, and be aware of regional differences. In Italy, for example, the horn is used frequently. In Germany, a driver signals irritation with a flash of their headlights—if you get honked at instead, you did something *really* bad.

Finally, know that most of the speeding tickets issued in Europe are from remote radar cameras, and you can accumulate four or five in a day without noticing. See that bright light flash? Be prepared to open your wallet.

210 EXPLORE BAJA

A thousand miles (1,600 km) long, stretching from the California border down to Cabo San Lucas, Baja is an incredible place to ride.

You can ride pavement down the entire length of the peninsula. But to really get the most out of the experience, you'll want to take a machine you can ride on dirt roads. And don't even worry about bringing a bike with a license plate—a pure dirtbike will do. So will big single-cylinder dual-sport or a twin-cylinder adventure bike.

What to bring? First off, plenty of tire-repair materials. If you're riding on a dirtbike, consider upgrading to a bigger "desert" tank, at least four gallons (15–16 liters). Never pass up gas when you get the chance to fill it. Gas stations are easy to find, but you may have to travel a ways between them. And take a spare air cleaner too—you'll need to service it every night due to Baja's dust, especially in the summer off-road. As for navigation, you won't need more than an AAA map, although a GPS is always worth packing.

Mexico will require you to have proof of ownership for your bike. And don't even think about bringing in guns or illegal drugs.

When to go? Well, it's hot in the summer and cold in the winter. The winter and spring are best for the east coast where it gets humid, the summer for the higher central spine, and the summer and fall for the Pacific coast.

211 RIDE THE WORLD'S LONGEST HIGHWAY

The Pan-American Highway is the most direct north/south route through Central America. Depending how one defines it, it runs from Prudhoe Bay above the Arctic Circle all the way down to Ushuaia at the tip of South America. By the most generous definition, you can cover close to 30,000 miles (48,000 km). The "official" route starts in Monterrey, Mexico and concludes in Buenos Aires, Argentina.

If you're thinking of an eight-lane Autobahn, think again. Most of the Pan-American is paved, but 50 miles per hour (80 kph) is about the maximum speed. And it will be mostly two lanes.

A notable missing link is the Darién Gap between Panama and Columbia, a 99-mile (160-km) section of mudfest and swampland that's defied pavement. The truly adventurous will try to battle through this area, while mere mortals will jump the gap by ferry.

212 SURVIVE LATIN AMERICA

Latin America (from Mexico all the way down to the bottom of South America) is one of the great underappreciated travel destinations for motorcyclists. One language (Spanish) will get you through almost all of it (and while not ideal, you can manage most of Brazil with it, too). The area encompasses more than 7 million square miles (18 million square km) and about 15 percent of the world's landmass, so there's plenty to explore. It's affordable, there are vast areas of nature to experience, and most regions are bike friendly and bike savvy. There's just enough infrastructure to provide support, and in general the governments are reasonable to deal with.

Riding in Latin America is tremendously rewarding, and for the most part the people are extraordinarily friendly. But the countries vary widely, and can change from year to year. Some can be war zones between drug cartels, local governments, leftist guerrillas, and rightist paramilitaries. Others (notably Costa Rica) are so peaceful the country doesn't even have an army.

As for motorcycles, a solid adventure-touring bike is a great choice, although most streetbikes will make the trip. You can camp, but accommodations in Latin America are generally affordable and let you lock your bike up safely at night—theft is an unfortunate but real issue.

213 EXPERIENCE VIETNAM

The best way to see Vietnam is by bike, and there's plenty to see. There's enough infrastructure to make this trip doable, the weather's warm year-round, and a bike is the chosen form of transport for the locals, especially in the larger cities.

Honda's world-famous C90 Cub may be all the bike you need—a 250 twin is about the biggest thing you'll ever want. If you're intent on bringing your own bike, a 250-class dual-sport will be about right; most riders rent or buy a bike in-country. Know ahead of time that the bureaucracy of travel permits and bike importation will require some patience.

Vietnamese traffic may seem crazy, but it isn't, really—once you learn to embrace the chaos and go with the flow.

Be prepared to deal with unimproved roads—another reason why an indigenous bike will be the best choice: the locals know what works here. November to February are the coolest and driest months—the monsoon season in all of Indochina is legendary.

214 RIDE LONG (NO, REALLY LONG) DISTANCES

Every two years, the aptly named "Ironbutt" race takes place in the U.S over eleven days and 11,000 miles (17,700 km). Riders must hit a series of checkpoints in a very tight timeframe. Why does this matter to you, if you never plan to subject yourself to this kind of fun? Well, these folks know about surviving a really long ride. Here are some of their key hints.

KNOW YOUR LIMITS If the longest you've ever ridden is 250 miles (400 km), don't plan on a string of 1000-mile (1600-km) days. Eliminate all irritants. Something that's a minor annoyance can finish you off after that great a distance.

BE PREPARED Prepare your bike before the trip. We're all short of time, but if you can't get your bike right before you start, on the road is no place to try and make repairs. Don't make any big repairs or changes (accessories) just before the trip. Upgrade your tool kit . . . and join a towing service, just in case.

BE SAFE Forget about high speeds. Slow and steady wins this race. And really, really, really forget about drugs. Not even coffee. If you're tired, stop. Get into your rain suit before it starts raining. Get gas before you need it. Never ride faster than you can stop. Stay away from long-haul trucks.

GEAR UP Pack wisely. Less truly is more in this race. Keep the things that you will need easy access to (flashlight, eyeglasses) in a tank bag where you can reach them with a minimum of trouble. Do make room

215 CROSS AFRICA

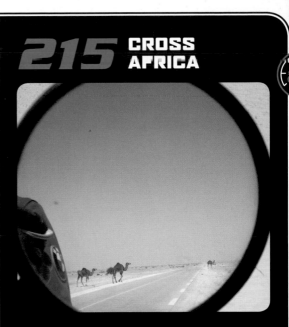

Africa has to be the ultimate adventure-bike destination. In the north, you have the Sahara desert to contend with. Below that the continent has a full catalog of animals which are happy to eat you like a leather-wrapped snack. And snakes like the mamba are fine with killing you just for sport. Even the lowly mosquito or tsetse fly can take you out.

If you're looking for the beginner's route, choose South Africa. It's easy, and you can be out in the bush country while just a short ride from any of the major towns.

Tanzania, Kenya, and Uganda offer spectacular wildlife viewing and plains riding. Morocco in the northwest blends African and Arabic influences while Algeria, Libya, and Tunisia return the classic Sahara experience. And of course Egypt is incomparable.

The first of two traditional trans-African routes runs from the Mediterranean south to Cape Town, generally along the west coast. The second route runs from Cairo through Sudan and Ethiopia, into Kenya, and south from there. At the time of this writing, Sudan is politically unstable, and that's a point worth mentioning of any African country—stability.

It's a big continent, and there's no reason to take a political risk when there's so much to see. Treat unstable countries like you would potholes in the road, and ride around them.

for an electric vest, though. Carry a flat-repair kit and know how to use it.

REST RIGHT Know when to stop. Tired? Pull over now! And remember, it's often the case that a rest stop can make you go faster.

BE HEALTHY If you can't eat right, at least eat light. Be sure to stay hydrated, and when outside of well-populated areas, carry at least a half gallon (2 liters) of water. Carry vitamins and aspirin, too.

BE AWARE Be careful crossing county lines. Road maintenance can change quickly when one county runs out of money. That nice two-laner can become a potholed mess within a few short moments.

ISLE OF MAN

NUMBER OF TURNS: **200+**

FAST FACTS

OFFICIAL NAME The British Crown Dependency of the Isle of Man

LOCATION The Irish Sea, United Kingdom, off the west coast of Great Britain and the east coast of Ireland

TRACK LENGTH 37.75 mi (60.73 km)

NUMBER OF TURNS Over 200

DATE OPENED 1907

FAMOUS FEATURE Guthrie's Memorial, an S-turn corner between the 26th and 27th milestone markers on the highway that makes up part of the course. Formerly known as "The Cutting," this turn was named after the famed Scottish motorcycle racer and six-time Isle of Man TT winner, Andrew James Guthrie.

TRIVIA Not technically a track established for formal racing, the Isle of Man is a self-governing region, with an open-course touring trophy-style road race on public roads.

The IOM TT is a time-trial type of race. Riders typically start off at 30-second intervals, and the winner completes the course in the shortest elapsed time.

While a popular locale for races, the Isle of Man has also had more than its fair share of riding casualties. From 1907 to present, there have been at least 239 fatalities on the course.

The official currency is the Manx Pound, while the official languages include English, Manx, and, due to the large influx of riders, Biker.

FAMOUS POINTS ON THE TT COURSE

A BRAY HILL
B QUARTERBRIDGE
C BALLASPUR
D CRONK-Y-VODDY
E BALLAUGH BRIDGE
F WATERWORKS
G WINDY CORNER
H CREG-NY-BAA
I GOVENOR'S BRIDGE

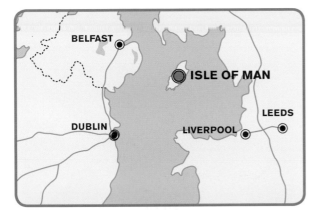

218 RIDE LIKE MAD

Imagine that you go to a race at Daytona or Le Mans or Suzuka and they let you drive (or ride) onto the track and have at it. That's exactly what happens on Mad Sunday, when the course is thrown open to anyone on a bike. Imagine *Mad Max* meets *Apocalypse Now* with a touch of Steve McQueen's *Bullitt* thrown in for good measure, and you'll get the picture. Of course you have to do it once.

219 EAT LOCAL TREATS

MANX KIPPER
Locally caught herring, salted and smoked with oak chips. Perfect with a beer or a glass of single malt.

MANX QUEENIES
Special Manx scallops, served with a white or cheese sauce.

BONNAG
A scone-like crumbly cake served in Manx tea rooms.

217 KNOW THE GREATS

JOEY DUNLOP
From Northern Ireland. 29 TT wins between 1976 and 2000. Known as "Yer Maun."

MILE HAILWOOD
Called "Mike the Bike," a 12-time TT winner. Brought the fledgling Honda Motor Company their first wins in 1961 in both the 125 and 250 classes.

STANLEY WOODS
Dubliner who rode between 1923 and 1939, racking up 10 victories.

220 SHAKE A LEG

What's up with that three-legged symbol you see everywhere on the IOM? It's a triskelion dating back to the 13th century. The island's motto is *quocunque jeceris stabit* (Latin for "whichever way you throw me, I shall stand")—which we think is perfect if you're a bike rider.

I HAVE TWO QUOTES ABOVE MY TOOLBOXES.

The first is from the nineteenth-century Scottish philosopher Thomas Carlyle's *Sartor Resartus*: "Man is a tool-using animal . . . without tools he is nothing, with tools he is all." The second quote is in Latin, from the Roman poet Virgil: *Felix qui potuit rerum cognoscere causas.* "Happy is the person who understands how things work."

You don't need to be a great mechanic to be a proficient rider, but understanding how your bike works will probably help you understand why it acts the way it does, and how you can get the most out of it. Mechanical skills can also help you to spot a problem before it escalates. Motorcyclists have much more intimate relationships with their machines than car drivers do, and a little change in the bike can translate into a big change in the way it performs or handles.

Doing your own mechanical work can also save you some money. And off-road riders really need some mechanical proficiency because it can be a long, lonesome walk out when you're a couple of hours' ride from the nearest pavement.

This chapter can never be a complete substitute for a real shop manual specific to your bike, but it can introduce you to the first principles. We all have to start somewhere, after all. And if nothing else, you won't look and sound completely ignorant if you have to take your bike to a garage and a service manager tries to explain something to you.

221 SET UP SHOP AT HOME

Some of us have workshops that would make a NASA engineer envious. Others end up working under a shady tree, in a carport, a drafty barn or shed, or on the street in front of our house. But no matter where you set up, getting organized is the first step toward doing a good job.

You'll want a safe, secure place to work. It needs to be level, so the bike doesn't fall over—especially on you. And pick someplace where kids, pets, or spouses aren't likely to come and trip over a half-assembled engine or kick over a parts box scattering everything.

Keep your most used tools where they're easy to access; your specialized tools can be stored under benches, in cabinets, or even in the rafters. And clean your shop before you even start to take the bike apart—any dirt or debris is bound to find its way into the places where it can do the most damage.

Safety should always be your first concern. Plenty of houses have burned down because someone was using a torch in the garage, or left solvent-soaked rags in a heap. Ask yourself what could go wrong—because if it can, it probably will.

222 ORGANIZE YOUR PARTS

The best tools to organize your parts aren't in your Snap-On dealer's truck, or in any shop catalog. They're in the kitchen department of your local supermarket.

MUFFIN PAN These get five stars when it comes down to organizing small parts. They're available in several sizes, and the metal cleans up easily.

COOKIE SHEET After they get too gnarly for kitchen use, out they go to the garage. Perfect for oily parts. Also great as a drip pan under a leaky engine.

PAPER CUPS An old standby. Easy to label—just write on them. Toss them when the job's done.

ZIPLOC BAGS The quart or liter size are best. Write on them with a marker, or label the parts on a piece of paper to put inside, too.

RUBBER BANDS Just to bundle parts together and tag them (you can use masking tape, too). Works best with cleaned parts.

CARDBOARD BOX Turn the box over, punch holes, and put little parts in them. Best for things like side cover screws; knowing which one fits where is important.

223

EQUIP YOUR SHOP

Every motorcycle workshop needs the following items. If you don't have the space or resources to do it all yourself, a few friends can go in together to rent a garage, or one friend can supply the space while the rest supply tools and fixtures.

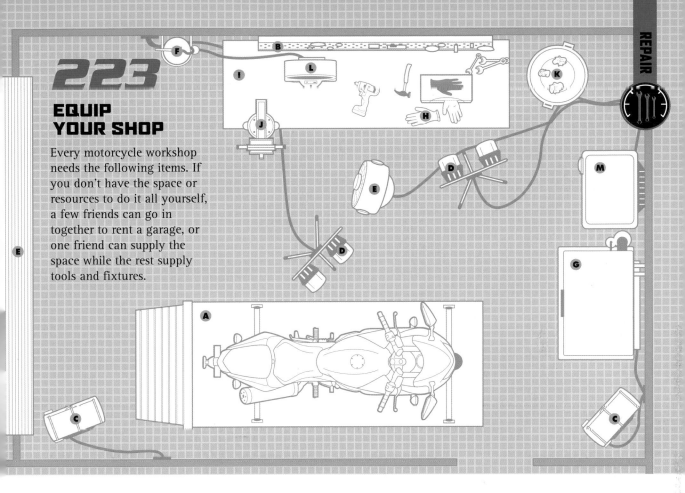

A. WORKSTAND Critical. This needs to be a long, sturdy bench about knee high, strong enough to support a bike. Fit it with tie-down hooks and/or a front-wheel chock to hold the bike upright.

B. PEGBOARD Hang your most frequently used tools where you can get to them easily. Start with combination wrenches, hex keys, and socket sets to fit your bike. Include pliers, hammers, and screwdrivers. Add more specialized tools as needed.

C. HEAT Lots of wrenching goes on at night or in the winter when it's too cold to ride. It's no fun working in an unheated garage, so at least plug in a couple of space heaters.

D. LIGHT Get as much light in your workspace as possible. Big fluorescent lights overhead are a necessity—you can easily find used ones for cheap. Add some drop lamps on extension cords for when you need special spot illumination.

E. VENTILATION Solvents and fuel mean nasty fumes. Be sure you have adequate ventilation. An open garage door is a start; a couple of box fans are even better.

F. FIRE EXTINGUISHER A no-brainer. Keep it close by.

G. PARTS TANK A dedicated parts-cleaning tank is a real luxury, but once you've used one you'll never go back. Benchtop models are available. Use rubber gloves and eye protection.

H. GLOVES Latex or (better) blue nitrile gloves are a great choice when you're working around grease or oil.

I. WORKBENCH Along with the bike stand, a waist-high workbench lets you do your best work easily.

J. VISE Mount it to the end of your workbench. About 10,000 uses. Maybe more.

K. TRASH CAN Metal, with a tight-fitting, fire-resistant lid. Empty it often.

L. SOUND SYSTEM A lot of maintenance is tedium, and a radio or iPod speaker system can make those long hours more bearable.

M. FRIDGE For beer or your drink of choice—but stay sober and safe, whether riding or wrenching.

COMBINATION WRENCH SET Either metric or standard, depending on your bike. Really old British iron uses a third system (Whitworth). If you're low on cash, get only the sizes you need, but it's usually cheaper to buy a complete set.

SOCKET SET Get a kit with drive handles and extensions. Buy the best set you can afford—you'll probably use it more than any other tool. If you can only get one drive size, pick up a ⅜-inch set.

HEX KEYS Again, available in standard or metric. The best have a ball drive on one end that lets you use them at an angle.

SCREWDRIVERS The most misused tool ever. Buy some cheap ones to loan out or for when your kids use them to pry open cans or punch holes in the wall; hide the good ones for proper bike work.

PLIERS You'll need several pairs: needle-nose, wire-cutting, adjustable-jaw, and locking.

ZIP TIES The "tool" of a thousand uses. Keeps cables tidy and routed, holds wiring in place, temporarily repairs broken turn signals, and more.

FEELER GAUGES These thin metal strips are essential for setting valve clearances.

DRAIN PAN Something that will hold at least a gallon (4 liters), for changing oil.

BATTERY CHARGER Also called a trickle charger. Keeps your battery topped up if the bike is parked for a long time. If you go riding every day of the week, you can skip using one of these.

HAMMER Smaller is generally better. Get a second soft-faced hammer or rubber mallet for delicate work.

IMPACT DRIVER A necessity for removing torn-up case screws.

FLASHLIGHT It won't replace real shop lighting, but a handheld light is good for peering down into the dark recesses of your engine.

MULTIMETER OR TEST LIGHT Tracking down any electrical gremlins without one is going to be pretty much impossible.

CONTACT CLEANER A consumable, but one of the most useful tools in the shop. Blasts out crud with a powerful solvent, and dries instantly.

SHOP MANUAL Forget the booklet that came with your bike. If you're into serious work, shell out for the encyclopedia-sized version from your dealer.

225 ADD IN SOME EXTRAS

While they're not essential, having these next few items will make your life a lot easier.

QUALITY TIE-DOWNS I've owned a pair of Ancra straps (A) for more than 30 years now, and they're still going strong. There are about a thousand bad ways to transport a bike, but with a pair of tic-downs you're well on your way to doing it right.

SAFETY-WIRE PLIERS Nothing says professional like a good pair of these (B). Most riders won't need them, but if you ever need to prep a racebike, they're a must.

EPOXY Crack an engine part in the middle of nowhere and you're sunk—unless you have this magic stuff (C). The best are metal-filled (like the J-B Weld brand), but if they leak in your tool bag you'll never get the mess cleaned up. Easiest to carry is the putty type that you knead to activate.

KNIPEX COBRA PLIERS I try to avoid specific brand names, but these little grabbers (D) are the best. Small enough to carry with you (get the 7.5-inch/180mm size).

T-HANDLE SET This tool set (E) is what the factory race mechanics use. Fast and foolproof.

226 PACK A TOOL KIT

We don't mean a rollaway filled with a ton of shop tools here—this kit is a compact set that fits under your seat or in a daypack. In the old days, your bike probably came with one; now you may have to assemble one yourself.

A tried-and-true method of learning what to pack is to use your on-bike tool kit to perform routine maintenance. Need a 5mm hex key? Can't get the fairing off without a Phillips screwdriver? Oil filter need a special 17mm socket? Use the take-along kit for service at home and you'll learn what you need for your particular bike.

Street riders can get away with just a credit card and a cell phone to call a towing service; dirt riders need something more extensive. Everyone should carry these items at the very least.

- ☐ HEX KEYS
- ☐ SIX-IN-ONE SCREWDRIVER
- ☐ PLIERS
- ☐ SPARK-PLUG SOCKET (OEM PARTS ARE BEST)
- ☐ SHOP RAG
- ☐ OPEN-END WRENCHES

Dirtbike riders should add tire-repair equipment and a chain-repair tool.

At the very least, bring a tow strap!

227 GET IT ON VIDEO

Worried you won't be able to reassemble what you've taken apart? Use your phone to shoot short videos showing how everything went together. When it's time to put everything back, just review your "notes."

228 PICK A MULTITOOL

Combining the versatility of a Swiss Army knife with a pair of pliers, a good multitool is like having a whole toolbox in your pocket. They're not the best at any one job, but they're handy, versatile, and the perfect solution for a motorcyclist who needs to travel light. But what should a motorcyclist look for in one of these tools?

Strong pliers are the number-one feature, without a doubt. Long-nosed or short-nosed is up to you—we prefer something in the middle. Wire cutters come next. Integral with the pliers, you don't need them to chop heavy barbed wire—find a pair that can cut small-gauge electrical wire and cable ties. A metal file is a big boost; multitools with this feature will thin the list quickly. Screwdriver functions are last on the list, and probably the weakest point of any current design. Finally, look for solid construction and comfortable handles. Paying a little extra for a brand-name tool is generally worth it. Whether you carry the multitool on your belt, under the seat, or in your riding jacket is up to you. But make sure you have it on every ride.

229 MAKE AN IMPACT

This tool can be the motorcyclist's best friend, especially if you're trying to remove a damaged sidecover screw. An impact driver transfers a blow from a hammer into rotational torque. It can help jar a stuck fastener loose, but just as important, it can also keep the screwdriver tip from camming out of the slot, which will further damage the screw head. Here's how to use one.

STEP 1 Set the driver to the tighten or loosen setting. This idea is pretty obvious, but if in doubt practice on another screw that's already loose.

STEP 2 Ensure the screw head and driver tip are clean and degreased. Use a shot of contact cleaner. A little grit on the driver's tip (like fine sand) helps it grip even better.

STEP 3 Hold the driver perfectly perpendicular to the bolt, take a breath, and give it a whack with a good-sized hammer (one with a head that weighs approximately 32 ounces, or 1 kilogram).

STEP 4 Check to see if the screw has turned after each blow. It'll only move a few degrees, and it's usually easiest to see if the impact-driver tip moves.

230

GET GRITTY

Got a Phillips screw whose head is so chewed up that the screwdriver keeps slipping out? The solution is an impact driver, but lacking that just stick the tip of the screwdriver in some dirt and give it another go. The grit often helps the tip get some extra bite. And when you get a chance, replace that screw!

231
USE A TORQUE WRENCH

Torque, in this instance, is the measure of how tight a nut or bolt needs to be. The great dirt bike writer Ed Hertfelder once opined that there were three torque levels: White knuckles, grit your teeth, and break wind. This is usually followed by a fourth—the bolt snapping off.

You can be more precise with a torque wrench—a special wrench that measures how much rotational force you're applying to a bolt. There are two types: The beam type with a pointer indicating how tight the nut or bolt is, and the click type which uses a calibrated clutch (usually set by turning the handle to the desired torque setting). Both work well, although the beam type is usually less expensive.

Torque is measured in foot-pounds or newton-meters. Really small bolts are measured in inch-pounds or newton-centimeters—don't confuse the two. When you use a torque wrench, be sure the nut or bolt is clean. The specs will tell you whether it should be dry or lubricated.

With critical bolts (like engine connecting rods) there should be no guesswork—refer to a detailed shop manual. But for other fasteners (handlebars, axle nuts, switches) some general guidelines are in the following entry. Note that these are for the bolt-shaft diameter, not the measurement across the flats on the bolt head.

232
TIGHTEN IT RIGHT

FASTENER TYPE	FOOT/POUNDS	NEWTON/METERS
5mm bolt and nut	3.6	5
6mm bolt and nut	7	10
8mm bolt and nut	16	22
10mm bolt and nut	25	34
12mm bolt and nut	40	54
5mm screw	2.9	4
6mm screw	6.5	9
6mm flange bolt (8mm head, small flange)	7	10
6mm flange bolt (8mm head, small flange)	9	12
6mm flange bolt (10mm head)	9	12
10mm flange bolt	29	39
Spark Plug (12mm thread)	10	14
Engine Oil Drain Bolt (12mm thread)	22	29

233
IRON IT OUT

Sure, you can use a couple of big screwdrivers to change a tire—if you don't mind tearing up your rims, puncturing your tire's inner tube, and eventually paying someone else to do the job for you. But with a good pair of tire irons (also called tire spoons), you can easily change or repair a tire yourself.

Ideally you'll get two sets. For shop work, you need a pair of long irons, about 12 inches (30 cm), with a curved spoon in one end. The thinner the spoon, the better. A comfortable handle on the other end is a big plus. For the trail, shorter 8-inch (20-cm) irons are a lot easier to carry, but harder to use due to less leverage. Look for a thin, curved tip on one end, and a flatter blade on the other. Thick metal tire irons are heavy and tougher to get into tight spaces.

Several companies make a combination tire lever/axle wrench (tire spoon on one end, hex-wrench head on the other). They're light and save you from carrying an extra tool to remove your axle nut.

Try using two long irons and one short one: The short iron keeps the tire from walking on the rim, while the long irons do the serious work. Hook one end of the short iron under the sprocket or disc rotor to keep it in place—the third hand makes the job easy.

234 USE A BIKE LIFT

Hunching over to work on your bike gets to be a drag pretty quick. If you're lucky, you'll be able to build a knee-high platform in your garage. But the real deluxe setup is a bike lift.

There are two kinds—small, portable, foot-operated dirt-bike lifts that fit under the engine cases, and larger, deluxe, full-bike platform lifts. Either one is surprisingly affordable; some even store vertically, saving space when not in use.

You need power to lift the bike: electric, compressed air, or hydraulic. Hydraulic lifts often use a foot-pump jack to actuate either parallel or scissor arms under the platform.

Lifts are a piece of cake to use. Roll your bike up onto the platform, put the front wheel into the chock provided, put the bike onto the sidestand or centerstand, or use tiedowns to secure the machine. Then use the power source to raise the stand to working height, engage the locking mechanism, and be sure the bike and stand are level and secure.

The most important thing about any bike lift is to use one that's up to the job. A lift designed for a small-sized dirt bike is unsafe with a massive Harley.

235 GET SOME AIR

Compressed air is your friend. In fact, it's been so widely used in industry that it's often known as the fourth utility (behind electricity, water, and natural gas). In Europe, 10 percent of all electrical power goes to running air compressors. No shop is really complete without a compressor, because it can do all of these things and more.

CHANGE YOUR BIKE'S GRIPS To install or remove a grip, float it on a cushion of compressed air instead of struggling with a knife or glue.

CLEAN YOUR AIR FILTER Blow the filter clean from the inside out—don't just blow dirt deeper into the filter.

DRY YOUR BIKE Blow the water off your bike after you've washed it to prevent spotting.

DUST OFF GEAR After a dirt-bike ride, use compressed air to clean your boots, gloves, backpack, etc. by blowing away dust and dirt.

CLEAN YOUR SHOP If you work in a garage with an open door, compressed air will blow the shop clean way faster than a vacuum.

FILL YOUR TIRES You can fill a tube-type tire with a bicycle pump, but setting a bead on a tubeless tire requires a lot of air fast. A compressor is just the ticket.

REBUILD BRAKES Use compressed air (gently!) to push the pistons out of your brake caliper so you can change the seals during a rebuild.

CLEAN CARBURETORS
Carbs are full of tiny air passages that fill up with varnish. Soak the carb or the jets in carburetor cleaner and then blow out with compressed air. Also use compressed air to blow out carburetor/fuel tank vent lines that are plugged by dirt, spiders, and so on.

HOLD VALVES CLOSED
In a major rebuild, you can hold the valves in a closed position by blowing compressed air into the spark-plug hole if the cylinder head is on the bike.

236 FIND A GOOD MECHANIC

A good motorcycle mechanic is a treasure, but like most treasures, they're hard to find. With the time, training, and inclination, you may learn enough to do all your own work. In the meantime, here are the things that you should look for.

EXPERIENCE Your buddy who "knows a lot about bikes" may only know slightly more than you do. And if you know nothing, then he knows next to nothing. You can do better than that.

TRAINING Some people are naturally gifted. But it's safer to trust someone who's graduated from a certified training program, or who has extensive experience working in shops or for race teams.

PROFESSIONALISM He says he'll work for beer? Pass. A real mechanic is a professional. He offers a guarantee, keeps accurate records, and doesn't try to do stuff he's not trained to do.

PERSONALITY I've known plenty of great bike mechanics who related better to machines than to people. The smarter mechanics hire someone with a more sociable personality to work the front office while they stay in the back. And remember: He's your mechanic first, not your friend.

237 GET THE ANSWERS

When you're searching for a good mechanic, be sure to know what to ask him about his background, his skills, and what he can do to help you and your machine. Have him try these questions on for size.

- ☐ Have you ever worked on a bike like mine?
- ☐ Can you tell me how long the work will take?
- ☐ What's the guarantee on the work?
- ☐ Can you give me a written estimate?
- ☐ Can you give me some references from satisfied customers?
- ☐ Where were you trained?
- ☐ How long have you been working as a mechanic?

If you don't know much about bikes, don't be shy about taking someone along who's less intimidated to get a second opinion on your new (potential) mechanic.

238 USE THAT CENTERSTAND

Conspiracy theorists will tell you that the lack of centerstands on today's bikes is a plot to make you take it to a dealer for service. In reality it's for cost savings, weight reduction, and increased ground clearance. If you do have one, here's how to use it.

Start by standing to the left of the bike, and take hold of the left handlebar grip with your left hand. Straighten the front wheel, put your right foot on the centerstand tang, and push down until the stand touches the ground.

Gently rock the bike toward and away from you until you feel both of your centerstand's feet contact the ground. With your right hand, grip the horizontal frame under the seat. Some bikes often have a special handle here to make lifting the bike easier.

Move your body as close to the motorcycle as possible. Keep your back straight and your head up. Don't lean over the bike or push your butt away from it. Next, straighten your right leg (the one on the tang) and lock your knee. At the same time pull up (not out) with your right arm. The bike should pop right up.

If you're still having trouble, you can practice by first rolling the bike's rear wheel up onto a ¾-inch (19mm) piece of wood, or even a one-inch (2.5 cm) block. Practice with lighter bike or even a scooter to help you get your technique dialed in.

239 START IT UP

The number one reason bikes don't start—and we've seen it thousands of times—is because the kill switch on the right handlebar is in the "off" position. Sounds dumb, but it happens over and over. Switch set to "run"? In that case, there are several systems you need to check, generally in this order.

FUEL Is there enough fuel in the tank? Is the fuel valve on or on reserve? Is fuel getting to the carburetor or fuel injectors? (With a carb, you can pull off the fuel line to check.) Next, check the float and jets, especially if the bike has been sitting around for a couple of months.

ELECTRICAL Is there spark at the plug? (Test by pulling off a plug wire, putting in a spare plug,

grounding it, and cranking the engine.) If not, check your ignition switch or CDI unit.

COMPRESSION Remove a sparkplug and use a tester to see if your engine has enough compression. If not, the valves may need to be adjusted, or it could be the decompression mechanism (if any) needs adjustment.

If the engine feels and sounds like to wants to start but doesn't, and the bike has a carburetor, check for the choke function. If the engine runs for a minute, then dies, your fuel-tank vent may be plugged; try again with the gas cap open. If the engine doesn't crank at all, you may have a dead battery or faulty starter motor. Charge the battery first and check the connections.

240

GIVE YOUR BIKE A BUMPSTART

Dead battery? No worries; it's still easy to get your bike started so you don't have to hitchhike home. If your bike has a kickstarter, you're in luck, but not many modern bikes do. Still, you can do it—roadracers bumpstart their bikes all the time. Just follow these instructions.

STEP 1 Switch the key to the "on" position and make sure the kill switch is set to "run".

STEP 2 Stand on the left side of the bike and hold both handlebar grips.

STEP 3 If there's a hill around, point the bike downhill.

STEP 4 Put the bike in second or third gear.

STEP 5 With the bike in gear, push it forward until it doesn't want to move any more. The bike will probably move only a few inches.

STEP 6 Pull in the clutch.

STEP 7 Holding the clutch in, run forward, pushing the bike as fast as you can. If you have a helper, have him or her push the motorcycle from behind at the same time as well.

STEP 8 After about eight steps, swing up over the saddle and sit down hard. As soon as your rear hits the seat, snap the clutch lever out fast and give the bike some gas. If the bike doesn't start, repeat these steps until it does, or until you pass out from exhaustion.

241 GET THE JUMP ON YOUR BIKE

Jumpstarting a bike, especially one that's been sitting for a long time, is the easiest way to get going with a dead battery, and it's no different from jumpstarting a car. You'll need to use a pair of jumper cables to connect your battery to another vehicle's battery.

First, remove the seats or sidecovers to give you access to both bikes' batteries. Connect the positive (+) terminal on the dead battery to the live battery using the red cable ends. Next, connect the black cable end to the negative (-) terminal on the good battery. Finally, connect the remaining black cable end either to the chassis,

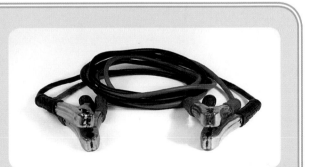

the engine, or the negative terminal on top of the dead battery.

Start the dead bike. As soon as the engine starts, remove the negative cable first, then the positive cable. And *never* let any two cable ends touch each other, especially not a positive and a negative lead.

242
START A SUBMERGED BIKE

Bikes end up under water for two reasons: floods and tipovers in streams. If yours was thoroughly submerged (like days in a flooded basement) don't even try to start it; it'll need a full disassembly. If it's underwater briefly, there's hope.

If you're the one riding and you know the bike's going down, flick off the kill switch before it goes completely under. If the engine is running, you risk bending the connecting rod, since the water in the cylinder can't be compressed.

Get the bike onto dry ground, and remove the air cleaner and spark plug. Drain the airbox and exhaust pipe. Lay the bike over on its side if you have to; with a light two-stroke trail bike you can even turn the whole thing upside down.

Put the bike in gear, lift the rear wheel off the ground, and give it a spin. The engine will turn over slowly and pump any water in the cylinder out the plug hole. If your bike has a carburetor, remove the float bowl or the bowl's drain screw, drain the gas, and reinstall.

Reinstall the spark plug, dry the contacts, wring the air cleaner out and reinstall, and try to start the bike. With luck, it should run fine. As soon as possible, change the oil in the engine and gearbox (and final drive if your bike has a shaft). And don't let it happen again!

243 GIVE IT A KICK

Just like old cars used to have a hand crank, until the 1980s, most motorcycles had a kickstarter too. Some dirt bikes still do. So, if you need to start your old classic, here's how.

First, get the toughest, gnarliest pair of boots you have. Kickstart a big single in your flip-flops or shower shoes and you'll end up in the hospital with a collapsed arch when it kicks back. At least boot up your right foot when you try this.

Second, be sure the ignition switches are on, gas is on, choke is set, etc. Turn the ignition switch off, kick the bike through a few times slowly to free up the clutch plates and to get some oil to the top end. Three or four times will do. With the ignition still off, find the compression stroke by slowly pushing the kickstart lever down until it's very hard to press.

Turn the handlebar all the way to the left—that way if the kickstart lever kicks back, it won't drive your knee into the bar end. Release the lever and let it travel all the way back up.

Turn on the ignition. Take a deep breath, and kick the lever down to the bottom as hard and as fast as you can. With some bikes you'll need to open the throttle a little at the same time. Others like having the throttle closed. Only experience will tell you what to do with yours.

244 LEARN ABOUT PRELOAD

All vehicle suspensions have two general parts: a spring, and a shock absorber or damper. These two parts are placed between some component that moves (a swingarm for the rear and a fork leg for the front) and some component that doesn't (the frame/chassis). The suspension controls wheel movement for rider comfort and better handling. Even the most basic motorcycle suspensions usually allow for some adjustment, especially to the rear suspension's preload.

Motorcycle suspension springs are designed so that they're always under compression—and how much compression is a function of preload. Measure an uninstalled spring with no compression on it—that's called the spring's free length.

When you have to compress that spring to install it, you're pre-loading it. At the rear, a ramped-collar adjuster is the simplest method—turning the collar in

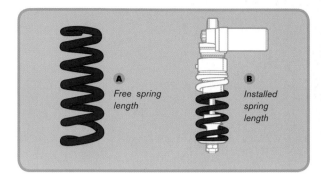

A Free spring length

B Installed spring length

one direction pushes it down harder on the spring, pre-loading it more. Another method is to use a collar that screws down the shock body, compressing the spring. For fine-tuning, some sportbike shocks use a hydraulic adjuster—in that case, you can just spin a knob to adjust your preload.

Why should you adjust your bike's preload? To set your suspension's sag—read on to learn more.

245 SET YOUR SUSPENSION SAG

A motorcycle's suspension works in two directions. When you hit a bump, the suspension compresses (the wheel moves closer to the chassis), and then rebounds (the wheel springs back, farther away). Your suspension needs to be set to work properly in both directions with the amount of weight your bike is carrying; setting your bike's sag is the first step in getting it right.

Sag is how much your machine settles on its suspension at rest. To measure the sag, have a helper lift the rear of the bike as high as possible—if you have a centerstand, just use that to lift the rear wheel off the ground. Now measure from the rear axle to a reference point straight above—the seat, fender, etc. Do the same with the front suspension. This measurement is the suspension

value with zero sag—for our example, let's say the number was about ten inches (250mm). This measurement is called unloaded or free sag.

Now, let the bike stand normally on both wheels, with no rider. Push down on both the handlebar and the seat a couple of times, and let the bike return to normal. Have your helper hold the bike upright, and repeat the measurements you've taken; you'll see that the weight of the bike has settled and compressed the suspension. The difference between this number and zero sag value is called static sag.

Finally, sit on the bike in your riding gear, both feet on the pegs and keeping the bike vertical. Repeat the same measurements, and you'll see the bike has settled even lower. This measurement is the ride height.

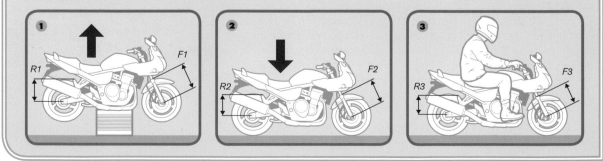

246 ADJUST A SPRING

You usually need to change your preload because you're adding a passenger, carrying a lot of luggage, or have simply put on weight. If you use all your preload adjustments and still can't get to the desired numbers, then it's time to use a stronger or weaker spring.

Aim for 0.2-0.6 inches (5–15 mm) of static sag at the rear, and 0.8–1.2 inches (20–30 mm) of static sag at the front. In terms of ride height (sag with the rider on the bike) your basic setup should be 1–1.4 inches (25–35 mm) at the rear and 1.2–1.6 inches (30–40 mm) at the front (free sag minus loaded sag). If you don't have enough sag, decrease your spring preload until you get the desired value. Too much sag? Increase the preload.

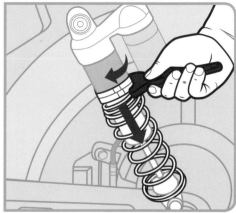

247

TIGHTEN A SPOKE

How do you know if a spoke is loose? You can grab each pair of spokes where they cross and give them a squeeze. But the time-tested method is to put the bike on a stand, spin the wheels, and let a wrench lightly tap each spoke as it goes around. A properly-tensioned spoke makes a satisfying "ting" sound; a loose spoke will make a dull "thud." It's a lot like tuning a guitar, and if you're tone deaf it pays to strong-arm a musician friend who has a good ear and get them to give it a listen for you.

A proper spoke wrench is a must. Just tighten the nipple down on the spoke in ¼-turn increments until it sings in tune with its friends. You're trying to screw the nipple down farther on the spoke, so in this picture you'd be turning it counter-clockwise. While you're at it, you can give the wheel a quick check to see if it's in true. Be sure to test both sides of each wheel.

248 BALANCE A WHEEL

The correct way to balance a wheel is, of course, on a dedicated wheel-balance stand. But you can even do a rough job on your bike—the principles remain the same.

For the front wheel, you'll want to loosen the axle pinch bolts and axle to reduce binding, but leave the axle in place.

Remove the brake caliper or push the pads back in the caliper body. For the rear, remove the chain and take off the caliper or push the pads out of contact with the disc.

Slowly spin the wheel and note where it comes to rest. With a piece of tape, chalk, marker, or crayon, mark the 12 o'clock position on the wheel (the light spot).

Turn the wheel 90 degrees to both the 3 o'clock and 9 o'clock positions and see if the light spot returns to the 12 o'clock position on its own. If so, tape a wheel weight onto the rim at the light spot.

Repeat the above step until you've added or removed enough weight that the wheel remains motionless when the light spot is turned to both the 3 o'clock and 9 o'clock positions.

Spoked wheels use crimp-on fishing-sinker-type weights, while cast wheels use adhesive-backed lead weights. An old-school substitute for spoked wheels is a string of lead solder wrapped around the spoke and crimped on with a pair of pliers.

Reinstall the chain, pump the brakes, tighten the axles, and you're done.

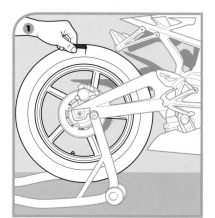

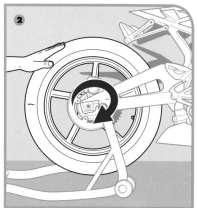

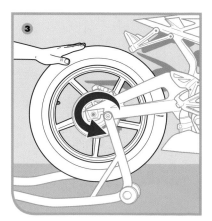

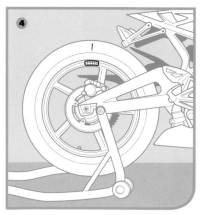

249 GET IN LINE

Proper wheel alignment is a fundamental for good handling. It can also affect your bike's tire wear. And getting it right is simple: You just need a good eye, some string, and a few tools. This technique works for streetbikes and dirt bikes.

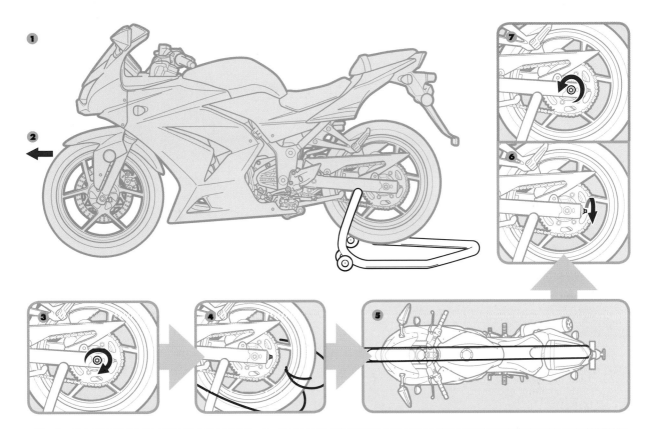

STEP 1 If your bike has a centerstand, use it. If not, use a trackstand, or shims under the bike's sidestand—or a patient helper to hold the bike upright.

STEP 2 Point the front wheel straight. Just get it as close as you can—you'll make the fine-tuning adjustments later.

STEP 3 Loosen (but don't remove) the rear axle nut.

STEP 4 Get a long piece of string or fishing line—about 15–20 feet (4.6–6 m). Find the center point. Wrap the string around the rear tire with the midpoint in the center of the tire. Pull the string toward the front tire. You should have one piece of string leading forward from both the left and right sides of the bike. The string should touch only the rear tire—nothing else. Adjust up or down until that's the case.

STEP 5 Kneel in front of the bike and pull the string tight so it forms a straight line from your hand to the front and rear edge of the rear tire. For hands-free adjustments, you can tie each string end to a weight.

Straighten the front tire, and check the distance between the string and the front and rear edges of the front tire's sidewalls. If the wheels aren't parallel, the four measuring points won't match up.

STEP 6 Loosen or tighten the rear wheel's adjusters to bring the rear wheel parallel with the front. Turn the bolts 1/6 turn at a time. Check the chain tension to ensure it's not tight or loose.

STEP 7 Tighten the rear-axle nut, and sight down the chain to ensure the sprockets are in line.

250 RIDE THE INSIDE LINE
NÜRBURGRING

NUMBER OF TURNS: **16**

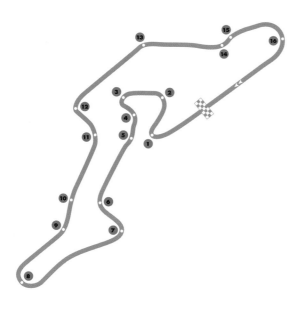

FAST FACTS

OFFICIAL NAME Nürburgring Großer Preis-Strecke

LOCATION Rhineland-Palatinate, Germany, encircling Nürburg

TRACK LENGTH 3.199 mi (5.148 km) (GP-Strecke); 12.93 mi (20.81 km) (Nordschleife)

DATE OPENED 1984

FAMOUS FEATURE The Carousel, a sweeping, berm-style, 180-degree hairpin. Although it's among the slower turns on the Nordschleife, the "Karussell" is perhaps one of the most iconic curves on this road.

TRIVIA This track was originally made of the much larger Nürburgring Nordschleife ("North Loop") and Sudschleife (the "South Loop," which fell out of use by the 1970s), built in Germany's Eifel mountains in 1927, encircling the city of Nürburg.

After the German MotoGP was held for the last time in 1980 on the older Nordschleife, the "GP-Strecke" ("Grand Prix Course") was built around the old pit area northeast of the Sudschleife. Nürburgring now shares MotoGP hosting privileges with the nearby Hockenheimring track.

Although notorious for its share of fatalities over the years, and some controversy in part due to fans' criticism of the GP-Strecke's smaller size, Nürburgring remains a well-known destination for both amateur and professional racers, and is also a popular filming location for the TV series *Top Gear*.

251 KNOW YOUR RUBBER

Once, I asked a rep from one of the big motorcycle tire companies to tell me all he knew about tires. "They're round, black, and sticky," he said. I told him to give me the graduate course. "Some are stickier than others. Let's go to lunch."

The right tires can make a huge difference in how your bike handles. So can the wrong ones. But how do you keep from making an expensive mistake? With a little more knowledge than my lunch-loving pal ended up imparting to me.

First, let's talk about street tires. You can divide them into two classes: tube type and tubeless. If your bike's wheels have spokes like a bicycle, you probably need tires that take an inner tube; if your bike uses cast wheels, you'll probably use tubeless tires.

Next, a vocabulary lesson: tread and pattern. Tread is the part of the tire that comes in contact with the road. The grooves and channels cut into that tread comprise the pattern. Racing slicks have 100 percent tread, but no pattern. Tread is what gets the work done; on a street tire, pattern exists only to channel water away and keep a tire from losing its grip when wet.

Third, we come to profile. Viewed from behind, a car's tire has a square profile: horizontal where it contacts the road surface, connecting to vertical sidewalls. Motorcycles have vertical sidewalls too, but the tread is rounded—this shape lets a motorcycle's tires stay in contact with the road and keep traction when the bike leans through a turn.

Contact patch is the part of the tread that's on the road at any time.

Profile is the shape of that curved tread section. Is it a gentle curve, or more of a triangle? Or is it broad in the center, and curved only towards the edges?

Compound is the material that makes up the tire. Racing tires use soft compounds that only last 100 miles (160 km), but that offer tremendous, sticky grip. At the other extreme, hard-compound touring-bike tires trade maximum grip for longevity that can be as high as 20,000 miles (about 32,000 km).

252 WRAP YOUR HEAD AROUND THE TREAD

Your average motorcycle tire has more arcana etched on it than a copy of *The Golden Bough*. If you're confused by all this code, here's a handy guide to what it all really means.

TUBE DESIGNATION Tires are used with an innertube (Tube Type or TT) or without (Tubeless or TL). The tread and sidewalls may be made of differing numbers of layers, and include various materials (sometimes steel or fiberglass; usually nylon, kevlar, aramid, or other resilient fabrics).

LOAD/SPEED INDEX The number indicates how much weight the tire can bear. The letter denotes the maximum speed rating for the weight borne by that tire, when that tire is inflated to maximum pressure.

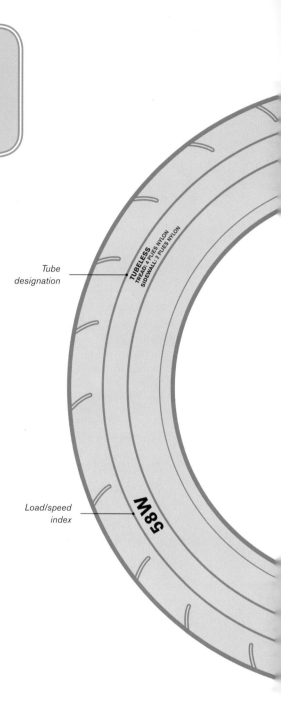

Tube designation

Load/speed index

MAXIMUM WEIGHT*		
	LBS	KG
45	364	165
46	375	170
47	386	175
48	397	180
49	408	185
50	419	190
51	430	195
52	441	200
53	454	206
54	467	212
55	481	218
56	494	224
57	507	230
58	520	236
59	536	243
60	550	250
61	567	257
62	584	265
63	600	272
64	617	280
65	639	290

MAXIMUM SPEED		
	MPH	KPH
J	62	50
K	69	100
L	75	110
M	81	120
P	95	130
Q	100	150
R	105	160
S	113	170
T	118	180
U	125	190
H	130	210
V	150	240
W	168	270
Z	>150	>240

(*the numbers for the maximum weight are only a partial range of the full load index.)

WHEEL ROTATION To perform safely, a tire has to rotate in the right direction and grip properly. If mounted backward, the tire's tread might peel or tear.

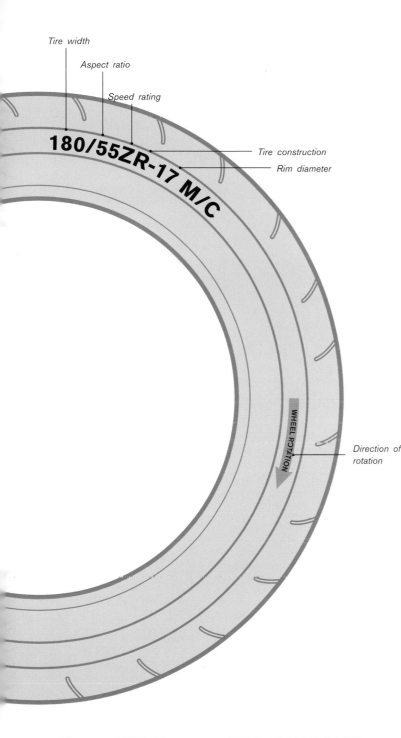

Tire width
Aspect ratio
Speed rating

180/55ZR-17 M/C

Tire construction
Rim diameter

WHEEL ROTATION

Direction of rotation

TIRE CODES

This complex set of numbers and letters (called the metric tire size system) carries a wealth of useful information.

TIRE WIDTH This is measured in millimeters; aspect ratio is the tire's height as a percentage of its width. Low-profile tires can lower seat height and deliver a firmer ride, and are most often found on sportbikes; high-profile tires yield more tire flex and a softer ride, especially on dirt bikes and touring machines.

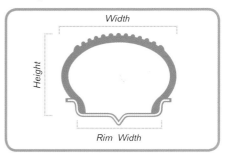

Width

Height

Rim Width

SPEED RATING Uses letters derived from the speed index to indicate the tire's safe speed (which could differ from its maximum speed). If there is no speed rating, an M is placed before the width/aspect number, to show it is simply a motorcycle tire.

TIRE CONSTRUCTION Either "B" for belted (parallel to direction of travel) or "R" for radial (at a 90 degree angle, which most bikes use), or unlettered (for bias-ply tires, often found on dirt bikes).

RIM DIAMETER Measured in inches (to fit the proper wheel size).

PRESSURE RATING Tires often have a maximum tire pressure rating (which differs based on whether the tire is hot or cold). Your bike's manual often has your suggested safe pressure rating, too.

OTHER INFORMATION Your tires might also bear some other markings: manufacture date, tread wear indicators, or mounting dots (for balancing or placement near the inflation valve on the wheel).

Other tire coding systems include: Alphanumeric (used on touring bike tires; letters and numbers denote width, aspect ratio and other info); Standard Inch (on older bikes and gradually being phased out; aspect ratio is always 100 percent); and Low-Profile Inch or 82-Percent Series (all of these tires have an 82-percent aspect ratio).

253 THE INSIDE LINE
MISANO

NUMBER OF TURNS: **16**

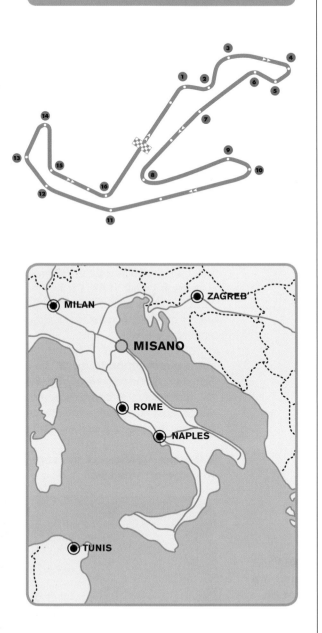

FAST FACTS

OFFICIAL NAME Misano World Circuit Marco Simoncelli

LOCATION Rimini Province, Italy, South of Misano Adriatico

TRACK LENGTH 2.626 mi (4.226 km)

NUMBER OF TURNS 16

DATE OPENED 1972

FAMOUS FEATURE This entire track is fully lit to afford a view of the circuit and its racers, no matter the time of day or night.

TRIVIA First opened in 1972, this track gained fame as the host of the San Marino MotoGP races from 1985 to 1987. Its layout has been altered on and off since 1993 to add facilities and to allow alternate race loops. Despite its multiple curves and hairpin turns, it's a fast ride; in 2007, Ducati racer Casey Stoner set a track record of 1 minute, 33.918 seconds.

Originally Circuito Internazionale Santamonica, named for the region in which the track was built, this course was renamed Misano World Circuit in 2006. The name of a local racer, Marco Simoncelli, was added in 2012 as a memorial after his death during a Malaysian GP race the previous year.

Open 320 days out of the year, Misano not only offers a complex racetrack and space for 60,000 spectators, but also the Santamonica Sporting Restaurant, an elegant dining establishment complete with its own swimming pool.

254 KNOW YOUR KNOBBIES

Streetbike tires rely on rubber coming in contact with the road to generate grip. A dirt bike's tires depend on aggressive knobs and tread blocks to dig into the dirt surface. The height, hardness, and spacing of these knobs or tread blocks determines how a tire will perform.

Big adventure bikes or dual-sports ridden primarily on the pavement benefit from hard rubber compounds and large tread blocks spaced closely. This design increases tire life and grip on the street, but the tires' performance in the dirt will suffer. Hard-compound knobbies work better in the dirt, but their street performance—especially under hard braking—suffers dramatically, and they wear out faster too. Soft, open-pattern knobs are the choice for soft soil and mud, but they are a terrible choice for the street.

Most tire manufacturers rate their dual-sport tires by percentage of street/dirt use. For example, a tire like the venerable Dunlop 606 is really 80/20 dirt/street, while a skin like that same company's TR91 Trailmax is just the opposite, designed to be used on the street 80 percent of the time, and only 20 percent on the dirt.

255 PATCH A TUBE

When I'm out dirt riding and I get a flat, I don't patch a tube by the trail—I just throw in a new tube and patch the old one at the lunch stop or in the evening. But three flats in a day? It's patch city, baby.

STEP 1 If the leak is obvious (big nail sticking out?) you might not even need to remove the whole tube—just lever off that section of the tire with the wheel on the bike and fish out the damaged part. Otherwise locate the leak by looking for the hole, listening for air, or getting it wet and watching where the bubbles are coming from.

STEP 2 Clean and dry the area around the hole. Roughen the area with a bit of sandpaper, the grater-like tool from a patch kit, a metal file, or even a rock.

STEP 3 Spread glue over the hole. The total glue coverage should be slightly larger than the patch.

STEP 4 Let the glue dry until tacky. In really cold temperatures, setting the glue on fire for a few seconds may speed the process.

STEP 5 Lay the patch on smoothly and evenly, and hold it in place for a minute. Cover the patch with a handkerchief, and use a smooth stone or stick to burnish it down.

But what can you do about a giant hole or tear? It's possible to use a needle and thread to sew the hole up. Apply glue liberally and make an extra-large patch out of a scrap piece of old tube.

256 CHANGE A TIRE

There's a difference between changing a tire and repairing a tire. For our purposes, changing a tire means replacing it with a new one.

OPTION 1 Get out the credit card. With wide, stiff, low-profile sportbike tires, especially the rear, a professional job is your best option. A tire shop has specialized machinery to do the job right without scratching the rim or damaging the bead.

OPTION 2 With smaller streetbikes and all dirt bikes, mounting a new tire is well within the average mechanic's skill level.

STEP 1 First, use a bike stand to get one or both wheels off the ground, and remove the wheel by following your owner's manual instructions. Let all the air out of the tire.

STEP 2 Breaking the bead means getting the tire loose on the rim. Use your boot or a chubby friend to push the tire down into the center of the rim. Repeat on both sides.

STEP 3 Use your tire irons to lever one side of the tire up over the rim. If you've never done this, try practicing on a bicycle tire first—the idea is exactly the same, but the motorcycle tire requires better technique, tools, and strength.

STEP 4 Flip the tire over, and lever the other side off the rim. This idea seems counterintuitive, but it will let you push the rim out sideways, especially if you use a little lube on the tire.

STEP 5 Lever the new tire onto the rim, being careful to note the proper rotational direction. If you're using a tube, inflate the tube partially (just enough so that it holds its shape) and slide it into the tire.

STEP 6 Finally, using two tire irons and taking small "bites," lever the tire on to the rim. Plenty of lube helps. Line the balance dot up with the valve stem on the rim.

Inflate to the recommended pressure.

257 MAKE YOUR STAND

An empty five-gallon bucket makes a great poor-man's tire-changing stand. An empty 25-gallon steel drum with the head cut out of one end is even better. Cover the sharp edge with a bead of automotive heater hose sliced lengthwise.

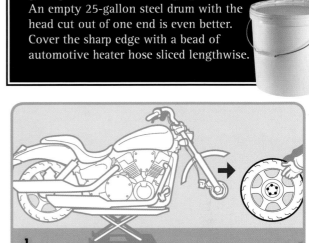

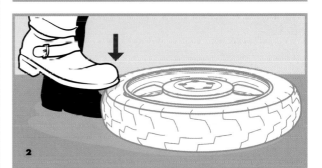

258 PLUG A TIRE

How should you repair a tubeless tire when you're out on the road? First, if the nail or screw is still in the tire, and the leak is slow enough, the best solution may be to simply leave the offending object in place, monitor the situation, and just keep adding air. But for a really bad leak, you'll need to plug the tire, or call for a tow truck.

METHOD 1 Pull out the nail, and ream the hole out with the tool from the plug kit. This usually looks like a short, rat-tail rasp with a "T" handle attached to it. Then, take a strip of the plug material, peel off the backing, and thread it into the insertion tool the same way you'd thread a big sewing needle.

Cover the material with glue, to act as both a bonding agent and a lubricant. Insert the plug material until it's completely through the tire's carcass, and then slowly withdraw the tool. The plug should stay in; trim it flush with the tire.

METHOD 2 This method gives better results, but will require a special gun-type tool in order to "shoot" a mushroom-shaped plug into the hole. The first step is the same as in the above method—pull out the nail and ream out the hole.

Next, insert the mushroom plug into the gun, lube the gun's insertion tip with glue, push it into the hole, and operate the gun's handle. The plug is injected into the hole, and the mushroom-tip head positively locates the plug inside. Slowly withdraw the gun, leaving the plug behind. Trim the plug to flush with the tire's surface, and then reinflate the tire.

Both of these plug methods work best when the damage is in the center section of the tire. The closer you get to the sidewall, the less your chance of success. Should you trust a plugged tire, or bite the bullet and buy a new one? The choice is up to you, but if the tire leaks still slowly after you've plugged it, then it's wise to just replace the whole thing.

259 PUMP IT UP

STREETBIKES

How much air pressure should you put in your bike's tires? Start with the recommendations in your owner's manual—but that's just the beginning.

Running a lower air pressure increases your tire's contact patch (good), but if it's too low, you increase the rolling resistance, raise the tire's operating temperature, and eventually encounter handling problems due to carcass deformation—which is why flat tires handle so poorly. High air pressure reduces grip, but also lessens rolling resistance.

At the track, tire techs measure carcass temperature using something called a pyrometer, looking for optimal rubber temperature. On the street, however, you need to keep careful notes about how your bike handles with varying pressure.

One thing's for certain though: Probably 90 percent of a tire's problems come from underinflation. When in doubt, use the stock settings, but monitor the pressures regularly and closely. And always use a cold tire as your baseline.

DIRTBIKES

Here the issue is traction, and two things will dictate your pressures—the trail surface and the type of tire you're using. In mud and sand, some riders run pressures as low as ten pounds in the rear, and 12 up front. In the desert where speeds are high and hardpack and rocks increase the danger of pinch flats, you may nearly double those pressures.

Most of the time, start around 15 psi front and rear (1.03 bar), and work your way up and down from there. A softer tire works best in softer terrain, and sometimes reducing the air pressure can make a tire with more tightly spaced knobs grip the ground better.

260 RETIRE YOUR OLD TREADS

Most streetbike tires have wear bars just like car tires. When the tread surface wears away to the top of these wear bars, it's time for new rubber.

Other factors enter the decision too. Even with plenty of tread, if a tire is worn flat in the middle, the bike won't turn as well. Any cracks in the sidewall? Get new tires. Excessive cupping on the front tire (lots of hard braking in city traffic) will make the tire vibrate and compromise grip. Finally, tires just age out, especially in hot climates. If your tires are hard as granite, shell out the cash for some new skins.

261 TREAT YOUR TIRES RIGHT

WARM UP YOUR TIRES

Tires get softer and grip better as they heat up—this is why racers use those tire warmers (really, glorified electric blankets), so their tires grip well from the very first lap. You don't need them for the street, but the lesson is the same—when your tires are cold, don't ride as aggressively or lean your bike over as far. As the tires warm, your bike will ride smoother and be able to grip the road better.

MIND YOUR TIRE PRESSURE

Inflation: Your owner's manual probably lists recommended inflation pressures for your tires, and the same information should appear on a sticker by the swingarm or chain guard. This info is a good starting point, but heavily-loaded bikes may require more air pressure. Regardless, frequently checking your air pressure means your tires last longer, your bike handles better, and fuel economy improves.

PLUG A TIRE?

Is it safe to plug a motorcycle tire? That depends. The best repairs use a combination plug/patch that you need to install from the inside of the tire. Mushroom-head plugs, injected into the hole with a special tool, also give good results. But if the hole is anywhere but the center of the tread, it's best to consider a plug of any kind a temporary fix to get you home.

WHEEL ROTATION

Mounting your own tires? Pay attention to the little arrow on the sidewall. If you can't figure this out, you probably shouldn't be riding.

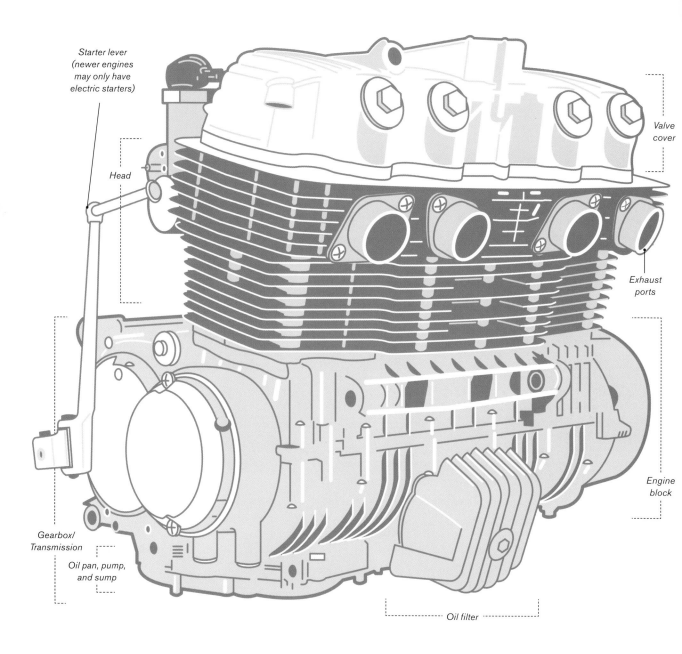

Starter lever
(newer engines
may only have
electric starters)

Head

Valve
cover

Exhaust
ports

Engine
block

Gearbox/
Transmission

Oil pan, pump,
and sump

Oil filter

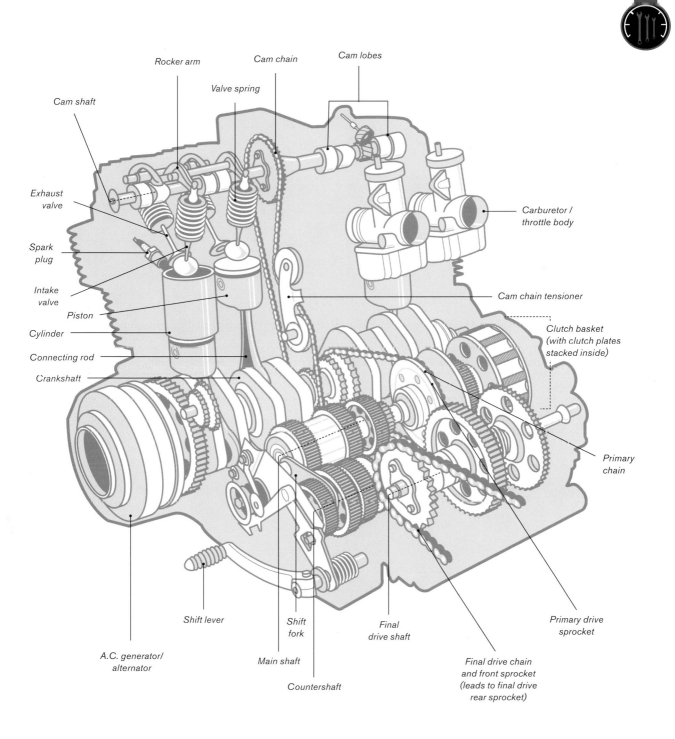

Rocker arm

Cam chain

Cam lobes

Cam shaft

Valve spring

Exhaust valve

Carburetor / throttle body

Spark plug

Intake valve

Cam chain tensioner

Piston

Cylinder

Clutch basket (with clutch plates stacked inside)

Connecting rod

Crankshaft

Primary chain

Shift lever

Shift fork

Final drive shaft

Primary drive sprocket

A.C. generator/ alternator

Main shaft

Countershaft

Final drive chain and front sprocket (leads to final drive rear sprocket)

263 IDENTIFY THAT ENGINE

1. SINGLE
Examples: Most dirt bikes, scooters, Honda CBR250R.
Characteristics: Light, narrow, simple. Good bottom-end torque. May vibrate significantly.
Good Choice For: Off-road riding. Economy.

2. PARALLEL TWIN
Examples: Classic old Triumphs. Kawasaki Ninja 300.
Characteristics: Narrow, light, responsive. May vibrate.
Good Choice For: General riding, commuting.

3. V-TWIN
Examples: Most Ducatis, Harley-Davidsons, and Moto Guzzis.
Characteristics: Good balance of torque and horsepower. Narrow. Low center of gravity.
Good Choice For: Cruisers.

4. BOXER TWIN
Examples: Many BMWs.
Characteristics: Smooth. Lots of torque. Sometimes limited lean angles.
Good Choice For: Pretty much a BMW exclusive.

5. TRIPLE
Examples: Triumph Speed Triple.
Characteristics: Perfect balance with a 120-degree crankshaft. Halfway between a twin and a four.
Good Choice For: Triumph sportbikes.

6. INLINE FOUR
Examples: Honda CB750, most Japanese sportbikes.
Characteristics: A universal engine architecture. Smooth and powerful, but typically wider than a twin.
Good Choice For: Road riding with a 600cc and up.

7. V-FOUR
Examples: Yamaha V-Max, Honda VFR.
Characteristics: Smooth, lots of torque, narrow. Complex and typically heavier than an inline four.
Good Choice For: Sport-touring.

8. OPPOSED (FLAT) SIX
Examples: Honda Gold Wing.
Characteristics: Heavy, complex, but smooth and reliable.
Good Choice For: Luxury Touring.

9. INLINE SIX
Examples: Honda CBX, RC166, BMW K1600 .
Characteristics: Smooth. Fast. Wide. Complex. Unique.
Good Choice For: High-performance touring. Making a big statement.

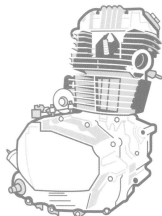

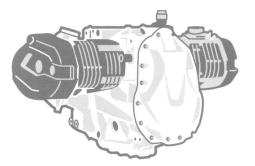

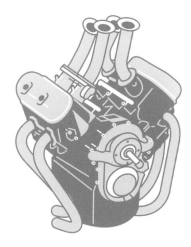

2

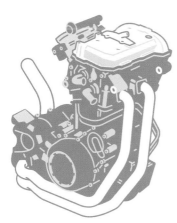

3

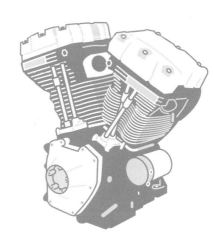

5

6

8

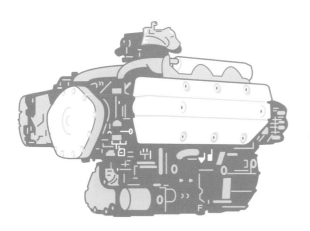

9

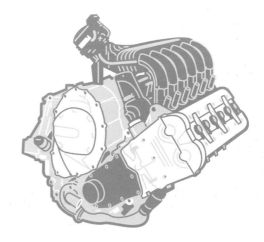

264 PROTECT YOUR WINDSHIELD

Automobile windshields are easy to care for—a little water, a little ammonia, and you're done. Motorcycle windshields are another story. Their windscreens are plastic, and if you're not careful, you can make a bad windshield a lot worse.

STAY SHADY Sun is a windshield's worst enemy. Park your bike out of the sun, or at least cover the windshield, especially if your anti-UV coating is damaged or gone. If you use a bike cover, look for one with a soft cloth lining over the windshield area. Alternatively, cover your windshield with a clean towel before deploying the cover.

KEEP IT CLEAN Clean your windscreen with warm water, lots of it, and a drop or two of mild soap. For dried-on debris (like squashed bugs), soak a bath towel in warm water, drape it over the windshield, and wait 10 minutes. If you need to scrub, use only a soft towel, and plenty of running water.

BE GENTLE Clear plastic windshields often have an anti-scratch coating that also helps prevent UV damage. Aggressive polishing cuts right through the coating. If your windshield is in good shape but a little glazed, a light touch, a clean cotton or microfiber rag,

and a plastic cleaning compound are all you need. Use small circular motions when polishing—circular scratches are less apparent than long, linear scratches.

265 FIX AN OLD WINDSHIELD

If the protective coating on your windshield is peeling, you'll need to take drastic measures. Start with a product designed for deglazing plastic headlight lenses, which often comes in a kit with two or three grades of polish—start with the most aggressive; finish with the finest. Regular coats of clear polish after that can keep your windshield looking good. Use a fresh, clean pad for each new polish grade. You can also wet-sand the finish with 1200-grit paper. Be very careful not to sand any more than is needed. Then, follow the polishing steps we just discussed.

GRIOT'S
CAR CARE

PLASTIC
POLISH
Restores Optical Clarity

266 POLISH OUT A SCRATCH

Whether your beloved bike has its first scratch or its fiftieth, they can all be unsightly. Fixing them, though, can be easy enough.

Surface scratches just put a mark on your paint (or plastic) that won't go all the way through. To get rid of these marks, a mild polish like a dab of toothpaste on a wet fingertip is often all it takes.

If the scratch cuts through the paint down to the primer or metal below, there's little to do but touch up or repaint it. Progressively finer polishing compounds can also reduce the scratch's sharp contours. But you have to use a *very* light touch: The paint is already so thin under the scratch, it's very easy to cut through.

With plastics, you will want to reduce the sharp "V" of the scratch profile. Using fine sandpaper (800 grit, and then 1,000 grit) along with plenty of water, sand lengthwise along the scratch. You want to soften the edges—you'll never remove them, but the scratch will be less apparent.

Whichever method you use, finish up with some plastic polish or wax to restore your paint or plastic's shine—otherwise you'll end up with a large, dull area that may look worse than the original blemish. When in doubt, practice on a part of the finish that can't be readily seen—like the underside of your gas tank.

267 FIX YOUR FAIRINGS

With a car, you have to deal with dents. But with a motorcycle, fairings and windshields crack from vibration, tipovers, and runaway shopping carts. What can you do about it? It depends on how bad the damage is.

  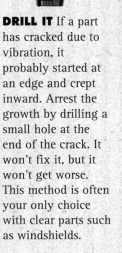

GLUE IT Don't laugh—those sticky cyanoacrylate glues (aka Super Glue, Krazy Glue, etc.) can do a fair job on small cracks. Back up the repair with some fabric soaked in more glue. Avoid cotton: combining the glue and that fiber can actually cause fires.

WELD IT Many plastics can be welded just like sheet metal, but you need special equipment for it. Still, if your fairing is only cracked and not too scuffed, plastic welding may actually be cheaper than new parts.

DRILL IT If a part has cracked due to vibration, it probably started at an edge and crept inward. Arrest the growth by drilling a small hole at the end of the crack. It won't fix it, but it won't get worse. This method is often your only choice with clear parts such as windshields.

268 REMOVE A DECAL

Behold the sticker—the tattoo of the motorcycle world. Racers get paid to put them on their bikes. Wannabes put them on their bikes to look like real racers. And just like a bad tattoo, in the morning you're faced with regret. Thankfully, stickers are a lot easier (and less painful) to remove than ink.

Gentle heat is your friend, so pull out a hair dryer and get to work. Use just enough heat to soften the glue that's holding the sticker on—too much and you risk melting or blistering your paint, too. Start with the hair dryer several inches away and keep it moving. Keep trying to lift the sticker's edge with a fingernail. Gradually move the heat closer until an edge gives way. When it does, aim the hair dryer between the lifted edge and the sticker itself, getting a direct shot at the adhesive.

After the decal is off, clean up residual glue with a petrochemical product (like lighter fluid), then use wax or plastic polish to restore the finish.

269 CLEAN YOUR BIKE

Washing your car is simple—you just clean the glass and paint. Washing your bike? There's a lot more to contend with. Dirt bikes don't need much more than a blast with the powerwasher. They lead a rough life, and who'll notice a dull finish? A high-priced streetbike needs a little more attention. At every step, of this process, gravity is your friend. Washing, drying, detailing—work from the top towards the bottom.

STEP 1 Treat painted surfaces (gas tank, fairings, fenders) gently—use mild detergent, a soft clean cloth, and warm water.

STEP 2 Chrome parts can be treated like paint, but follow up with chrome polish.

STEP 3 Wheels invariably need brushwork, just like your teeth. Brake dust is tenacious, but soap, water, and a cleaner with a brush will do the job.

STEP 4 Bikes have plenty of nasty, greasy parts, too. Here, the solution is chemical warfare. Some of your best friends aren't cleaners at all, but oils and solvents like WD-40. Spraying down really manky bits like final-drive sprockets, the underside of the engine, the swingarm, etc. can help loosen that nasty black grime. Follow up with a power washer and a solvent-based cleaner. If you need to do any localized scrubbing, use brushes you've reserved only for this purpose—never use the gunk brushes on the cleaner parts of your bike.

STEP 5 Dry off smooth, painted surfaces with clean towels or a chamois. With all their nooks and crannies, most bikes will look better if you first blast them dry with compressed air. If nothing else, the exhaust hose from a shop vac (an industrial vacuum cleaner) will blow most of the water off. A leaf blower works great for this.

270 GET A GRIP

Changing a grip looks like such an easy job, but often proves more frustrating than trying to give an angry Siamese cat a bath. But it doesn't have to be that way if you try these pro tips.

The easiest way to remove an old grip is to slice it off with a razor blade. Want to reuse it instead? Pull it away from the bar and spray a healthy dose of contact cleaner in the gap. Work fast, and push the straw from the can's spray nozzle in as deep as you can. Twist and pull the grip off. If it sticks halfway, spray in some more contact cleaner.

Shade-tree mechanics use hair spray, glue, gorilla snot, friction tape, and special adhesive to put on new grips. We just use more contact cleaner. Spray it into a new grip, liberally coating all the inside surfaces. Give it a really good shot, a couple of seconds' worth. Then immediately slide the grip on to the bar end. Then walk away for 20 minutes and let the tacky rubber bond to the bar end.

Want more security? Wrap some stainless-steel lock wire (about 0.030-inch-diameter, 0.7 mm or 20 gauge) around the grip at each end and in the center, and twist it tight. Most dirt-bike grips even have special grooves for the safety wire. It'll squeeze the rubber down and create a seal to keep moisture from getting under the grip and loosening it from the handlebar.

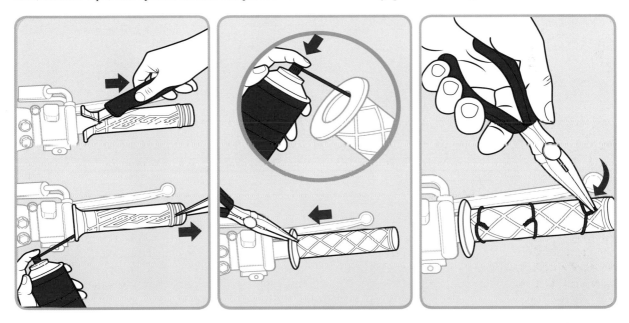

271 REPAIR A TORN SEAT

Nothing looks as bad as a strip of silver duct tape on a black seat, covering up a tear. What to do short of this unsightly fix?

For really minor tears, try a super-glue product. Also, for black seat covers, black gasket sealant can work.

Larger tear? Try sewing it closed with close, fine stiches, then sealing with the gasket goop.

Big hanging tear? Three choices: a new seat

(costly); a professional re-upholstery fix (this can be surprisingly affordable if you bring only the seat into an auto shop); or easiest of all, a new seat cover. These items are available online, and usually only need a heavy-duty stapler to install.

272 ADJUST YOUR CHAIN

Adjusting your bike's chain won't make it any faster, but it's critical if you want your chain to last. It's fast, easy, and next to checking your own tire pressure it's one of the first things any home mechanic should learn. Too tight is as bad as too loose, but it'll only take minutes to get it right. You should check and adjust your chain every 500 miles (805 km), and more often for a dirt bike. It's also a great time to look for kinks or rust, and to give your chain a quick cleaning and lubrication, too.

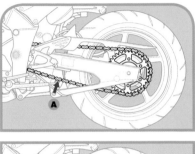

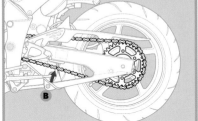

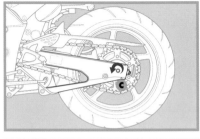

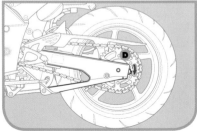

STEP 1 Read the owner's manual for the correct amount of drive-chain slack. Most streetbikes also have a sticker on the swingarm.

STEP 2 With the engine off, put the bike on its sidestand or centerstand, and shift the transmission into neutral.

STEP 3 Find the midway point of the chain between the front and rear sprockets [A]. Push up on the bottom of the chain and note the distance between the full-slack (lower) position and the no-slack (upper) position on the bottom [B]. 1.2–1.6 inches (30–40 mm) is typical for streetbikes, while dirt bikes may need 1.4–2.0 inches (35–50 mm) of slack.

STEP 4 To adjust the drive chain, loosen the axle nut a couple of turns [C]. If all you have is a short wrench, you can stand on it to get the nut loose.

STEP 5 Most streetbikes and some dirt bikes feature bolts that you turn to increase or decrease the chain slack. Adjust them a quarter turn at a time; be sure you make the same adjustment on each side of the swingarm, so the rear wheel stays aligned [D]. Measure and adjust until your chain is within spec.

STEP 6 Whatever system you have, when you have the correct chain tension, remember to tighten the axle nut back to the correct torque (check your manual, but usually to 65 foot-pounds or 88 newton-meters).

273 FIX A STRIPPED BOLT

Screw up the threads on a bolt? First, try slowly and carefully running a nut up and down in the threads. If you're having a tough time getting the nut started, try to run the bolt backward, then forward.

No joy? Then break out a thread restoration tool, like the one shown here. This device clamps around a bolt and straightens/cuts new threads. It's pretty much universal, and a tightening system allows you to vary the pressure you need.

Stripped out the part that the bolt screws into? That's a tougher situation. Sometimes the easiest fix is just to use a longer bolt and put a nut on the end. If not, you can just drill out the hole and tap in new threads for the next oversized bolt. You can also drill out the hole and install a new (steel) threaded insert. Next time, use a torque wrench!

274

MASTER YOUR BIKE'S CHAIN

Motorcycle chains are efficient devices, but there is one infuriating aspect: the master link.

Your factory stock chain links were created equal. But if you have to remove your chain for any reason (replacement or breakage), you need some way to rejoin the two loose ends—which requires a master link.

There are two types: the rivet-on and the clip-on. With a rivet-on link, you need a special tool for installation, like the silver one above. It lets you break the chain open, and press on the new master-link plate to rivet the ends together.

With a clip-type link, you often hold the two loose ends the right distance apart while you try to insert the new link. A tool like the second one (orange in our photo) helps with that job. When installing a clip-type link, remember that the open end of the clip faces opposite the chain's direction of travel.

275

READ A WORN SPROCKET

Chains are costly, and you need special tools to replace those without master links. So how do you find out if you'll need a new one?

First, be sure the chain is adjusted properly. Then, with the engine off and the bike in neutral, grab the chain with your thumb and forefinger at the very back of the rear sprocket. (Be sure the chain is cool to the touch first.) If you can lift any link more than about halfway off its sprocket tooth, it's time to say adios to that old metal snake.

If the chain is finished, the front and rear sprockets may be, too. Look them over for a hooked or wavy appearance, as in this illustration. Putting a new chain onto a worn sprocket will ruin the chain pronto; the same goes for changing the sprockets but using a clapped-out chain.

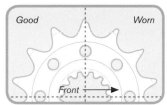

Good / Worn / Front →

276 MAKE LIKE A SNAIL

Some dirt bikes have "snail-cam" adjusters, with notches on their outside edges. Loosen the axle nut, and then tighten or loosen the chain one notch at a time, the same on each side. The notches are usually numbered (if not, then you can number them using a permanent marker); be sure each side ends up on the same number.

277 SET YOUR VALVES

There's no way to give a step-by-step method for every engine out there, so get your hands on a shop manual. But you'll need surprisingly few tools for this job, and most of them are inexpensive: some wrenches and a set of feeler gauges (thin metal strips of varying thickness).

No matter what kind of engine you have, the work will go easier if you remove the spark plugs—this makes it easier to turn the engine over. What you want to do is get each cylinder to Top Dead Center (TDC), where the piston is at the top of its stroke. On most engines, this means turning the crankshaft until each piston rises in turn. When it's in the correct position, you'll use the feeler gauge to measure how much

clearance there is between the valve and the valve-opening mechanism.

Some systems will let you adjust this clearance by turning a screw. Other (high performance) systems require you to replace shims—that usually involves removing the camshafts.

How often should you adjust your valves? Your owner's manual will tell you—bikes' typical inspection intervals are between 3,000 to 16,000 miles (4,800 to 26,000 km). And some engines use hydraulic adjusters. How you adjust them? You sit on your couch, open a beer, and watch the ballgame—they adjust themselves automatically every time you ride.

278 CLEAN THE RUST OUT OF A GAS TANK

Need a low-cost way to salvage a vintage metal fuel tank with severe interior rust? Take the tank off the bike, and seal off the petcock hole. Pour in a couple of quarts of kerosene. Add a handful of nuts, bolts, and sheet-metal screws, and start shaking. The nuts and bolts knock the rust off from the inside, and the kerosene helps the rust flake loose. Keep shaking until your arms give out. Dump the nut, bolts, and rust out, refill with clean kerosene, rinse the bolts, dump them back in, and repeat over and over until the tank is clean. Rinse with solvent and coat the inside of the tank with a sealant.

279 MIX TWO-STROKE FUEL

The engine in your car is a four-stroke. And while most of today's motorcycle engines are four-stroke types as well, there are still some two-stroke engines out there, especially when it comes to scooters and off-road bikes. Chainsaws, outboard engines, and weed-whackers also use two-strokes.

This sort of engine needs to have oil mixed in with the fuel. How much oil? Most owner's manuals will tell you, but ratios between 32:1 and 40:1 are common. Thus, your mix is 40 parts gasoline to one part oil.

If you're working with the metric system, it's easy: 10cc of oil to 400cc of fuel. Imperial measurements are a little less intuitive: an ounce of oil (think shot glass) to a quart of gasoline is about 32:1. A gallon of fuel is 128 ounces. At a 40:1 ratio, that means you'll need 3.2 ounces of oil.

Pour the correct amount of oil and gasoline into a bottle or can, shake vigorously, and pour it into your fuel tank. No separate bottle or measuring cup? Pump the straight gas into your fuel tank, add what you think is the correct amount of oil, fit the gas cap and slosh the bike as violently as you can to mix it together. Too little oil will result in engine damage; too much will foul the plug and stop the engine, but without doing permanent damage. No oil at all? You're out of luck.

280 DON'T BE FUEL-ISH

Two-stroke premix doesn't like to sit around—if the mix is older than a week, mix up a new batch. And avoid fuel with high alcohol/ethanol contents. So-called E85 fuels (up to 85 percent ethanol, 15 percent gasoline) often mix poorly with two-stroke oil, and the oil falls out of suspension quickly.

281

CHANGE YOUR JETTING

Carburetors mix fuel and air in a precise ratio (by weight, about 14 parts air to one part gasoline). The problem comes because there's less air (by volume) at higher elevations, and because some engine modifications (new exhaust pipes, new air cleaners) change the amount of air flowing through your engine.

Jets are small brass nozzles inside your carburetor that spray liquid gasoline into the moving air, mixing them together. These small, removeable fixtures have a hole in the center that's precisely sized. When you change how much air flows through your engine (or if high-altitude operation changes it for you), you'll often have to change your jets to match, fitting new nozzles with larger or smaller holes as needed.

It's not tough. Most engines have two jets, one for low-speed operation (the pilot or idle jet) and one for high-engine-speeds at large throttle openings (the main jet). A long, tapered needle controls the fuel/air mix at throttle openings between ¼ and ¾.

If your engine is too lean (too much air), it will often pop and backfire on you. If it's too rich (too much fuel), it stumbles and burbles. The best way to judge is to read your spark plugs or run the engine on a dyno.

Changing the jets is a trial-and-error adjustment method that simply involves screwing in larger or smaller nozzles (jets) or moving the needle higher or lower (richer or leaner) in the throttle slide.

282

SYNC YOUR CARBS

Engines need to mix gas and air together to run properly, and they use either carburetors (old school) or fuel injection (more common on newer engines). Motorcycles using carburetors often feature one carburetor per cylinder. This design helps to optimize performance—if everything's working right. And in order for them to work right, the carburetors need to be synchronized—that is, they all need to work together.

Most of the time, you adjust them by measuring intake-manifold vacuum. If your engine has a small screw plug between the carburetor and the cylinder head, you start the engine, remove the screw, fit a tube, and measure how much vacuum that cylinder is producing, usually measured in inches or millimeters of mercury. A dial gauge or vertically graduated tubes gives you the readout. To make the job easier, four gauges (or four tubes) let you measure two, three, or four carbs at once.

Usually adjusting them is as simple as turning a screw. When all the carbs give you the same readout, your little symphony is in tune—it's time to go riding!

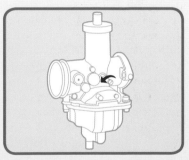

283 PULL THE PLUG (AND READ IT)

Spark plugs provide the discharge needed to fire each cylinder in your bike's engine. But over time they can be subject to all sorts of nasty wear and tear. The result is a bike that won't go, or at least one that delivers on the expression "not firing on all cylinders"—an unsafe and potentially engine-damaging issue.

The eyes may be the windows to the soul, but sparkplugs are the windows to your engine. Removing a spark plug and inspecting it can tell you plenty about what's going on in your engine. Is it running rich? Lean? Burning oil? Pull a plug and find out.

FOULING The end of the spark plug can be covered—or the gap between electrodes can be bridged—by dry or wet carbon (from fuel or oil leakage), ash (from excessive combustion deposits), or yellowish stains (from leaded fuels).

GLAZING When a spark plug overheats, deposits on the insulator or electrodes may melt and cover the surfaces, giving them a 'glazed' look.

MELTING Excessive heat or premature ignition can also burn the ceramic insulator or lead to the electrodes' surfaces melting and becoming pitted and uneven.

EROSION The spark plug's electrodes may become oxidized, corroded, or react with leaded fuel, and grow pitted, leading to a wider gap—thus drawing more voltage for ignition.

BREAKAGE The end of the plug may suffer damage from being struck by the piston (if the plug is too long), foreign objects in the chamber, or thermal shock from sudden heating or cooling.

DETONATION The insulator may be damaged if the electrodes' gap is improperly set or if the fuel is causing engine knocking.

TIME Gradually, the ignition cycle does wear at the electrodes, widening the ignition gap and burning out the ceramic insulator.

284 GET THE SPARK BACK

Caring for your bike's spark plugs is an easy task. A few tools and a little work keep your engine firing right.

First, remove the spark plug's cap and examine its terminal end, then remove the spark plug with a spanner to take a look at the electrode (see above item). If it's shot, then replace it. If it's just in need of a cleaning, give it a thorough rinse in kerosene or gasoline, then wipe it down with a clean cloth.

Check the electrode's gap with a gauge, and adjust if necessary (your manual usually indicates a gap between 0.8 and 1.2 mm).

Carefully screw the plug back in—not too tightly, so as to avoid damaging the threads—and you're set!

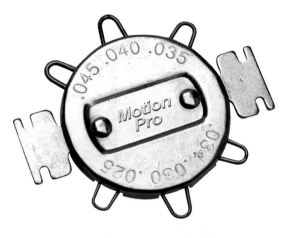

285 MAKE A QUICK FIX

Bodges. Band-Aid fixes. Field repairs. When your bike breaks and you're out on the road (or trail) you might not have the tools, parts, or time to fix it correctly. You might just need something that will get you home—because walking (or worse, pushing) stinks.

FLAT TIRE No pump? No patch kit? No tube? No problem! Just pry off one tire bead and start stuffing anything you can find into the tire carcass: rags, newspapers, sage brush, hay. Jam in as much as you can—you want the tire really filled. Ride slow on a repair like this; you won't have much traction, but you won't destroy a rim and you might even preserve the tire. On dirt bikes, a handful of giant cable ties can secure a knobby to the rim, even without the stuffing.

LOOSE HANDLEBAR Most handlebars are ⅞-inch (20-mm) tubing held by a pair of clamps. But time, vibration, and worn clamps can cause the bar to slip. The fix? Remove the clamps, cut shims from an aluminum beer can, place them between the clamp and the bar, reinstall, and tighten. The aluminum is soft enough to grip both the bar and clamp tightly.

CRACKED CASE A common occurrence when dirt-bike riding in rocks. Lay the bike over on its side, clean the crack with gasoline or (better) contact cleaner. Knead up some two-part epoxy and patch it over the crack. Wait 20 minutes and ride off. No epoxy? Look for a pine or spruce tree and use some pitch mixed with charcoal.

RADIATOR HOLE Some pepper or a plug of potato can close the hole (epoxy works too). But what to do about the lost water? Your hydration pack is the first solution. Avoid using any soda-pop in the cooling system though. No water in your canteen? Then it's time for every male in the group to step up, unbutton, and let fly down the radiator. Not a pretty sight, but you'll make it home—if your bladder is big enough.

286 CHARGE IT!

Your motorcycle's electrical system charges your battery when you ride it. But if the bike sits for a long time without being ridden, bad things start happening in that little black box of lead and acid. At the least, it will be discharged when you want to go for a ride. At worst, it will have turned into a heavy, toxic lump. What can you do to resuscitate your battery?

If the battery's completely flat, remove it from the bike (or at least disconnect both positive and negative cables). Check the electrolyte level and top up with distilled water if needed. Make sure the top of the battery is clean. Hook it up to a charger in a well-vented area. Don't just use a full-power automotive charger—you want one with a 2-amp setting.

Not going to be riding for a while? A trickle charge is a great way to maintain your battery. These chargers (some are even solar-powered) feed your battery a small amount of current, keeping them topped off. The best models monitor the battery so they don't overcharge it. The very best even feature a desulfation mode. You can also pre-wire your battery with a pigtail, making it easy to hook the charger up without removing the seat or any of the body panels.

287 BOX YOUR MOTORCYCLE

Sometimes a big adventure requires you to ship your bike. Or maybe you have a race bike going to Daytona. Either way, you can work with a roll-on/roll-off shipper, or crate your bike. Crating offers the most protection—especially if your machine might end up sitting on a loading dock for a week.

You can either build a crate yourself, or buy one from a shipping company or motorcycle dealer. Some even have a steel framework and cardboard cover for added protection. Even if your dealer won't sell you a shipping crate outright, he may "rent" one to you for a modest deposit.

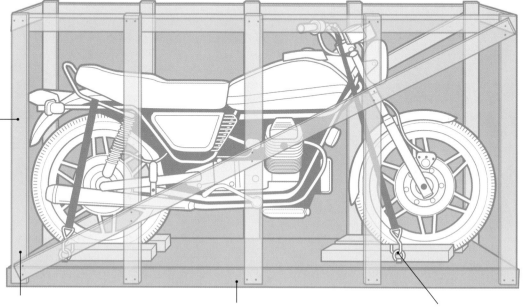

The skeleton of the crate is built with wooden 2x4s or steel framework to keep its shape, and that of the bike inside.

STURDY PANELING *The crate should be built to withstand the rigors of shipping—be it harsh weather, rough handling, or mishaps with forklifts.*

STURDY BASE *The crate's floor has to bear the weight of your bike plus the crate itself, and have gaps to allow a forklift or other equipment to hoist it up.*

STRONG ANCHORS *Heavy-duty steel eyebolts or similar points should be built into the crate to let you securely tie down your bike.*

288 LOAD YOUR BIKE INTO A VAN

YouTube is full of clips of bike-loading mishaps. But if you follow this plan, you won't be in one of them.

First, park the vehicle with its rear wheels in a low spot to lower the ramp angle. Try backing the van/truck up until the rear wheels stop where the street and driveway meet, in the gutter.

While loading the bike, you'll need to step up into the bed of the vehicle. Place a sturdy box about one foot (30 cm) high between the pavement and the bed, so you'll have a step to climb up on. Be sure it's strong, so your foot doesn't crash through.

Use the longest ramp possible, to reduce your

angle of approach and thus your chance of smacking the engine case where the ramp and the vehicle's bed meet up.

When you push the bike up, go from the left side. Get your movie-making friends to help—put them on the right side and have them push, too.

289 TIE DOWN YOUR RIDE

We bet as many motorcycles are damaged by bad tie-down jobs as are crashed on the road. It's a tragedy that never needs to happen. Here's all you need to know.

STEP 1 Hook the tie-downs to the handlebar or (better) the upper or lower triple clamp. The triple clamp anchor point is easier if you use a pair of nylon loops (soft ties). Loop the soft tie around the clamp first, load the bike, then attach the tie-down hook. Attach the other end of the tie-down hook to the anchor point in the truck bed.

STEP 2 Put the bike on its sidestand and tighten the left tie-down. It doesn't need to be drum-tight yet—just remove the slack.

STEP 3 Push the bike over to the right side. With the left tie-down already snug, the front suspension will be compressed. This spring force is what's going to keep everything snug and in place. When the bike is upright, snug down the right tie-down.

STEP 4 Keep the bike straight up and down, not leaned over to either side, and don't pull the tie-downs too tautly; compress only about half the travel in the front suspension.

STEP 5 To keep the rear end of the bike from bouncing around, take a second pair of tie-downs and run them from an anchor point in the bed, around the rear wheel, and over to an anchor on the right side. All you're trying to control is lateral movement here.

Be sure to use quality tie-downs with thick webbing, strong hooks, and aggressive spring buckles. The ratcheting types are overkill for bikes. Two pair will give you four anchor points—a really bombproof setup.

290 GET A TWO-WHEEL TOW

Motorcycle give up the ghost while you're out with your friends? Or maybe you just ran out of gas a couple of miles before the fuel stop?

First, get 12 feet to 20 feet (4 to 6 m) of rope, tie-downs hooked together, a bit of fence wire or phone cable, or best of all, a one inch (2.5 cm) wide flat nylon strap.

One method keeps the towline down low. On the lead bike, wrap the line once around the right footpeg (if the drivechain is on the left). The rider firmly holds the line in place with his foot. The rider being towed does the same thing using the opposite footpeg (left in our example). If the tow goes wrong, either rider can easily let go.

Another method starts with the line tied to the frame of the lead bike as high as possible. Alternately, make a "Y" in the end of the line and tie each end to a footpeg; the fork should rest in the center of the seat above. The end leads back to the trailing bike, and goes under the headlight, on the centerline of the bike. The loose end wraps around the handlebar once or twice, and is held by the left (clutch) hand. The towing rider operates the front brake normally, and if he needs to get free, he can simply let go.

Either way, the more experienced rider should be on the trailing bike, and should keep all the slack out of the line; the trailing rider can run over a slack line and get it caught up in the front wheel. All braking should be done by the trailing rider, and the lead rider should keep the speed down.

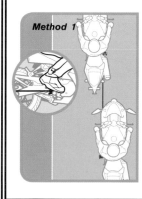
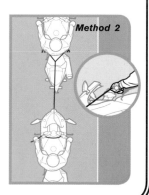

Method 1 *Method 2*

291 WINTERIZE YOUR BIKE

Winter can be cruel to both a bike and its rider. Until the Big Thaw comes, here's what you can do to put the machine into storage.

CLEAN IT Give the bike a thorough wash and wax. Don't just wax the paint—apply wax and/or polish to all the metal areas, especially the chrome. You're trying to defend against moisture here. Dirt attracts moisture and reacts with it. The result? Rust.

PARK IT It's time to keep your machine indoors. If you don't have a heated garage or can't park in the kitchen, find a place protected from rain and rodents.

DEAL WITH FUEL Fill the tank, add a fuel stabilizer, and run the engine (ride several miles) to let the mix work through the fuel-delivery system; this method is best with fuel injectors. Or drain all of the fuel and run the engine dry—with carburetors this can help keep the system from varnishing. If you have a metal fuel tank, spray inside it with WD-40 or other rust inhibitor.

CHANGE THE OIL Change it before you park the bike, and again before you begin riding. Moisture from condensation gets into the oil and compromises it. Oil's cheap; new bearings aren't.

PREP THE ENGINE Ride briefly to warm the bike. Then remove the spark plugs and squirt engine oil (25cc or so) into each hole. Slowly turn the bike over with the plugs out (put the bike in gear, raise the rear wheel, and spin it a few times). Replace the plugs.

PROTECT THE BATTERY Disconnect it and store it where it won't freeze. Or, put it on a trickle charger.

SAVE YOUR TIRES Put the bike on stands front and rear (at least the rear) to get both tires off the ground.

USE ANTIFREEZE With a liquid-cooled bike, make sure it has the correct ration of antifreeze in the cooling system. Check with a hydrometer.

SHIELD YOUR PIPES Keep critters out of the airbox or tailpipe with plugs or a sheet of plastic stretched over the openings and secured with rubber bands.

COVER IT UP You'll prevent scratches and keep your clean bike cleaner, even indoors.

GLOSSARY

ADVENTURE BIKE A motorcycle built with on and off-road capability. Often with a tall frame and high seat height, along with luggage/cargo capacity.

AIRBOX Compartment where air is drawn into an engine through its intakes; contains a filter to keep indrawn air clean.

AMA American Motorcyclist Association, a nonprofit motorcycling organization founded in 1924.

BAGGER A motorcycle equipped with hard saddlebags and a fairing. Often a cruiser.

BORE AND STROKE The diameter of an engine's cylinder and the length of the piston's travel in that cylinder. The volume of this, multiplied by the number of cylinders, gives you the engine's size.

BURNOUT The act of revving a motorcycle engine's throttle to very high rpm while controlling the clutch and brake in order to generate tire marks and smoke.

CAMSHAFT The camshaft is the device which opens and closes an engine's valves. SOHC means Single Over Head Cam, and DOHC means Double Over Head Cam.

CARBON FIBER A strong, lightweight plastic composite reinforced with carbon filaments. Often used in riding gear (e.g. knuckle guards on gloves) or body-panel accessories for motorcycles.

CARBURETOR The part of an engine that mixes gasoline and air together.

CBS (COMBINED BRAKING SYSTEM) A braking system that links or combines both the front and rear brakes (standard practice is to have front and rear brake systems separate).

CENTERSTAND A retractable stand under some motorcycles which lets them stand straight up and down when parked or for service, compared to the more common sidestand, where the bike is leaned to the left side.

CHOPPER A cruiser-class motorcycle with minimal bodywork, a long wheelbase, and often with an extended front suspension.

COMPRESSION RATIO The mechanical ratio of how much an engine compresses the fuel/air mixture before ignition. Typically, higher compression ratios produce more power.

COUNTERSTEERING A dynamic phenomenon wherein the rider pushes on the left handgrip to initiate a left turn, and vice-versa.

CRUISER A type of motorcycle built for relaxed street riding, and with specific and often traditional styling elements such as chrome parts and custom paint.

CURB WEIGHT The weight of the motorcycle alone and without the rider or passenger, usually including a full tank of fuel.

DAMPER A mechanism to slow or reduce the force of a moving part. Usually it refers to a suspension shock absorber, or a device fit to damp steering movements.

DIRTBIKE A motorcycle specifically designed for off-road activity, with high suspension and knobby tires.

DISC BRAKE A type of brake where a caliper grabs a disc (or discs) to slow the motorcycle. Typically more powerful than a drum. Easy to see on the front of most modern bikes.

DRUM BRAKE A type of brake externally resembling a drum, with most of the brake mechanism inside.

DUAL-SPORT A type of motorcycle designed (and legal for) riding in both the dirt and on the street.

DYNAMOMETER A machine used to measure an engine's the torque and power output of an engine. Often abbreviated to "dyno."

EFI Electronic Fuel Injection.

ENDURO Technically, a specific type of off-road motorcycle competition. More often used to describe a type of dirtbike which is also street legal (more correctly called a dual-sport) or an off-road-only bike designed for trail riding.

ENGINE BRAKING Decelerating by closing an engine's throttle, thus leading to a vacuum effect from reduced air intake, as well as drivetrain friction, which combine to slow the motorcycle.

ERGONOMICS The dynamic fit of a motorcycle and its rider; how a bike or its parts fit a human being.

FAIRING Bodywork on the front or sides of a motorcycle. May cover the handlebar or engine. Often features a windscreen.

FINAL DRIVE The mechanical connection between a motorcycle's transmission and rear wheel. Usually a chain or a shaft; less often a belt.

FOOTPEGS The footrests on most motorcycles. Often folding. Contrast with floorboards on some custom motorcycles and scooters.

FORK The two legs of the front suspension assembly. So called due to the resemblance of two tines on the common table utensil.

FOUR-STROKE ENGINE One of two fundamental engine designs (see also "two stroke engine,"). Requires four cycles of the piston through the cylinder (induction, compression, power, exhaust) for every power impulse.

FUEL INJECTION A type of fuel-delivery system for an engine where a precise amount of measured fuel is delivered to each cylinder by a small injection pump.

FULL-FACE HELMET A type of motorcycle helmet with a chin bar that covers the lower jaw area. Often equipped with a flip-up face shield.

GVWR Gross Vehicle Weight Rating: The maximum allowable weight of motorcycle, rider, passenger, fuel, luggage, etc.

HIGHSIDE A crash in which the motorcycle flips over to fall on the side opposite of the direction it was leaning in. The rider is often flung over the bike.

HOLESHOT Achievement in dirtbike racing wherein a rider is the first to enter the narrow initial turn on a track, thus gaining an advantage over other riders.

INLINE-FOUR A motorcycle engine configuration where four cylinders are disposed in a row.

KICKSTAND A retractable prop stand on the left side of the motorcycle which lets it lean over in a stable attitude when parked.

LANE SPLITTING Riding between lanes of cars which are stopped or moving slowly.

LOWSIDE A crash in which the motorcycle falls over in the direction it is leaning. Its rider usually lands on the ground behind the motorcycle in this fall.

MASTER CYLINDER Part of a motorcycle's brake system. When a rider squeezes the front-brake lever (or presses down on the rear-brake pedal), fluid is compressed in this cylinder, and the pressure generated

the angle of the fork away from vertical and toward the rider—i.e., the angle that pushed the front wheel away from the bike. Choppers and customs often feature much rake, sportbikes less. Typically, more rake results in a longer wheelbase.

REDLINE The maximum rpm at which an engine can operate without causing damage to itself. Traditionally shown on a tachometer in red numerals. Also used to describe the act of engaging an engine in such maximum effort ("redlining").

RISING-RATE Typically a rear-suspension design where the force required to deflect the wheel increases with wheel travel to resist bottoming.

travels through a brake line and exerts stopping force on the brakes themselves.

RPM Revolutions per minute, the standard measure of engine speed.

MOTOGP Short for Motorcycle Grand Prix. More formally known as Road Racing World Championship Grand Prix. The premier championship of motorcycle road racing. Various MotoGP events are held worldwide every year.

SCOOTER A small motorcycle, typically with a step-through design, and often featuring full-coverage bodywork and a one-speed automatic transmission.

O-RING CHAIN A type of final-drive chain where each link is sealed with a small rubber ring for superior lubrication properties.

SHOCK/SHOCK ABSORBER A mechanism to slow and/or reduce the force of a moving suspension component. In the front suspension, the shocks(s) are incorporated into the fork legs.

PARALLEL TWIN An engine configuration where two cylinders are placed parallel to each other (compare with V-twin).

SISSY BAR A bar extending vertically behind the passenger; sometimes equipped with a backrest.

PILLION Passenger seat. "Riding pillion" means riding as a passenger. A somewhat outdated term.

SPORTBIKE A type of motorcycle built for more active street riding, often with an aggressive or hunched seating position and aerodynamic bodywork.

PORT A passage in an engine's cylinder-head which leads either from the throttle to the intake valves, or from the exhaust valves to the exhaust pipes.

STEERING HEAD The part of a motorcycle's frame about which the steering pivots.

POWERBAND The range of operating speed in which an engine is able to operate the most efficiently. Often expressed on a chart as a curved line showing the relationship between torque and engine rpm.

STANDARD The classic format for a motorcycle, with a neutral seating position, minimal bodywork, and a sometimes slightly old-fashioned appearance.

PRIMARY DRIVE The mechanical connection between an engine's crankshaft and its transmission. Usually either gears, belt, or chain.

SWINGARM Part of the rear suspension which directly connects the rear wheel to the frame.

RADIAL A type of modern tire construction where the reinforcing belts of a tire's carcass run directly side to side with no angle.

SUPERBIKE A modified version of a production sportbike used for track racing; also the abbreviated name of the actual event series, the Superbike World Championship aka SBK.

TACHOMETER An instrument which shows engine speed in rpm. Often abbreviated as "tach."

RAKE Part of a motorcycle's steering geometry. Rake is

TANKSLAPPER An uncontrolled oscillation of the handlebars that happens when the front wheel of a motorcycle loses control; may result in a crash. Also known as a speed wobble.

TARGET FIXATION The act of becoming overly focused on an obstacle in one's field of vision, rather than trying to avoid it.

TEXTILE An alternative to leather for motorcycle riding gear; denotes a range of fabrics including nylon, aramid and Kevlar. Each type varies in waterproofing and abrasion resistance.

THROTTLE The twist-grip on a motorcycle (usually on the right side of the handlebars) which controls fuel delivery, and consequently speed and power.

TOP END A motorcycle's top speed; the upper ranges of a motorcycle engine's powerband; or, the upper parts of a motorcycle engine, i.e., the cylinder head, valve train, etc.

TOURING BIKE A motorcycle built for leisurely long-distance riding, with a long, stable wheelbase and comfortable accommodation for rider (and often passenger).

TRAIL Part of a motorcycle's chassis geometry. Trail is the distance on the ground between a vertical line dropped straight down from the center of the front wheel and a projection of the fork extended until it touches the ground. Typically, greater trail increases steering stability, while less trail increases responsiveness.

TRAIL BRAKING The act of braking while entering a turn, and gradually releasing them as the rider reaches the turn's apex, to adjust speed more smoothly and accurately.

TRICKLE CHARGER A battery charger which delivers a steady, low-level current to a battery in order to keep it charged for extended periods of time.

TRIPMETER An instrument on the motorcycle's speedometer which records mileage travelled, and which is resettable.

TWIN An engine with two cylinders.

TWO-INTO-ONE PIPES Exhaust pipes which join two cylinders' exhaust and route them to one muffler, like the letter Y.

TWO-STROKE ENGINE An engine design that requires

only two cycles of the piston through the cylinder (one down, one up) for every power impulse. Current two strokes are generally limited to smaller engines due to pollution issues.

UNSPRUNG WEIGHT The weight of a motorcycle's components below the suspension springs (tires, wheels, brake discs. etc.) Less unsprung weight typically improves handling and suspension compliance.

VIN Vehicle Identification Numbers, appearing on a motorcycle's registration papers and stamped on the frame,

VTEC Variable valve Timing and Electronic Control. A Honda-designed system which allows an engine to run on two valves per cylinder at lower engine speeds and four valves per cylinder at higher engine speeds for superior performance. The system may also change valve timing, lift, and duration.

V-TWIN A type of engines with two cylinders set at an angle to each other like the letter V. Popular configuration for cruisers.

WHEELBASE The distance between the center of the front wheel and the center of the rear. Typically a bike with a longer wheelbase offers stability, while one with a shorter wheelbase is more responsive.

WSB World Superbike; a popular racing class.

INDEX

D

Daytona Beach Bike Week, 145
Daytona International Speedway, 144
dealerships, 3, 8, 185, 186, 190
Dean, Paul, 72
decal removal, 268
desert, riding in the, 118–119, 210
dirtbikes, 6, 11, 14, 82
  choosing, 20
  types of, 19
  See also under names of dirtbike types
documents, travel, 204
Dolomites, riding in the, 202
downshifting, 84, 85, 88, 92, 155
drag bikes, 70
dragging knees and elbows, 179–181
D-rings, 47, 49
dual-sports, 11, 19, 21, 254
Dunlop, Joey, 217
dust, riding in the, 122, 125
dyno charts, 72, 73

E

earplugs, 38, 50
eating while riding, 193
Edwards, Colin, 139
emergency stops, 165
enduro bikes, 19
engines, 13, 65–66, 68, 72, 73
  adventure-bike, 22, 68
  breaking in, 79
  components of, 262
  cooking on, 195–196
  cruiser, 16
  dirtbike, 68
  and dragstrip launching, 177
  dual-sports, 21
  four-stroke, 66, 279
  maintaining, 79, 277
  sportbike, 17
  standard-bike, 15
  starting after malfunction, 239–243
  and swamp riding, 140
  touring-bike, 18, 68
  two-stroke, 66, 279
  types of, 263

and winter storage, 291
environment, protecting the, 121
Europe, riding in, 202, 205, 207–209
exhaust systems, 13
  adventure-bike, 22
  dual-sports, 21
eye protection, 37

F

faceshields, cleaning, 192
fairings, repair of, 267
fenders, 13
field repairs, 285
fire. *See* campfire
flat tires, field repair of, 285
flat-track riding, 139
food, 193–196, 219
footpegs, 13, 15, 93, 143
  forward-set, 16
  on used bikes, 29
four-stroke engines, 66, 279
frames, sportbike, 17
France, riding in, 202
fuel injection, 282
fuel stabilizer, 291
fuel tanks, 13, 278, 291
  adventure-bike, 22
  standard-bike, 15
  touring-bike, 18

G

gasoline
  carrying spare, 135
  filtering dirty, 137
  mixture for two-stroke engines, 279–280
gearing, 83
  dual-sports, 21
Germany, riding in, 207, 208
Globe of Death, 170
gloves, 37, 44, 54, 58, 60, 62
goggles, 37, 40, 46, 62, 64, 125
GPS, 26
grips, changing, 270
group, riding in a, 191, 203
Guthrie, Andrew James, 216

ABOUT THE AUTHOR

Mark Lindemann was an Associate Editor at the late, great *Cycle* magazine between 1982 and 1987, and has been in the motorcycle industry ever since. Proficient on both streetbikes and dirtbikes, his notes show he's ridden over 750 machines on four continents, of which only a handful have actively tried to kill him. In 2012 he was the recipient of *Cycle World*'s prestigious Joe Parkhurst Award for embodying the spirit of the sport. In addition to his efforts at *Cycle*, his work has appeared in *Cycle World, Motorcyclist, Cycle World Travel and Adventure, Supercycle, Garage,* and *Outrider Journal*.

Career highlights include outrunning a low-flying aircraft at Bonneville, a citation for riding at 134 miles per hour in a 25-mph zone, and being stitched together by a veterinarian after a streetbike crash. His garage is filled with more tools than should be allowed by law. Compared to his former fearless self, today he rides about as fast as an advancing tectonic plate.

ABOUT THE MAGAZINE

Cycle World is the largest motorcycling publication in the world, with articles on street, dirt, and competition riding around the globe. The magazine was founded in 1962 by Joe Parkhurst who, as a result, was inducted to the Motorcycle Hall of Fame as, "the person responsible for bringing a new era of objective journalism" to the US. Readers enjoy the magazine for its stunning photography, practical, hands-on information, and insights into the sporting world, as well as the high quality of its writing and guest contributes from expert riders to cultural icons such as Hunter S. Thompson. Over 310,000 bike enthusiasts read the magazine each month.

FROM THE AUTHOR

Thanks to Rick Loveitt and Dick Wedeen, my first motorcycling role models. To the band of brothers from Cycle magazine, but especially Ken Lee and Mark Homchick—every ride with them is still a treasure. To Dirk Vandenberg and Bruce Ogilvie, who had to leave too soon but who taught me so much. To Kevin Cameron, Gordon Jennings and Jewel Hendricks, who unlocked the mysteries of the mechanical world. And to a whole string of English Composition instructors (especially Mitchell Marcus) who taught me to write good. Thanks to Mark Hoyer at *Cycle World* and Roger Shaw at Weldon Owen books for the faith they had in me—what the hell were they thinking? To my editor, Mariah Bear, for cracking the whip and providing the adult leadership a project like this requires—every writer should be so lucky.

But most of all, thanks to my wife Sybille for her support and understanding, not only during the writing of this book but for all the time I've spent behind the handlebar of a dirtbike or burning through the tires on an endless string of sportbikes. Why she puts up with me is a great mystery, but one I happily accept.

weldon**owen**

PRESIDENT, CEO Terry Newell
VP, PUBLISHER Roger Shaw
EXECUTIVE EDITOR Mariah Bear
PROJECT EDITOR Ian Cannon
CREATIVE DIRECTOR Kelly Booth
ART DIRECTOR William Mack
DESIGNER Allister Fein
ILLUSTRATION COORDINATOR Conor Buckley
PRODUCTION DIRECTOR Chris Hemesath
PRODUCTION MANAGER Michelle Duggan

Weldon Owen would also like to thank Bridget Fitzgerald, Robert
F. James, and Andrew Joron for their editorial expertise and
Daniel Triassi, Sarah Edelstein, and Lou Bustamante for design
and production assistance.

© 2013 Weldon Owen Inc.

415 Jackson Street
San Francisco, CA 94111
www.wopublishing.com

CYCLE WORLD

EXECUTIVE VICE PRESIDENT Eric Zinczenko
EDITORIAL DIRECTOR Anthony Licata
PUBLISHER Andrew Leisner
EDITOR-IN-CHIEF Mark Hoyer
EXECUTIVE EDITOR Andrew Bornhop
MANAGING EDITOR Matthew Miles
TECHNICAL EDITOR Kevin Cameron
FEATURE EDITOR John Burns
ROAD TEST EDITOR Don Canet
SENIOR EDITOR Blake Conner
EDITOR-AT-LARGE Peter Egan
EDITOR-AT-SPEED Eric Bostrom
EUROPEAN EDITOR Bruno dePrato
DESIGN DIRECTOR Sean Johnston
ART DIRECTOR Maria L. Bereni
DEPUTY ART DIRECTOR Pete Sucheski
ASSOCIATE ART DIRECTORS Kim Gray, James Walsh
ASSISTANT ART DIRECTOR Christina Pendón
PHOTOGRAPHER Jeff Allen
www.cycleworld.com

Cycle World and Weldon Owen are divisions of

BONNIER

Library of Congress Control Number
on file with the publisher
Flexi Edition ISBN 978-1-61628-607-1
Hardcover Edition ISBN 978-1-61628-633-0
10 9 8 7 6 5 4 3 2 1
2013 2014 2015 2016
Printed in China by 1010 Printing International